Vestiges of a Philosophy

OXFORD STUDIES IN WESTERN ESOTERICISM

SPIRITUAL ALCHEMY
From the Age of Jacob Boehme to
Mary Anne Atwood, 1600–1910
Mike A. Zuber

MYSTIFYING KABBALAH
Academic Scholarship, National Theology, and
New Age Spirituality
Boaz Huss

OCCULT IMPERIUM
Arturo Reghini, Roman Traditionalism, and the
Anti-Modern Reaction in Fascist Italy
Christian Giudice

THE SUBTLE BODY
A Genealogy
Simon Cox

RETAINING THE OLD EPISCOPAL DIVINITY
John Edwards of Cambridge and Reformed Orthodoxy
in the Later Stuart Church
Jake Griesel

VESTIGES OF A PHILOSOPHY
Matter, the Meta-Spiritual, and
the Forgotten Bergson
John Ó Maoilearca

Vestiges of a Philosophy

Matter, the Meta-Spiritual, and the Forgotten Bergson

JOHN Ó MAOILEARCA

OXFORD
UNIVERSITY PRESS

Oxford University Press is a department of the University of Oxford. It furthers
the University's objective of excellence in research, scholarship, and education
by publishing worldwide. Oxford is a registered trade mark of Oxford University
Press in the UK and certain other countries.

Published in the United States of America by Oxford University Press
198 Madison Avenue, New York, NY 10016, United States of America.

Library of Congress Cataloging-in-Publication Data
Names: Ó Maoilearca, John, 1965– author.
Title: Vestiges of a philosophy : matter, the meta-spiritual, and the
forgotten Bergson / John Ó Maoilearca.
Description: New York, NY, United States of America : Oxford University Press, [2023] |
Series: Oxford studies in Western esotericism |
Includes bibliographical references and index.
Identifiers: LCCN 2022029948 (print) | LCCN 2022029949 (ebook) |
ISBN 9780197613917 (hardback) | ISBN 9780197613931 (epub) |
ISBN 9780197613948 | ISBN 9780197613924
Subjects: LCSH: Bergson, Moina, 1865–1925. | Mediums. | Spiritualists. |
Science and spiritualism | Mysticism. | Materialism. | Bergson, Henri, 1859–1941.
Classification: LCC BF1283.B4645 O53 2022 (print) |
LCC BF1283.B4645 (ebook) | DDC 133.8—dc23/eng/20220729
LC record available at https://lccn.loc.gov/2022029948
LC ebook record available at https://lccn.loc.gov/2022029949

DOI: 10.1093/oso/9780197613917.001.0001

1 3 5 7 9 8 6 4 2

Printed by Integrated Books International, United States of America

Contents

Illustrations

Figures

Table

Acknowledgments

I want to thank many people whose thoughts, shared either in conversation or in print, have helped this book emerge from its darkness: Paul Atkinson, Lucy Bolton, William Brown, James Burton, Alastair Cameron, Jimena Canales, Howard Caygill, Dennis Denisoff, David Fenton, Matthew Goulish, P. A. Y. Gunter, Emily Herring, Lin Hixon, Ian James, Wahida Khandker, Katerina Kolozova, François Laruelle, Beth Lord, Catherine Malabou, John Meechan, Markus Rajala, Filipa Ramos, Diarmuid Rooney, Anne-Françoise Schmid, Anthony Paul Smith, Iris van der Tuin, Catherine Wheatley, Amanda Wilkinson, and Yaron Wolf—all have helped light a path for me without which it would have been far harder to see a way through the work. I've also been remarkably fortunate to meet with individuals along the way who have been generous enough to share with me whatever was needed to offset the many gaps in my knowledge when writing a book such as this: Mark Price, for his crucial understanding of the Kabbalah's Tree of Life; Ties Van Gemert, who shared both his paper on Bergson and psychical research, as well as insights into some of the oddities of Henri Bergson's vocabulary; Owen White, who shared his time with me each week for well over two years as we both schlepped away at our respective projects; and the late Pamela Sue Anderson, who shared kindness with me from when we first met in 1994 until I last saw her talk in late 2016, speaking on Bergson in fact—a true spirit of Isis. Without the ongoing advice and collegiality of Charlotte de Mille and Juliet Chambers-Coe, two very real and creative spirits, this would certainly have been a lesser work.

Louise Pichel at the Museum of Freemasonry, London, and the officers at the Museum of Witchcraft, Cornwall, were commendable in allowing me access to and copies of materials in their archives (when this was possible before the pandemic). The Gladstone Library in Hawarden, Wales, was the perfect residence in early 2020 to allow me to begin the writing process—peace and quiet are rare things to find in a library nowadays, and it has it aplenty. The trail of friends helping me track down various rights and permissions—Nicola Levy, Michael O'Byrne, and Lisa Power in particular—proved indispensable when navigating the labyrinthine world of music publishing.

I am especially grateful to Henrik Bogdan for his initial acceptance and subsequent guidance of the book through its publication in the Oxford Studies in Western Esotericism series—he has been, as is said, a "marvel." In addition, I would like to thank those at Oxford University Press who have borne this project along—and Rachel Ruisard and Cynthia Read, in particular, deserve my appreciation. The production and copyediting skills of Narayanan S. and Leslie Anglin, respectively, improved the book greatly, as did two anonymous reviewers of the manuscript, whose suggested amendments also helped to advance it in significant ways. Lindsay Seers was kind enough to provide help in sourcing some of the images in the text.

Finally, I must pay a debt to my family: James, Eoin, and Aoife first, who deserve much sympathy for all the nights that their Dad stayed awake at work on the book (with some resulting grumpiness the next morning perhaps, after too little sleep); my sister Margaret, for demonstrating the patience and stoicism of an older sibling; and, finally, my partner Laura Cull Ó Maoilearca—my co-conspirator in all things spiritual and material, a mystic and a woman of action, but most importantly the *élan* that has given this work life from its initial gestation through to its eventual materialization. That *élan* comes to Laura from her late father, Roger Cull, who was a mix of science and art, earth and ether as well, and to whose spirit I dedicate this book.

Prologue: A Reciprocity of Acceleration

Among the many challenging ideas found in the works of Henri Bergson, one of the strangest, and most difficult, concerns what he called "complete relativity." This concept appears in his penultimate monograph, *Duration and Simultaneity*. This text gathered ideas concerning Bergson's infamous clash with Albert Einstein at the Société française de philosophie in 1922.[1] At the center of their disagreement lies a difference in attitude toward "Langevin's paradox," or the "twin's paradox," first put forward in 1911 by the physicist Paul Langevin in his own exploration of Einstein's special theory of relativity (STR). This paradox concerns a thought experiment where one "voyager," Paul, sends his twin brother, Peter, off in a rocket at a speed just less than that of light.[2] After a year, the rocket turns around and heads back to earth at the exact same velocity. Peter gets out after what has now been a two-year journey in the rocket only to discover that Paul has "aged" two hundred years "and has long been in his grave."[3]

This is a predicted result from STR due to Peter traveling close to the speed of light, which retards the aging process (following Einstein's theory).[4] Understood as two (biological) clocks, Peter's velocity relative to Paul allows him to age more slowly than Paul. Peter cannot reverse time, but he does retard it, at least relative to Paul. Yet it might still be asked: why is it *Paul's* aging alone that quickens relative to Peter? After all, in a consistent relativism of time, surely Paul could be seen as traveling at near to the speed of light *relative to Peter*—their speeds are reciprocal and covary—in which case, there would be no age difference between the two at all.[5] So here is the paradox: the answer to whose aging slows down and whose speeds up all depends on which frame of reference you decide to treat as immobile (and take your measurements from), and which is taken as being in motion relative to this frame. And, as this decision is entirely contingent, it leaves STR looking somewhat perverse as a theory.

Moreover, for Bergson, separated twin siblings are more than interchangeable clocks; they are living beings that cannot be substituted for each other without losing something in the process. From this vantage point, a clock is an impersonal abstraction of our lived experience of time (*durée*). Indeed, it is one that privileges only one frame of reference at a time in what Bergson dubs a "single" or "half-relativity" (*la demi-relativité*)—the frame of reference of the immobile measuring the mobile. In contrast to this seemingly flawed approach, Bergson proposed a "double" or "complete relativity" (*la relativité complete*) where there are no privileged reference frames and where no perspective can be completely represented by another in an act of substitution.[6] Every frame or perspective is equalized as *completely* individual. It is impossible for Paul to represent the personal experience of Peter fully, because experience is *more* than the representation of experience. For one to represent fully another's lived time, one must experience it in every detail, in person. *But this is impossible without actually being that other person*: "if I want to actually measure Peter's time, I must enter Peter's frame of reference; I must become Peter. If I want to actually measure Paul's time, I must take Paul's place."[7] Otherwise, all I am left with is my virtual image of Paul, not his actuality. Ultimately, STR is predicated fallaciously on "a time or a space [that is] always virtual and merely imagined, never real and experienced." Its "essence" is to "rank the real vision with the virtual visions" or to hide "the difference between the real and the virtual."[8]

Let's pause for a moment to think this through, because, in one way or another, it is crucial for everything that follows in this book. Fulfilling the counterfactual, "if I had been you . . ." entails me being *all* that you are, and hence *not* I-being-you (which would only bring along non-you baggage with it), but *you*-being-you (which even includes all of *your* kinds of self-alterity, auto-differentiation, etc.). We need a *complete* history (material, psychological, and social) to "transform" one person genuinely into a real other person (rather than merely an abstraction of that other): this would be an exhaustive factual analysis of that person-there-and-then that only *that* person-there-and-then can embody.[9]

This emphasis on haecceity, on the *thisness* of this temporal perspective (a real time that is always lived by an actual someone, somewhere) is not to reinstate a totalizing logic of self-identity, hermetically sealed off from all alterity, however. Indeed, to circumvent the dichotomies associated with STR, it is precisely the logic of separation (Peter *or* Paul) that must be overcome. The scene is thereby set for alternative logics, logics based on objects that are not *only* solid, hard bodies impervious to substitution with each other, but also fluid ones, watery and gaseous ones, or even sonic ones. This will involve performative, imagistic, and diagrammatic thinking, where some things can indeed be this *and* that, here *and* there, but not through a transcendent act of substitution (*my* representation of you standing in for you), so much as an immanent act of *partial* self-expansion, alteration, or bifurcation. To follow this work, we will need different logics that *come from* different kinds of things. Some of these logics will appear standardly "philosophical" or rigorous in a "hard" material sense; but some others will appear (or will be named) "mystical," "occult," or "spiritual." As if that's a bad thing.

Therefore, the stipulation that *this* is not *that* (that Peter is not Paul) need not be seen as an immovable obstacle but a creative constraint, because to voyage or travel—be it in time or space—is not a matter of mere representation between solid bodies. Transport involves a transfer of being, too—a qualitative change subtends (and "supertends") every quantitative one. If the voyaging siblings *could be* ontologically interchangeable, it would not be as wholes, but as moving, fluid, and luminous parts, within other "wholes" that are themselves mutating. They would be alter egos altering each other mutually within "larger" processes. These "parts" are not separate, impenetrable things, but lines of moving continuity which flow heterogeneously. And, finally, these "heterogeneous continuities" would embody the *thisness* or *thatness* of each partial perspective—nonsubstitutable from the outside precisely because they are mobile, moving *inside* duration (at various foliated levels). Following an alternative way of thinking, this logic might also be called a "Tattwa Vision," the hermetic practice of perceiving "thatness" in order to undertake another kind of cosmic voyage.

This book is dedicated to the strange voyages taken by two figures from history whose reciprocal accelerations took them far apart from each other on one level, and yet who also remained within an ongoing, "covarying" change, a continuous movement of alteration.[10]

Strange Memory

An Introduction in Five Parts

> I believe precisely that, at the base of all our mystical states, there are techniques of the body which have not been studied. . . . I think that there are necessarily biological means to enter into "communication with God".
>
> —Marcel Mauss, "Body Techniques"[1]

Zelator

A lifetime ago in 1990, I shared a London house with a ragbag group of fledging academics. Like me, they were working in the city at various part-time jobs such as "desktop publishing," proofreading, or legal services, while waiting to begin their doctoral studies in the autumn. I was going to work on Bergson at University College, London—at that time an exotic endeavor, both for me and the College (Bergson Studies has become more mainstream since then). One evening in and around March time, I ended up in the unenviable position of trying to explain Bergson's ideas about time and memory to a friend of a friend. This was at our own house party and, despite loud music playing, I did my best to educate the fellow. I should add that this chap was already a philosophy graduate, but he clearly needed the benefit of my learning nonetheless (he was also taller than me, better looking, and much more successful with the opposite sex, but there was nothing I could do about all that). Having rehearsed my clarification of Bergsonism a number of times previously, its dénouement was always at the point when I would explain how, ordinarily, "we think that memory is the mental faculty that allows *us* to recall the *past*, whereas, for Bergson . . ." But here, my listener interrupted and finished the sentence for me: "whereas with Bergson, memory is when the *past* recalls *us*. Yes, yes." He was also a clever clogs.[2] This episode must have grated

Vestiges of a Philosophy. John Ó Maoilearca, Oxford University Press. © Oxford University Press 2023.
DOI: 10.1093/oso/9780197613917.003.0001

on me for a while as it is one of the few things I can easily recollect from that period of my life.

This thesis of memory as ontological, as a *real* persistence of the past in our psychic lives, obviously did not come to life with Bergson alone: in various forms it harks back to the Renaissance (the spheres of the universe as memory system) and then ever further to Plato's *anamnesis* (recollection not merely as knowledge *of* the past but knowledge from a past life abiding within us as the soul travels from one life to another—metempsychosis). The idea that memory is a form of (mental) time travel can be understood cognitively rather than ontologically, of course, wherein it is only a representation of the past, albeit one that has real effects in the present.[3] This is the way it is understood in numerous psychological studies, the most well-known possibly being Ellen Langer's "Counter Clockwise Study" in 1979. This experiment involved eight elderly men living for a week in a residential retreat that re-created the social and physical environment of 1959. After the week was over, all eight appeared to have grown younger as a result, be that understood in terms of cognitive or physical health. Their attitude—conditioned within a kind of "Proustian space"—reversed the effects of the aging process to render them younger, as measured on a number of levels (physical strength, perception, cognition, taste, hearing, and visual thresholds). The house they entered was a figurative time slip of sorts: Perry Como played on a vintage radio; *The Ed Sullivan Show* shone from a black-and-white TV; all the books and magazines in the house were period correct. Nor were there any mirrors in the house that might break this spell. Moreover, the eight men in the experimental group were instructed to behave, to act, just as if it really were 1959 now, rather than to reminisce *about* 1959 from the current year of 1979. Meanwhile, a control group in another house "remained" in 1979 and only had to recollect the life they had in 1959. In them, no significant changes were detected at the end of the exercise.[4] The eight in the experimental group, however, exited the house as different people, analogically de-aged.[5] Yet, of course, beyond the confines of this house, everything was still in "1979": though the effects of some of the men's advancing years might have been tempered, nobody conducting this experiment was claiming that time itself was really put in reverse, inside or outside of the house.

The idea of a real (psychological) time machine—one where *you*, or some aspect of you, *are* the machine—was not being entertained in this experiment. Some films, on the other hand, have flirted with this idea. One of them is Jeannot Szwarc's *Somewhere in Time* (1980), which was filmed at about the same time as the "Counter Clockwise" experiment. The protagonist of the story, played by Christopher Reeve, travels from 1980 back to 1912 through sheer force of will—achieved through self-hypnosis, a prepared environment in an old hotel (another "Proustian space"), and performative acts (dressing and behaving as though it actually were 1912). This story can also be compared, therefore, with Bergson's thesis that memory is a moment in which the past in itself returns. The first thing that connects them is the use of "Proustian space"—environmental stimuli that facilitate the return of the past. Indeed, is it merely a coincidence that the cousin of Bergson's wife, Louise Neuberger, and the best man at their wedding, was Marcel Proust? What mutual influence Proust and Bergson may have had has frequently been debated over the years in terms of the similarities and dissimilarities between their approaches to memory and the past. The verdict has usually been that there is indeed some connection between them, but that Bergson's is a more voluntarist theory: through an amplification of perception, more of the past enters into the present and extends it. That amplification does not come primarily through involuntary happenstance as with Proust (an unanticipated taste, smell, or sound), but through active work upon our attention toward *both* the environment and our "inner" experience of it.[6] This extension is not "all in the head" as a mental set of representations either, *pace* the cognitivist approach in modern psychology. And this is where Bergson's stance is both more complicated than some, and quite novel (for any "clever clogs" still reading).

The following quote from Bergson's 1911 lecture at Oxford, "The Perception of Change," captures a sense of this:

> Let us reflect for a moment on this "present" which alone is considered to have existence. What precisely is the present? [...] My present, at this moment, is the sentence I am pronouncing. But it is so because I want to limit the field of my attention to my sentence. This attention is something that *can be made longer or shorter*, like the interval between the two points of a compass. [...] Let us go further: an attention which could be extended indefinitely would embrace, along with the preceding sentence, all the anterior phrases of the lecture and the events which preceded the lecture, and as large a portion of *what we call* our past *as desired*.[7]

One year later, in a lecture given in Paris on "The Soul and the Body," Bergson attempts to "push the argument to its limit" by imagining a single sentence "lasting for years": "well, I believe that our whole psychical existence is something just like this single sentence, continued since the first awakening of consciousness, interspersed with commas, but never broken by full stops. And consequently I believe that our whole past still exists."[8] Attention is the time machine for Bergson. Indeed, one might even say that each of us suffers from some degree of attention-deficit disorder, only it is one which is species-specific, with (perhaps) only a few artists, mystics, and so-called madmen, as we will see, being less "disordered" than the rest of us.

In extending this attention (by whatever means) what we call our "past" is embraced within what we call our "present." The former distends the latter. So far, so "merely" psychological, perhaps. After all, it is only a matter, for now, of what we *call* "past" and "present." Yet Bergson seems to hedge his bets between psychology and ontology by remaining unclear as to what is being maintained here—my past as I remember it, or *the* past itself. Ordinarily, we would say that there is a major difference between the two, yet Bergson invariably fails to make the distinction, speaking interchangeably about "my past," "memory," and "the past."[9] On one page of his 1907 book *Creative Evolution*, for instance, he writes that "the piling up of the past upon the past goes on without relaxation." Only then does he say on the next page that "it is with our entire past, including the original bent of our soul, that we desire, will and act," and later again that "from this survival of the past it follows that consciousness cannot go through the same state twice."[10] So, once more, though it is I who actively remembers from the present moment, what returns is not a recollection, but the past in which I reside (my past is the past).

Ultimately, most commentators agree on this one point as regards Bergson's theory of memory—for him the past is a real agent, alive and kicking, in one form or another: "it is we who are in time, rather than time that is in us" (Grosz); "we are not 'in' time, in the manner that objects occupy parts of space. We *are* time, unfolding at different speeds" (Khandker); "rather than conceiving of memory as a way of relating to the past from the perspective of the present, Bergson regularly equates memory with the totality of one's past as it is preserved in itself" (Perri); "the past is not in the past but in a present which exists virtually and which lies below and beyond the time of adaptation" (Mourélos).[11] I could go on (don't worry, I won't). Nicolas de Warren calls all this "Bergson's Copernican Revolution" whereby consciousness as a whole does not move from the present to the past, but "from the past to the present, from memory to perception."[12] When I remember, I do not reach from the present into the past, but a part of the past extends my present, that is, my attention toward reality. It *distributes* my perception in space and time. Consequently, the agency is twofold, belonging both to me (it is *my* act of attention-recollection) and the past (whence the recollection emanates).

Ipsissimus

Strange ideas to be sure, then, and yet, despite some appearances to the contrary, this is not a Bergsonian idealism that would render the world as being "for me," the real as *my* idea, or as an artifact of language, a product of desire, power, difference, or whatever else. Bergsonism has always proposed something between realism and idealism—ideas related to the world realistically. To answer the question, "What returns in memory?" therefore, with only ever one kind of part—an idea, a representation, or even more concretely, an affect, an attitude, or a bodily relation, would still confuse one part for the whole. What returns is the real past itself, in part. And ideas, too, are real, for of course they are parts of the real as well. The real past sometimes returns in part as idea, but oftentimes in many other forms. As *Matter and Memory* puts it:

> Between this perception of matter and matter itself there is but a difference of degree and not of kind . . . the relation of the part to the whole. . . .
> My consciousness of matter is no longer either subjective . . . or relative. . . . It is not subjective, for it is in things rather than in me. It is not relative, because the relation between "phenomenon" and the "thing" is not that of appearance to reality, but merely that of the part to the whole.[13]

Mereology. In this part-whole relation, complex though it must be (especially when understood as a *temporal* connection), we may find the solution to how "my past" and "the past" become so interchangeable for Bergson (where personal memory dovetails with the historical past), so that hopefully the mysterious idea of the past remembering (me) in my act of remembering the past becomes less perplexing. A part-whole relation, *but one that is taken in time rather than space*, creates a series of continuities: these are indivisible changes, ones that are themselves "within" another change that itself changes (that is, they are "in" *durée*). As Jean Hyppolite tried to explain as far back as 1949: "this duration—which is pure succession, the extension of the past into the present and therefore already memory—is not a series of distinct terms outside of one another, nor a coexistence of the past with the present. But rather, it manifests the indivisibility of a change, a change that, as Bergson notes in chapter four of *Matter and Memory*, undoubtedly endures."[14]

Change changes—so there is not one monolithic or *homogeneous* continuity for Bergson (as Gaston Bachelard liked to portray it in his never-ending critique of duration), but a range of continuities with different durations strewn throughout the cosmos.[15] Indeed, they are the cosmos: continuities of bodies, large and small, of spatial arrangements, of ideas, of affects, of species, of phyla, and so on—each enduring at different, changing, and foliated levels of tension (or "tone" as Trevor Perri puts it).[16] What unites these temporal parts, if only partially, is not containment within any one single, transcendent timeline, but this tone or level of tension. It is something immanently temporal that we will call "covariance." What makes one temporal part *that* part of *this* whole (which is itself another part of another whole) is the *durée* it shares with others, its covariance.

Admittedly, the phenomenology of grief, for instance, will offer a counterexample to all this talk of continuity, especially when it is phrased in watery metaphors of "flow," "streams," "fluids," or "waves." Grief, by contrast, blocks—it stops. Grief and mourning (or even more severely, trauma) are experienced by many as a *halt in time*, a stoppage of time in its supposed "flow." All the clocks are stopped, and time freezes within either a past traumatic event or a perpetual present of loss. These clocks are mechanical, of course, but to resort to that fact here would be a crude response. Nor do we need to invoke the truism that "time heals all wounds," or even retort that our biological clocks are immune, or at least indifferent, to the psychological phenomena of suffering (they are not, by the way). It is not a coincidence that the Indo-European root for memory is *(s)mer*—which means "to mourn," and that the Germanic root is *smerd*—which means "pain." As the psychologist Patrick McNamara notes in this regard, "memory's deep roots extend back into mourning."[17] In fact, such a wholly different experience of time, the seemingly complete restriction of its flow, is precisely evidence for exactly the multiplicity of times being put forward here. Time flows differently on different planes, sometimes in such felt experiences of endured *deceleration* that it indeed feels as if at a complete standstill. In truth, the intimate connections between grief, mourning, and memory are precisely some of the *different* ways in which the past survives within the present, or rather remains indivisible within *a* present.

This question of variances (fast, slow, flowing, blocked), of different parts, also demonstrates just how inadequate the language of "one *or* many" is when applied to time. And with that, the logic of separable solids proves itself unfit for discussing identity, individuality, or unity (*versus* their putative opposites in generality, divisibility, and multiplicity). To overcome this dilemma, Bergson invented assorted formulas for *durée*, such as "a *moving continuity* . . . in which everything changes and yet remains the same," or that which is "ever the same and ever changing."[18] Continuity versus discontinuity, therefore, is a false opposition when one thinks of time as coming in different varieties, with no one time transcending all others (Newton's "absolute" time that "flows equably without regard to anything external"—the putative one-dimensional clock-time of the universe). The error lies in assuming a certain *continuity of the same, of homogeneity, irrespective of whichever absolute measures out and orients that sameness (time as container, or as arrow, or as increasing entropy, or its opposite, increasing complexity, and so on).*[19] In what covaries, therefore, we will suggest that the things that do remain the same, that continue, do so in diverse ways. Only three of these will take up most of our investigative efforts here: historical (in ways that allude to what we call "influence" but also go beyond it), philosophical (a conceptual lineage of sorts), and psycho-physical (as material, spiritual, and even art-cultural covariances).

Undoubtedly, the term "covariance" has its technical meaning in mathematics and statistics (concerning the interrelations between two or more variable quantities that remain unchanging), but its literal sense as a complex relation of movements, as an echo of variability across temporal levels, is where it is put to use here. Bergson himself talks of a simple version of this covariance with an ordinary example of train travel:

> Movement is reality itself, and what we call immobility is a certain state of things analogous to that produced when two trains move at the same speed, in the same direction, on parallel tracks: each of the two trains is then immovable to the travellers seated in the other. But a situation of this kind which, after all, is exceptional, seems to us to be the regular and normal situation, because it is what permits us to act upon things and also permits things to act upon us: the travellers in the two trains can hold out their hands to one another through the door and talk to one another only if they are "immobile," that is to say, if they are going in the same direction at the same speed. "Immobility" being the prerequisite for our action, we set it up

as a reality, we make of it an absolute, and we see in movement something which is superimposed.[20]

Immobility is a complexity of mobilities. This is not a relationship between substances, the intentional subject, say, or its intended object, but between changes, variations. We heard earlier that, in the Special Theory of Relativity what is deemed to be moving or not is relative to the frame of reference one adopts. For Bergson, however, when two real movements are covarying, they *create an immobility, a seemingly invariant continuity between themselves.* There is a continuity between temporally separated processes, becomings that share the same vector but not the same time or duration. We must take note, nevertheless: the continuity is itself what Bergson elsewhere called a *"variation perpétuelle,"* constantly (invariantly) moving, albeit more slowly.[21] Nothing is perfectly still, absolutely immobile: if everything moves, though, it is not as *measured* within one transcendent time, but simply as experienced within a "larger" one, a different temporal scale.

Of course, the two trains in the quotation above are separated by space. But if the movements in our extended train image are "separated" in time, how would we connect them? And who are we to do so? If they are separate *in time*, then there is no transcendental simultaneity to measure and contain the covariance (a view from nowhen). Perhaps, therefore, the covariance is real but can only be experienced immanently, *within the phenomenon*, as the physicist and philosopher Karen Barad would say—in a well-formed appearance. Covariance: when the relation between two changes (variance) remains constant—a "changing with" or "with-change," *Mitveränderung, Mitvarianz* (perhaps it sounds better in cod-German?).

Theoricus

But I am getting far ahead of myself. To lay my cards on the table, the strangeness of Bergson that I mentioned at the outset is not restricted to a number of conceptual peculiarities or inconsistences found in odd corners of his work. It concerns the entire thrust of his thought as a philosopher, one following the best scientific data of the day from psychology, biology, and physics, and yet also enframing them within a context where the physical world is understood as movement, energy, and force, alongside of which lie many other forces that might be dubbed physical and "spiritual" as well. It concerns a philosopher who reputedly denounced magic and publicly distanced himself from mysticism for most of his career, only to dedicate his last major work to tackling both, with mysticism rerendered as a kind of activity or movement rather than intellectual contemplation or private ecstasy.[22] It also concerns a philosopher who increasingly withdrew from public life with age, not in order to stop his pursuit of philosophical knowledge so much as to conduct his enquiries in private, for they were, as he confessed, only "for me." And, finally, it must concern *Matter and Memory*, if not the best known, certainly the most peculiar of all Bergson's books. Published in 1896, the strangeness of *Matter and Memory* comes from two elements: a first chapter that performs a bizarre thought experiment that equates the entire universe, indeed all being, with light—a light that shines, reflects, and refracts upon itself within a set of images; and a third chapter that diagrammatizes memory as a great cone, or rather as a conical past in itself within which *my* past moves via expanded or contracted attention.

Yet all of these concerns only comprise half of our story. Most importantly, this strangeness must invoke Henri Bergson's sister, Mina Bergson, a.k.a. Moina Mathers (or Moina Bergson Mathers), spiritualist and mystic, skryer, astral traveller, and image-maker. Mina was at the height of her powers in the 1890s, running an important Occult society, producing mystical artwork, and by the end of the decade practising the Egyptian mysteries of Isis in Parisian theaters—all at precisely the same time that her brother Henri was writing *Matter and Memory* and later invested as Professor of Classical Philosophy at the Collège de France. He was already a leading figure within the French academy by this time, eventually becoming the most renowned European philosopher in the first years of the following century. She was his seemingly estranged sister, though in her own right already celebrated as a feminist and occultist. Brother and sister were living in Paris, working simultaneously through seemingly very different but nonetheless complementary approaches to questions concerning the nature of matter, spirit, and their interaction. These are the separated siblings at the heart of our enquiry, whose covarying ideas will be analyzed on the basis of a logic of reciprocal acceleration, a watery, endosmotic logic of two lives sharing many strange ideas.

In this book, then, I will be examining the writings and recorded practices of Mina Bergson/Moina Mathers, their rarity notwithstanding, alongside those of her sibling. With her husband, Samuel MacGregor Mathers, Mina Bergson led the "Hermetic Order of the Golden Dawn" all through the 1890s, and subsequently the "Rosicrucian Order of the Alpha et Omega" from 1903 (eventually taking over as its sole head a little after Samuel's death in 1918).[23] She did this while living in Paris and performing public rites as one part of the Order's activities, the other involving private rituals of initiation and advancement in occult learning. Such was her fame in the last decade of the nineteenth century that historian Dennis Denisoff has described her and Samuel as the "neo-pagan power couple" of the *Belle Époque*.[24]

What did they do, then—what was the purpose of such Orders as the Golden Dawn? This simple description from Christopher Armstrong initially sums it up well: "the acquisition of a certain 'gnosis' or private experiential contact with ultimate realities through the deliberate deployment of incantations and rituals, drawn from various sources, some genuinely ancient and associated with the historic Rosicrucian movement, some ostensibly archaic but in fact of very recent concoction."[25] *Pace* Armstrong's jibe about "concoction" by the Golden Dawn, their public performances were never intended to be historically accurate. They were creative and artistic invocations—a "performance art," according to Denisoff, with ceremonies that were, as Frederic Lees described them at the time, "artistic in the extreme."[26] Performed at the Théâtre La Bodinière and other secret locations in Paris, Mina Bergson, dressed as high priestess Anari, would invoke the goddess Isis materially, immanently, and in person.[27] (Parenthetically, whereas an *evocation* in Enochian magic brings a spirit into the world as a separate entity, in an *invocation* the spirit is channeled by the medium into another body, her own being a common choice for such embodiment: she is not a means of communication so much as an incarnation of spirit, a moving conduit that, as we will see, works through mimetic performance as well as symbolism.)[28] Isis, who is first recorded c. 2350–2100 BCE, is the Egyptian goddess of life, the all-encompassing mother, a moon goddess, as well as the goddess of nourishment, healing, and magic (in the Osiris Myth, she brings her brother, Osiris, partially back from the dead).[29] So important for the Golden Dawn were these Isis rites, moreover, that after 1900 Samuel and Mina would refer to all their work as part of the "Isis movement."[30] That a *goddess* was central to the Golden Dawn is not surprising given the feminist orientation of many of its principles: the Golden Dawn preached the equality of the sexes on all fronts, as well as other radical causes in that era, such as animal rights and vegetarianism.[31] In our efforts here to recover Mina Bergson's ideas, it will also be necessary to examine a number of specific facets contained within this image of a feminine, divine "movement," and thereby a means to see it equally as an assembly of continuities, of covariants.

Reconnecting Henri Bergson's peculiar theory of memory with his ultra-realism toward the past (it lives, it exists), while arguing for certain "spiritualist" and even occult underpinnings to this connection (that coincide with some of his sister's practices), is far from a novel type of enterprise in the history of ideas, however. Be it one within a philosophical lineage (G. W. F. Hegel's gnosticism, Gilles Deleuze's post-Kantian esotericism, or the mystical sources of existentialism, say), or a scientific one (Newton and alchemy, for instance), looking for such reflections in a dark mirror is not an uncommon form of investigation.[32] All the same, as Joshua Ramey cautions us, there remains a "contemporary ambivalence over the validity and significance of esoteric, let alone 'occult,' apprehensions of nature and mind" such that a certain "political risk" comes with any such reading, especially in the face of the materialist worldview that currently dominates philosophy and "theory" in general. If the risk is worth taking, therefore, it is, as he says, because the "marginalization of hermetic traditions . . . constitutes a symptomatic repression of the complexity of both the history of modern philosophy and the stakes of contemporary culture, which is, from the internet to the cinema, completely obsessed with magic and with the occult."[33] As Henri Bergson is increasingly being enfolded within the history of philosophy as a known quantity, a domesticated figure with a few odd views in the philosophy of mind and metaphysics of time ("memory is when the past recalls us," yes, yes), it remains important to remind ourselves of just how wild many of his ideas were and remain, even today. This is not to maintain a stance of perpetual outsider—a gratuitous heterodoxy or exoticism—but to reinscribe that strangeness within more mainstream philosophy. What Gilles Deleuze describes as "state philosophy," and François Laruelle as "standard philosophy," should be countered, or nonstandardized, with its estranged other, its alter ego. Following this imperative, we will introduce several overlooked covariants, some historical, others more contemporary in theme, at various junctures through the course of the book.

Philosophus

One of those contemporary themes is materialism. A good number of terms with seemingly *immaterial* connotations have already been offered here—the spiritual, the psychical, magic—and others, too, might be added, such as gnosticism, hermeticism, occultism, and mysticism. Unsurprisingly, most, if not all, are anathema to contemporary discourses around materialism. So, we ask, is this attitude justified? Undoubtedly, several approaches in both ontology and philosophy of mind (especially the mind-body relation) have gathered under the banner of a "new materialism" in the first two decades of the twenty-first century. Though this particular title covers a wide range of materialisms, variously espoused through biology, neurology, physics, and even mathematics, they were and for now remain unquestionably part of mainstream European thought in many circles. More broadly still, "materialism" as such—be it "new" or "old," "historical," "transcendental," or even "performative"—still today represents the received wisdom in much contemporary philosophy. Whereas small corners within Anglo-American "analytic" philosophy have of late attempted to rehabilitate the spiritual—or consciousness—through panpsychism (in the work of Galen Strawson and David Charmers, for instance), or the process thought of Whitehead and his heirs, the European approach seems happiest when keeping a safe distance from anything with even a hint of the immaterial about it. Yet, as we will see, there are even more heterodox models of mind available to us than these Anglo-American views, ones that might be sustained without necessarily being accompanied with such (incompatible) associates as the immaterial, the ideal, or the disembodied.

The most significant and current European materialism is undoubtedly this "new materialism." It is built upon two premises that are noteworthy for our study. The first concerns what counts as "new" in its understanding of matter. Though Christopher Gamble, Joshua Hanan, and Thomas Nail argue in their 2019 study of the movement that "there is currently no single definition of new materialism," they do add that they all share the view that there was a "perceived neglect or diminishment of matter in the dominant Euro-Western tradition as a passive substance intrinsically devoid of meaning."[34] Whereas modern materialism was defined by "the passivity of matter insofar as matter is what is caused or moved by something else: vital and causal forces or natural laws of motion," the new materialists emphasize how "matter is 'alive,' 'lively,' 'vibrant,' 'dynamic,' 'agentive,' and thus active."[35] In sum, this is a view of matter that is neither physicalist nor mechanistic in the senses taken by many of the eighteenth- and nineteenth-century *reductive* materialisms, with physics deemed the supervening science that treats of ultimately inert, passive, and atomistic quantities in calculable, determined motion. Wholes were deemed epiphenomenal in one way or another in this view, and only an analysis into composite parts revealed the truth of the matter. Indeed, such approaches more or less continued well into the twentieth century in positivist philosophies, with only very recent developments, such as "New Mechanical Philosophy" (or "New Mechanism"), tempering the views held by many in this tradition.[36]

By contrast, new materialism loosely follows Gestalt principles and deems matter to form complex, nonlinear, dynamic wholes that are not the sum of their parts. This focus on the *micro* by both old and new materialisms—in physics to be sure but also in biology (stem cells) and cognitive science (neural plasticity, embryonic epigenesis)—is what Sam Coleman calls "smallism": the idea that truth resides in the smallest particulars of reality (which may clump together to form larger wholes); that "the ontological truth is to be found with the small, or with all the "smalls" in all their innumerable multiplicity."[37] In the new materialism, however, wholes are also real, even though emergent—their properties constitute a genuinely different level of reality, albeit that they are generated by the complex interactions of their smaller, constitutive elements. This *emergence* of the larger from the smaller, one that is neither reductive (the large does not reduce entirely to the small) nor mechanistic (such small matter is not passive), is a crucial aspect for much of this thinking. The question of level and scale, therefore, both spatial and temporal, will be critical in what follows here, too.

Whether it be Quentin Meillassoux's "mathemic" valorization of contingency, the idea of "plasticity" in Catherine Malabou's neurophilosophy, entanglement in Karen Barad's philosophy of physics, or "vibrant matter" in Jane Bennett's neo-vitalism, we can also see a second, less explicit premise of new materialism in much of its work: namely, that whatever number of emergent, nonreducible properties are allowed to matter, the idea of *spirit* cannot be added to the list. Nonreduced materiality alone prevails, while a transcendent, Platonist notion of spirit—the only one deemed possible by some—remains the conceptual outsider to be either eliminated or simply ignored. As John Zammito writes: "one of the essentially contested issues surrounding the new materialism is how to conceive the relation of 'spirit' to the natural."[38] This is why the possibility of a *nontranscendent* (or immanent) spirit is rarely, if ever, entertained. This is where some historical research may be of use, in particular around the school of "French Spiritualism." This was a loose tradition of thought that lasted from the late eighteenth century up to Henri Bergson himself as its final representative. Despite its name, it was not a school of the occult, but what we might nowadays call a nondualist, nonreductive approach to mind and body. These earlier French philosophers, including Maine de Biran (1766–1824), Félix Ravaisson (1813–1900), and Émile Boutroux (1845–1921), were equally determined to find a way in which matter and spirit could be thought together, but without turning to either dualism or reductionism. The place of spirit was retained in their research through *movement, duration*, and *habit*.[39] Many of their ideas will return in what follows.

Without falling for something like biologist Gerald Edelman's straw man argument—that is, the idea that anything other than the most parsimonious, scientistic, and nonsubjective approaches is simply turning physics into a "surrogate spook"—we can still admit that matter is weirder than many would allow.[40] And that is precisely where the "new materialists" are correct, although also where they are less "new" than proclaimed. For example, the materialism of *contingency* forwarded in Meillassoux's *Après la finitude* from 2006, actually reinvents, one hopes unwittingly, the ideas of Émile Boutroux, whose *De la contingence des lois de la nature* from 1874 argued for a similar contingency in the laws of nature. Only, and here's the twist, Boutroux argued his case *in the name of spiritualism*, not materialism. This makes Meillassoux's valorization of the contingency of nature in the name of materialism even more ironic. For Boutroux, the contingent is a sign of spirit, not mathematized matter. Having said that, we are not here to correct new materialism or detract from its valuable contributions to European philosophy. We wish to add to them.[41] As Adela Pinch writes, modern-day "trends in the humanities that embrace panpsychism, vibrant matter, object-oriented ontologies, and extended or dispersed conceptions of consciousness, could benefit from an examination of Victorian debates about panpsychism."[42] Both the panpsychists and spiritualists (in the French sense of the name) offer us alternative models for thinking about matter and its interrelations with human and nonhuman life, mind, and spirit. Indeed, in the example of Henri Bergson, we see an attempt to naturalize spirit via his concept of *durée*, without reducing or eliminating it.

We asked earlier whether the attitude of much contemporary materialist thought toward the category of spirit was justified. Behind this possibly simplistic question lies another, more complex one, however: can the category of the spiritual (expanded in terms of its allied names, the esoteric, the occult, the mystical, and so on) provide an added dimension to "materialism" in such a manner that neither reduces it nor inflates itself, but simply shows how the difference between the two might be considered a matter of temporal scale, of level or plane? A recent work from Larry Sommer McGrath is illuminating in this regard. In *Making Spirit Matter: Neurology, Psychology, and Selfhood in Modern France*, he writes that the spiritualism that emerged in France in the late nineteenth century was not like the spiritualism that went before—this was a "new spiritualism," or at least it was significantly different from older varieties because it had taken a scientific, and even materialist turn. As he reports on this particular reading of the issue: "the new spiritualism is not a new doctrine," one author wrote in 1884; "it is spiritualism renewed by science." The characterization of this transformation as a turn to materialism took hold thanks to a critic of the movement. A defender of the old guard decried what he saw as its abnegation in the form of "neo-materialism."[43] For Sommer McGrath, this critic was actually right and a "materialist moment" had now "inflected the spiritualist movement by the turn of the century." Moreover, the chief protagonist of this turn, Sommer McGrath contends, was Henri Bergson: "the thrust of his oeuvre, I argue, was to steer a materialized spiritualism into the twentieth century."[44] Not only was Henri Bergson the most "successful representative of the materialist turn in spiritualism," according to Sommer McGrath he "led a movement that operated with much more expansive notions of rationality, positivism, and materialism."[45] And here we see a clear dovetailing between this new, turn-of-the-century spiritualism with what is new in the new materialism we have currently, and it concerns a shared nonreductive approach to both matter and spirit:

> The charge of "neo-materialism" was revelatory. The accused never ascribed the label to themselves; yet, it was hardly a misnomer. [. . .] Unlike reductive materialisms, which conceptualized matter as the substratum and final explanation of spirit, this "neo-materialism"—and its leading practitioner, Henri Bergson—reimagined matter to enter into a partnership with the spiritual powers of memory, creativity, and action.[46]

Sommer McGrath is not alone in his more ecumenical interpretation of the spirit-matter relations at play among these thinkers. Jeremy Dunham writes that the "new spiritualists" were "inspired by developments in the life sciences [and] developed a theory of nature as open, creative, and evolving," while Mark Sinclair and Delphine Antoine-Mahut have argued that "spiritualism in the first half of the [nineteenth] century should be seen as a plural and open-ended development of a programme rather than as the reproduction of a one-track thought," and even that we "have to reject as simplistic and superficial standard characterizations of positivism and spiritualism as diametrically opposed."[47] And to round out these new, revisionist histories, we can turn to Jean Gayon, who argues furthermore that

> Bergson was a "spiritualistic positivist." This is not retrospective interpretation, something that I would formulate because it sounds like a nice paradox. It is the plain expression of the historical fact. Around 1900, "spiritualistic positivism" was the current name of a living tradition among certain French philosophers, such as Jules Lachelier or Émile Boutroux. Like Bergson, who was directly influenced by them, they emphasized a conception of the mind founded on spontaneity, contingency and indeterminism.[48]

What we see, then, is a clear reciprocal acceleration between the flight of new materialism away from old materialism—a flight that was inflected by properties also associated with spirit (creativity and contingency)—and the flight of the new spiritualism away from the old, whose own trajectory was modified by elements from material science. So, instead of talking of matter *or* spirit, we might talk in terms of continua, of contingency, creativity, and vitality. But again, these continua are not homogeneous, but themselves replete with qualitative change, with mutation.

And here is where we can also make a further point about *covariance*. In his essay, "Scale Variance and the Concept of Matter," Derek Woods speaks about the difference between "scale variance" (things that change with scale) and "scale invariance" (things that do not).[49] This notion builds on the work of philosopher of science Mariam Thalos and her concept of "scale freedom," which Woods interprets in his own work to mean "freedom from the notion that any single scale is the master scale." What Woods takes from this is the principle that "there is irreducible activity at every scale," and finally that "*matter* may not be the best concept for what the new materialism works to address."[50] The covariance, and covariants, we will talk about here concern a continuity formed through movements changing in concert: not as the *same* activity *simpliciter* but as different activities (plural) in some form of temporal reciprocity. And neither a spiritualism devoid of matter nor a materialism devoid of spirit can accommodate such continua.

Practicus

In all of this—Henri Bergson's ultra-realism toward the past and Mina Bergson's mystic invocations, aligned as spiritualist alter egos to certain aspects of new materialism—is it all going just a bit too far? Have we stretched Bergsonism to its breaking point? Vladimir Jankélévitch's reading of Henri Bergson may help us here. First, he commends us to *reinvent* Henri Bergson rather than be faithful to him: "Bergson's intention was not that we do again *what* he did but that we do again *as* he did. It is Bergsonian to look in the direction he shows us but not at all to go on and on about Bergsonism, about the place it occupies, about the right drawer in which to stow it away."[51] *The Bergsonian direction, the Bergsonian movement (not "Bergsonism"), is what continues Bergson.* And this unfaithful fidelity is also a kind of love:

> Bergson, for the first time, gives us a sense that philosophy is an act that each of us undertakes on his own account, as if he were alone in the world, as if he were the first to do it, as if no one had ever done it before him. Naturally, that is not true, but one must act *as if*. In this respect, the philosophical act resembles love. The one who does it redoes what millions of human beings have done before him. And yet he experiences what he does as something entirely new, unheard of, original, spring-like. For him, redoing is doing; for him, to start again is really to start; the one who loves for the first time is in his own way a brilliant inventor and improviser.[52]

In Henri Bergson's own words, "one knows, one understands only what one can in some measure reinvent."[53] This Bergsonian movement does not begin or end with Henri Bergson either (nor even with Mina Bergson as an equal protagonist). Each reinvention begins *as if* anew, like an act of love (what Alain Badiou would call an "event"). New materialism is one example of a presently widespread movement that is both itself and a reinvention. Yet some may still ask, what is the subject of such movements? What is being reinvented, what is being remade in these hetero-continuities? And the answer, it seems, is *all* kinds of different, heterogeneous beings: spatial (covariance all the way up, and down), temporal, affective, bodily, and conceptual (to name a few). There is an indefinite number of continuities in this continuist stance. We, however, will look at it through five domains in the following order: history, psychology, biology, philosophy, and physics.

In her book *Vibrant Matter*, Jane Bennett discusses Michel Serres's own discovery of structural invariance in the historical birth of physics: as far back Lucretius's *De Rerum Natura*, we see a powerful isomorphism at work:

> The Book V, on the world and nascent humanity, is traversed by the same laws as the Book IV, on perception; and these are the laws of matter found in Book II. Always the same whole, a multiplicity of elements, and always the same operations at work on these wholes. The method by structural invariants, generalised to the global stability of flowing movements, establishes materialism.[54]

Matter, perception, humanity, and world. The title of Serres's five-volume history of ideas, *Hermès*, invokes the messenger of the gods to signify a communication between the sciences and the arts, a translator that enables us to commute between different domains. Similarly, the Hermetic orders of the Middle Ages and after also invoked a seemingly simple principle of covariance, "as above, so below." Yet, as we will see later, this basic scalarity concealed something more sophisticated. Significantly, the Hermetic literature of antiquity and the Renaissance is based around a fictional character, Hermes Trismegistus, who was actually "a human composite figure possessing characteristics of the Egyptian god Thoth and the Greek god Hermes."[55] In other words, *he was invented*: a cultural appropriation that has been reappropriated, and reinvented, many times since in different eras and by different groups of people, large and small, many of them often seeking, by fabulation, origin stories with continuities, lineages, or traditions of their own.

In our own reinvention of such esoteric thinking, the five aforementioned covariants (history, psychology, biology, philosophy, and physics) will be named after five of the grades or levels found within the Golden Dawn (for reasons that will soon become clear). These levels are numbered and named as follows: *1° = 10° Zelator Covariant; 10° = 1° Ipsissimus Covariant; 2° = 9° Theoricus Covariant; 4° = 7° Philosophus Covariant;* and *3° = 8° Practicus Covariant*. Both names and numbers concern the position of the grade on the Kabbalistic "Tree of Life" or *Minutum Mundum* ("little world" or "little universe"), a hermetic diagram popularized by the Golden Dawn that structured divine reality as well as our mortal position within it, and knowledge of it (see Figure 1). The equals sign between the numbers is not an equation, by the way, but a graphic marker indicating a student's progress through

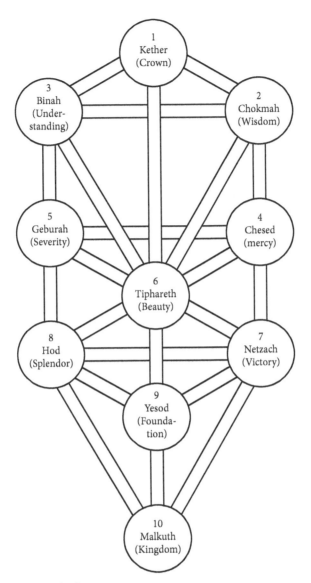

Figure 1 The Tree of Life

the system, how many grades have been completed (first number) and how many remain outstanding, in principle at least (second number).[56]

In this book, however, the diagram and its elements are used syncretically, bringing philosophical issues together with historical and spiritualist ones: for *Zelator*, the issue of discrete opposites versus continuities in the past relationship between spiritual/psychical research and its debunkers (zealots on both sides); while for *Ipsissimus* (or "superlative self"), we look at psychological studies of memory and the formation of identity. The remaining three grades are named after perspicuous issues among three particularly important figures associated with contemporary materialist thought: Jane Bennett (*Theoricus*)—studying the connections between seeing and unseeing as regards biological life, matter, and spirit; Catherine Malabou (*Philosophus*)— examining how a philosophy can remain "plastic" and continually mutate, even against its own ideas, and therewith open itself up to what Malabou calls "superstition"; and Karen Barad (*Practicus*)—the philosopher-physicist who relates subatomic theory to ethical and epistemological problems of identity, and so places practice and agency at the heart of reality—a gesture that we will extend further into art, and in particular what could be described as the "performance art" of Mina Bergson.[57] These staged encounters do not purport to be critiques, either negative or positive—I am not sufficiently expert on materialism to accomplish that—but they do orchestrate a number of salient ideas from these sources that should prove of interest for materialists and nonmaterialists of various hue.

It might have been noticed that these Kabbalistic grades are not in their original order on the Tree of Life. That is deliberate. Their disorder here reflects the fact that this structure of covariants is a philosophical experiment, an attempt to shape a set of ideas according to a nonstandard model, the hermetic one of the Golden Dawn. However, it does not share any of the ontological commitments of its source material. In this respect, we can think of this as an experiment in the spirit of François Laruelle's theory of "nonstandard philosophy." Laruelle's approach seeks to equalize different kinds of knowledge by flattening them: no one form is exemplary, *the* model of thought. Epistemic hierarchies are rejected because they are circular: be its authority based on logic, rigor, consistency, or scientific verification (through one or other privileged science), each model's claim to epistemic supremacy is ultimately question begging (or "auto-positional" as Laruelle would say) and can only ground itself through axiomatic presupposition.[58] Yet, for Laruelle, such flattening that does not make all philosophies equally *unreal* or *untrue* (the standard, albeit self-contradictory view of relativism), *but only equal.* At a minimum, they are equal as immanent parts of the Real (which is itself never defined, as that would simply establish a new authority, be it via materialism, idealism, even nihilism, and so on). In this Laruellean spirit, then, the hermetic grades of the Golden Dawn are only used by us as *a* model, and not *the* model; that is, they are adopted without any "religionist" commitment to their ontology, to what Wouter J. Hanegraaff describes as an "impossible dream of a 'history of truth.'"[59]

And this is why their grades are employed here in a disorderly fashion, or rather they are *flattened*: there is no hierarchy, teleology, or evolution of stages at work here. In one sense, however, the covariants themselves do "evolve" as they appear and reappear through the book: and that evolution is through their duration. Beginning quite small and almost as an aside from the structure of the main argument, they grow in scale until, by the end, the parts have virtually overwhelmed the whole. As such, the structure of the book performs a thesis that is sustained throughout (almost *ad nauseum*)—that any continuity harbors a discontinuity within itself, that is, a heterogeneity, an interference. Only, at this higher level, a new heterogeneous continuity of sameness and difference is thereby invented. I will leave the reader to discover any other elements that might covary (and so continue) between either the parts of the work or within each part. This is especially with regard to one *historical* covariance that hardly needs to be pointed out (though of course I will): that the three women and one nonbinary person who occupy most of these reflections comprise one spiritualist from the past and three materialists from the present.

$1° = 10°$ *Zelator Covariant*

In *The Bergsonian Controversy in France 1900–1914*, R. C. Grogin notes that the equivalent word in French for the English term "spiritualism" is not "spiritualisme," as one might expect, but "spiritisme." Spiritualism, as used in France, "denotes a system of belief in opposition to materialism."[1] Spiritism, however, dealt with the paranormal, the psychical, or the supernatural. Hence, the philosophical school of French Spiritualism, for instance, was one arguing for the irreducibility of mind to matter, or at least to a certain mechanistic conception of matter (as we already heard). Naturally, this raises the question as to what would be the equivalent English term for this French *spiritualisme*, if it is not "spiritualism." "Anti-reductionism" would be too antithetical, for there is also a positive account of mind rather than only a skeptical account of matter (or "opposition to materialism") running through this doctrine, albeit coming in different forms depending on whether one is looking at Maine de Biran, Ravaisson, Boutroux, Bergson, or any number of others. "Idealism," "immaterialism," or "subjectivism" would each also presume a common metaphysical monism that was not shared either. Even a "property dualism" would miss the mark in some cases. And this is especially true of Henri Bergson. As Jean Gayon writes:

> For Bergson, matter and mind are not substances. They are "tendencies" or "forces." These tendencies conflict and collaborate in many areas of human experience and, beyond, of reality. [. . .] For him, the mind/body problem (or more broadly the mind/matter problem) had to be examined in areas where these distinctions were obscure: phenomena of a high degree of material complexity, which can also be interpreted as "lower manifestations of the mind." The spiritualist/materialist debate is uninteresting and sterile if it focuses on the superior psychological faculties, understanding, reason, creative imagination.[2]

So let us leave names aside for now. In fact, even Anglo-French spiritualism/ *spiritisme* in the nineteenth century was not averse to the incorporation of

Vestiges of a Philosophy. John Ó Maoilearca, Oxford University Press. © Oxford University Press 2023.
DOI: 10.1093/oso/9780197613917.003.0002

the physical into its explanations of the paranormal, especially in the light of new scientific discoveries about the nature of matter. As Richard Noakes points out, new conceptions of "electricity, energy and ether offered possible physical explanations of telepathy, telekinesis and disembodied souls." In fact, a good amount of historical research has shown that in the nineteenth and twentieth centuries, "theories and ideas in psychology, biology, and physics flowed to and, occasionally, from psychical research"[3]

> X-rays seemed to behave like longitudinal and transverse etherial waves, radium emanations were startlingly more energetic than anticipated on the basis of energy conservation, and telepathic transmissions, spiritualistic levitation, and disembodied spirits defied fundamental notions of space, time, and matter.[4]

Such a seemingly powerful consilience between physics and psychics even left some "genuine" (read "old") spiritualists aghast. Those who claimed to be in contact with the spirits of the dead were up in arms, throwing doubt on the physicists' "brain wave" theories of telepathy in as much as they appeared to reduce the traces of departed spirits to merely latent powers of living minds.[5] Sometimes, scientific corroboration was the last thing desired.

More broadly still, a consilience of *ambition* between psychical and physical research was still recognized in some circles—and it was one concerning their *shared foundations*. As Mark Morrison observes, neo-alchemists, for example, were able to interpret the implications of "modern atomic theory in a way that emphasized the unity of matter (and even of energy)." In their view, it was oneness, rather than disunity and separation, that characterized the "major substratum of atomic theory," and all that was needed was to "spiritualize" this principle of fundamental unity. The idea of an "ever simpler and more basic unity" was never unique to the natural sciences, according to Morrison, and "unified field theories, and even the Theory of Everything in more recent physics" share a set of presumptions with hermetic and occult approaches.[6] (It is no surprise that the "God Particle" is as much a quasi-theological notion as it is a popular name for the Higgs Boson particle in modern physics.) That many ideas in physics involve statements about time, perception, the absolute, or individuality that sound not only metaphysical but mystical is not so interesting for us, however: what is significant are the different means through which mystics arrive at, and experience, their version of these views.[7]

And that *means* can cut both ways, either to re-enchant matter (inflate science) or reduce mind (deflate psychism). Richard Jones's work on the "philosophy of mysticism," for instance, concedes that an individual's mystical experience achieved through meditation (opening the "doors of perception," etc.), might also be realized through both more mundane methods (enjoying the beauty of nature, art, or music), as well as more pathological ones: emotional stress, grief, despair, illness, starvation, disability (e.g., epilepsy), brain injury, or sense deprivation.[8] And any of these ordinary methods can also serve to deflate one's spirits, in every sense.

Jones also points out that there are generally two types of reduction that can work to discredit mystical claims: *scientific* ones that see mystical states as "nothing but electrochemical activity in the brain or some other physical or biological phenomenon," and *sociocultural* reductions that interpret them as "social, psychological, or cultural phenomena."[9] Pamela Thurschwell's approach would be a sophisticated version of the latter. Following the example of Friedrich Kittler's work in media archaeology, spiritualism is read by her as a kind of "magical thinking" informed by the new kinds of reproduction and communication technologies that were emerging in the nineteenth century. Apparatuses like the telegraph and telephone "suggested that science could help annihilate distances that separate bodies and minds from each other." Suddenly, the claims of spiritualist mediums might be supported: "talking to the dead and talking on the phone both hold out the promise of previously unimaginable contact between people."[10] Yet the technology can also rebound on those employing it as a model. If mediumship is made analogous to a technology, perhaps the former's emergence as a cultural phenomenon at the same time as the introduction of the latter is more than just a coincidence. Thurschwell quotes Kittler to great effect on this matter:

> the tapping specters of the spiritualistic séances with their messages from the realm of the dead, appeared quite promptly at the moment of the invention of the Morse alphabet in 1837. Promptly, photographic plates— even and especially with the camera shutter closed—provided images of ghosts or specters which in their black and white fuzziness, only emphasized the moments of resemblance. Finally one of the ten uses Edison predicted . . . for the recently invented phonograph was to preserve the "last words of the dying."[11]

As Thurschwell then concludes, "there is always already a ghost in the machine, a telepath on the telephone wire": the spiritual is brought down to earth more with a tap than a thud.

Returning to Jones's work, it is notable how multilayered these reductions can be. Reductive approaches to mystical experience, "constructivists" as he dubs them, are wont to see mystical episodes as "genuine neurological events," but he adds that the "alleged cognitive content of all mystical experiences is *totally controlled* by the experiencer's *prior religious beliefs.* [. . .] No part of even a depth-mystical experience is unstructured—i.e., untouched by language or concept." Nature and nurture, brain and symbol, serve together against the supernatural. In the words of one such constructivist, Steven T. Katz:

> *there are NO pure (i.e., unmediated) experiences.* Neither mystical experience nor more ordinary forms of experience give any indication, or any grounds for believing that they are unmediated. That is to say, *all* experience is processed through, organized by, and makes itself available to us in extremely complex epistemological ways. The notion of unmediated experience seems, if not self-contradictory, at best empty.[12]

Katz puts it more pithily as follows: "what the Buddhist experiences as *nirvana* is different from what the Jew experiences as *devekuth.*" This is simply because "mystical experience is 'over-determined' by its socio-religious milieu."[13] Nothing is purely given—and all seeming givens are the product of selection and shaping. Yet where Jones refers to Katz and his followers as "constructivists," Katz himself prefers to describe his approach as "contextualist," and the crucial context for all experience, according to Katz, is *language*: "language," he contends, is "integral to mystical practice. This is not to exaggerate this fact or, yet, to attack the central issue of ineffability, but it is to begin to widen our parameters, to broaden our understanding, as to how language relates to mystical experience."[14]

However, these approaches can be double-edged, too. "Nonconstructivists" or "decontextualists"—arguing for the irreducibility of mystical experience—will reason that various cultural conceptualizations may indeed influence our interpretations of the spiritual, but that this "does not mean that they must be present during the depth-mystical experience itself."[15] There remains something that transcends every mediation. Against all such Kantian (constructive) approaches, "any postexperience intentional object is the product of memory and a conceptual scheme, but the experience itself is a direct awareness of a noumenon."[16] Memory here, funnily enough, plays the role of mediator and so introduces doubt because of its purported indirection. As the decontextualist Robert K. C. Forman argues, for instance, there are "PCEs [pure consciousness events]," which "show signs of being neither constructed nor shaped in either form, content, or process."[17] Forman sets out the initial case for these PCEs, not with accounts from mystics but with ordinary (though rare) psychological experiences. These are experiences anyone can replicate, and he turns to them simply to show that a pure, un-mediated experience *can* occur, and so therefore that not *all* experience is mediated, be it through language or any other social conduit. Forman's precedent PCE is that of a homogeneous perceptual field, or *Ganzfield*:

> Under conditions of steady or regular sensory input, in other words, senses and sensations are commonly forgotten. [...] just as the processes are parallel, the effect of such a recycling of a single subroutine is parallel with those of the *Ganzfeld* or the constant auditory stimulus. Not merely does the recycled stimulus itself ultimately fade, but there is a complete disappearance of any sense of thinking, perceiving, and so on. All perception and mental activity come to be forgotten. [...] Such an emptiness, it should be clear, is not like remembering something and applying it to form or reform visual information, rather it is more akin to a massive forgetting.[18]

The *Ganzfield* effect is interpreted by Forman as a "complete disappearance," "emptiness," or "massive forgetting." Whether the language of forgetting here is apt or not, it is significant that this liminal, yet ordinary nonmystical state is used to admit the possibility of extraordinary versions of these same states. As Forman continues in a later text:

> There are at least two epistemological modalities, or states of consciousness, available to the human being: ordinary and mystical. Ordinary experiences, thoughts, emotions, sensations, perceptions, and the like are intentional. Objects are encountered as distinct from the self. Their content is constantly changing. [...] Mystical experiences of the PCE type (and perhaps aspects of others) are, by contrast, nonintentional. One encounters or rests within awareness per se itself, however it is understood. The consciousness encountered therein is "experienced" as unchanging.[19]

Forman's final rehabilitation of decontextualism rests on the existence of these extraordinary mystical states, and the difference between them and their *linguistic expression*. Such expressions mediate the PCE in a language informed through various, ordinary "epistemological modalities."

This duality of experience versus expression is not new, of course, either among theorists of mysticism or philosophy: Henri Bergson himself also distinguished between the immediate experience of an intuition and its necessary distortion in any subsequent attempt to communicate that experience.[20] What Forman calls a "mystical PCE," Bergson called a "metaphysical intuition." In both cases, though, there is a special epistemological modality, one which Forman analyses as "our knowledge-by-identity of awareness" (which is nonlinguistic and nonconceptual)," and Bergson defines as "the *sympathy* by which one is transported into the interior of an object in order to coincide with what there is unique and consequently inexpressible in it."[21] Do note, though, the mundanity of the Bergsonian object in this immediate knowledge: it is not confined to religious states, or even liminal psychological ones, but is part and parcel of an everyday metaphysics of perception. An intuitive knowledge of *any perceptible object* is possible (which is then contrasted with a scientific/conceptual knowledge that analyses the object through its exterior appearances). In this respect, we might say that Bergsonian intuition propounds an everyday mysticism of object perception.

It may be said that we have been playing a little fast and loose in these last pages between different categories: the psychical (as parapsychological research), the spiritual (in both occult movements and mediumship), and the mystical (as an individual's private experience). Nonetheless, what they and indeed their opponents all share to some degree is a view of the *transcendent* nature of the putative reality underlying all these categories. As Jones puts it, from the mystical point of view:

> What is transcendent is not merely an *infinite amount* of something natural or some part of the natural realm that we cannot know, such as "dark energy," but something of another *type* altogether—something that in principle cannot be open to scientific study in whole or in part. Nor is it in a space beyond our spatiotemporal realm that encompasses it, although philosophers often treat it that way: it is something to which any phenomenal categories such as "space" would not apply. It is in an ontologically unique category.[22]

From the perspective of the practitioner of magic, this alternative ontology involves different sets of laws governing different kinds of objects. In *Persuasions of the Witch's Craft*, Tanya Luhrmann represents this stance as follows:

> The basic idea is that there are many different kinds of matter-like substances. Among them are psychic forces, granite rocks, imagined objects, spiritual essences and so forth. All of these substances interact with each other, but granite-like objects and spirit-like objects are governed by different natural laws. The point is that things which are normally thought not to exist (like a mental image of a polar bear, outside the imaging subject's mind) do exist, but in a different way, and under different laws, than do tables and chairs. Golden-hearted dragons are real, but not like brown-eyed anthropologists.[23]

Even though *different* versions of this general idea might be favored by different magicians, nevertheless, according to Luhrmann, "most of them view things imagined as a sort of stuff, which has an impact upon a tables-and-chairs reality."

This "magical realism," so to speak, raises another question from the Bergsonian vantage point, however: what if this alternative "stuff," these "different kinds of matter-like substance" that might not even fit our usual "phenomenal categories" like space—what if this stuff was not any kind of substance at all, within or without ordinary experience? In other words, what if it was rather a kind of temporal continuity that *always* operates immanently, only at different scales (be they *super-* or *sub-*), some of which, being so different from our own "norm," that they are taken as *para*-normal when all they are is *super*-normal—a continuation rather than an alternative? What we might call the "supernormal"—to give a new use to an old word—is the ordinary at a different temporal level, yet always in some *kind* of continuity with others.[24] Not one ulterior reality parallel to ours, but unattended aspects of a multilayered reality shared with indefinitely many others.

The *Zelator* grade, as its name would suggest, indicates all the energy of the initiate, the student, an absolute faith in the earth ("*Malkuth*" in the Tree of Life diagram), which, all the same, must not be taken as *unspiritual*.[25] Confidence in the power of the first name learned at the outset will soon give way to a continuism that sees names like "material" segue into the "spiritual" and "spirit," just as "psychical" research bleeds into "physics" research, spiritualism into "spiritisme," and so on. And such continuities represent what we will later call the "meta-spiritual."

1

Ordinary Mysticism, the Hyperbolic, and the Supernormal

Earlier, we heard Robert Forman discuss the difference between "ordinary" and "mystical" epistemological modalities. In addition, I have forwarded the idea that "*ordinarily*" we understand personal memory as a mental faculty of representation and the past as an impersonal, objective dimension of time that transcends mind, or, likewise, that we make ordinary distinctions between "my past" and "the past." I contrasted those ideas with Henri Bergson's strange views, especially the more alien versions of Bergsonism that often conflate or fuse such dyads. This has led to the suggestion that there may be something more outlandish still, even mystical, in his work. This is not, I should add, the same as the well-worn and rather tired refutation that all of his work is simply mystical nonsense (a basic name calling without any clarification as to what "mysticism" might mean in this or any context). It is instead a call to investigate some of the odd conflations operating in Henri Bergson's work, the "dynamic" monisms he utilizes in order to think through our ordinary dualities of thought and experience. We are not, then, pursuing an exercise in making Henri Bergson "spooky," or even spookier, but rather in comprehending the stranger elements of his philosophy within a *mundane* context—that memory is indeed a part of *the past*, but only a part of it. This is the proposal that a kind of real time travel through memory might be partially possible, but not in any *wholly impersonal* fashion (as in a machine traveling through time, for instance).

Elsewhere, I have written about a strategy of "supernormalization" that provides an exit from the stark duality of natural and supernatural, or of the normal and the paranormal.[1] It offers a paradigm that thinks only in terms of differences of *degree* rather than of *kind*. The category of the supernatural, as found in the arts, culture, philosophy, or even science ("spooky physics"), is rerendered as *structural*: a projected inconsistency or hyperbolic state of the

Vestiges of a Philosophy. John Ó Maoilearca, Oxford University Press. © Oxford University Press 2023.
DOI: 10.1093/oso/9780197613917.003.0003

"natural"; a placeholder for any "outside" whatever; or a liminal position that must be occupied by someone, thing, or property. For instance, as we know, Henri Bergson upheld an ultra-strong realism toward the past, arguing in *Matter and Memory* that the past persists as real, immanent *in* the present, and not merely as an *outside*, transcendent recollection of the past. In the same text, he describes how "when a memory reappears in consciousness, it produces on us the effect of a ghost," of a "mysterious apparition."[2] The past as specter as memory. Yet this paranormality is brought down to earth without reduction or elimination through a double maneuver: first, there is the seeming naturalistic reduction—the specter seen as merely a memory (reduction)—but then there is a second refraction whereby this ghost memory itself is inflated as a *real* part of the past. The reduction of the reduction. The part (memory) is not an unreal representation of the past, but an actual fragment of the past surviving in what looks like a hyperbolic state, as an *apparent* exception or inconsistency. The past as "merely" *my* memory, becomes my memory as *the* past (in part). Hence, this partiality is a difference of degree only, not a substantial one of kind.

Or take time travel again. Leaving aside any technological means that might make physical time travel theoretically possible and even mundane, the *experience* of being in a period of time outside of the standard, Newtonian "flow" of our natural lifetime—its "phenomenology," so to speak—can be reduced to a delusion or hallucination of some sort, perhaps with some underpinning pathology or at least anomaly of the brain.[3] Yet this reduction can itself be reduced so that we now see the brain hallucination *itself* as a kind of real time travel. Consciousness (experience) as mere brain event becomes the conscious brain part moving in a new time—a kind of panpsychic time travel. Deflation followed by reinflation. I have previously called this strategy a "refractive reduction," or "full anthropomorphism" (modeled on Henri Bergson's theory of "complete relativity" in *Duration and Simultaneity*). Such doubled reduction is also what I'm calling "supernormalization" here: a kind of low-key mundanizing of the supernatural; or an extraction of the supernatural by natural means.[4]

My usage of "supernormal" has a lot in common with that of the late nineteenth-century writer, Frederic W. H. Myers, who rejected the word "supernatural" altogether as meaningless. He coined this term "supernormal" instead, to apply to phenomena that are merely beyond what *usually* happens, basing it on an analogy with the term "abnormal." One study of Myers has described his life work as an attempt to develop a series that linked the "unknown to the already known," and so went from "normal to abnormal to supernormal psychological phenomena."[5] As he himself wrote in 1885, "when we speak of an abnormal phenomenon we do not mean one which contravenes natural laws, but one which exhibits them in an unusual or inexplicable form." The supernormal is the abnormal normal, so to speak—and both exist on a "continuum" or "spectrum."

In this way, we can think of supernormalization as pure immanentism: there is an immanent continuity such that the supernormal is always already the so-called normal: time travel is always already recollection (and not merely as "mental" time travel); the ghost is always already a pure memory. In other words, it was Kansas all along, Dorothy. Where we differ with Myers is as follows: he would think of telepathy or clairvoyance, say, as liminal versions of mental representation, that is, as mental states lying along the same spectrum as our normal psychical life, only far from where we ordinarily operate. We, however, simply take the corollary to heart: there is something *always already* "telepathic," say, in our ordinary, normal ability to "read minds" (such that, to those who supposedly suffer "mind-blindness," having a neurotypical "theory of mind" is a mystery).[6] Similarly, self-representation could be seen as a *kind of* out-of-body, or astral, experience, with so-called astral *projection* simply being the hyperbolic form of representation ("*hyperbole*" originally meaning "a throwing beyond"—from the Greek, *hyperballein*, "to throw above or beyond"). These states all exist on a *continuum*, as Myers puts it, but for us it is a *heterogeneous* continuity. Whereas Myers focuses on the unseen part of the "spectrum" in order to anchor its liminal status in the normal (going from mundane to extra-mundane), we, instead, enfold the extra-mundane into the ordinary without qualitatively altering the latter—everyday mental events are always already varied enough or sufficiently heterogeneous (if we could pay closer attention to them): Kansas metaphysics.[7]

This is why we will ask whether Mina Bergson's mystical practice, as found in performances such as the rites of Isis, scrying, or astral travel, might not be rendered both "ordinary" and epistemological through a supernormalization without reduction. Such an "ordinary mysticism" would change the way we see the extraordinary by enfolding it within the ordinary while also showing how esoteric knowledge might be equal (continuous) with supposedly more "accessible" forms of knowledge. Indeed, in her own occult practices, as we will see, we can sidestep both Mina Bergson's religionist commitments (and their assumed hierarchies) *as well as* any merely decorative and aesthetic interpretation of her work, *so as to then see* her use of costume, props, posture, dance, and other "movement arts" all playing a role as equalized *forms of knowledge* (what she herself will call an "occult science").[8] In other words, her methods of mysticism will be used, without religious or supernatural commitments, as a model of knowing.[9]

Some might suspect that any method of teaching and learning that emanates from a hermetic society cannot avoid some form of authority, some crypto-philosophical hierarchization of knowledge. Secret rituals, initiation rites, privileged access, and scaled grades of membership, do not bode well as regards any presupposition of an equality of knowledge (as we are entertaining here). And turning to the aesthetic dimensions of mystical ritual would not necessarily provide a "get out of jail" card with respect to authoritarian epistemology either. As Bruce Lincoln has shown, authority can operate through both language and, more subtly, a whole "theatrical array of gestures, demeanors, costumes, props, and stage devices."[10] So perhaps the suggestion that a hierarchy of knowledge is still at work here remains pertinent. This all remains to be seen. We will endeavor, nevertheless, to subtract the "religionist" element of even this aspect of the Golden Dawn, their arcane infrastructures and obfuscating bureaucracy notwithstanding, to leave only the raw material of their spiritualist approach in view, seeing their "emic" worldview, as it were, via an "etic" stance. And, ultimately, we will thereby try to show how mystical experience can be immanent within ordinary experience just as mystical thought is immanent within philosophy.

2

Meet the Bergsons

Henri and Mina were the son and daughter of Michal Bergson (1820–1898) and Katherine Levinson (1838–1928). They were born six years apart, in 1859 and 1865, respectively, and were the couple's second and fourth born, in a family with seven offspring. Their five other children were Juliette, Joseph, Philip, John, and Renée. Their father, a pianist of some repute, was born in Warsaw; their mother, in Doncaster, England. She was of Anglo-Irish extraction, though both she and Michal were also Jewish. The family was peripatetic, following Michal's musical career across Europe—Henri was born while they were based in Paris; Mina, while they were in Geneva. In 1869, four years after Mina's birth, the family left Paris for London, where they stayed thereafter. However, they left Henri behind in Paris (then aged about ten) to complete his education in the French system, visiting home in Britain only in the summer holidays. Indeed, while his family became British, Henri eventually adopted French nationality in 1878. Curiously enough, then, there is not a drop of French blood in Henri Bergson, supposedly the quintessentially French philosopher of his time, nor in any of his siblings, including Mina. As Henri Bergson's biographers conclude, the current Bergson family is British.[1] After their father Michal's death in 1898, their mother Katherine retired to Folkestone with her daughter, Renée. She died thirty years later in 1928. Within that period from the 1890s to the 1920s, as we well know, two of their children brought more than a little celebrity to the family name.

Henri's story is familiar to many: graduation from the École Normale Supérieure in 1881; a professor of philosophy at *lycees* in Angers, Clermont-Ferrand, and finally Paris all through the 1880s; the publication in 1889 of his doctoral thesis, *Essai sur les données immédiates de la conscience* (translated into English as *Time and Free Will*), followed seven years later by *Matter and Memory* in 1896. He held a chair at the Collège de France from 1900 onward and, in 1907, published his most famous work, *Creative Evolution*, which has defined Bergsonism ever since as a vitalist philosophy. World

Vestiges of a Philosophy. John Ó Maoilearca, Oxford University Press. © Oxford University Press 2023.
DOI: 10.1093/oso/9780197613917.003.0004

renown followed—though one that faded rapidly after the Great War—with the Noble Prize for Literature coming in 1927. Following the German occupation of Paris in 1940, Henri refused any special treatment from the new regime as a celebrated Frenchman rather than as a Jew: despite moving close to the Catholic faith in the late 1930s, at the end he wished to show his solidarity with the Jewish people. And, as Jewish, he was required to register at his local police station, which he did, contracting bronchitis while standing in line. He died on January 3, 1941, aged eighty-one and was buried at the Cimetière de Garches just outside Paris—"the most influential of all twentieth-century French philosophers," as Jean Gayon describes him.[2]

Mina's story is far less known. A talented artist from an early age, she studied at the Slade School of Art in London, where she became friends with fellow student, Annie Horniman (who would also later join the Golden Dawn). In 1887, she met the English occultist Samuel Liddell MacGregor

Figure 2 Henri Bergson (SPCOLLECTION / Alamy Stock Photo)

Mathers (1854–1918), one of the founding members of the Golden Dawn, and, from 1891, its leader. Mina herself joined the Golden Dawn in 1888, changing her forename to Moina—apparently to give it a more Celtic air.[3] She was its first female member.[4] In 1890—and against her family's will—Mina and Samuel married. In May 1892, the couple moved to Paris and founded the Ahathoor Temple for the Order. While the 1890s were its most successful period, with hundreds of members comprising artists, writers, and even civic leaders and socialites joining the Golden Dawn (culminating in MacGregor being commissioned to produce a replica Egyptian Temple of Isis for the 1900 Exposition Universelle in Paris), this success was not without some aggravation. By the turn of the new century there were also significant instances of political infighting, threatened schisms, and accusations of fraud.[5] A further infamous incident followed in 1901, involving a London trial concerning a separate Order's sexual violence against its own members, which brought extremely unwelcome publicity to Samuel and Mina (this "Horos" group having used instruction materials stolen from the Golden Dawn). This spelled the end of the core Golden Dawn group. Nonetheless, Samuel and Mina stayed on in Paris to set up its successor organization in 1903, the Rosicrucian Order of the Alpha et Omega. They continued their work, though now with more and more emphasis on the public side, with the "Isis movement" and its Egyptian mysteries becoming increasingly important. But Alpha et Omega never regained the heights of success the Golden Dawn enjoyed with its illustrious and influential membership. After Samuel's death in 1918 (possibly from the Spanish Flu pandemic of 1918–19), Mina eventually became the sole head of Alpha et Omega until her own death ten years later. By 1919, she had moved back to England to run their temple in London. She lived there until her death in 1928, at Saint Mary Abbot's Hospital, at the age of sixty-three. It is alleged that she died from voluntary starvation.[6] Mina's body was cremated. An unhappy ending? Perhaps. Yet we will insist that this is not only a tragic tale. On the merits of her own thoughts and practices, as well as in the reciprocal trajectories formed with her sibling Henri, we shall see covariances and continuities that manifest many signs of a fulfilling life.

There is no documentation of Henri's views of his sister's work (or vice versa), and indeed it is alleged that she was mostly estranged from her family (though others caution that this has been overstated).[7] However, we do know that Bergson visited the Mathers—when both lived in Paris from 1892 to 1918—and that at one point Mina lived within 800 meters of her brother's

Figure 3 Mina Bergson (also known as Moina Mathers, or *Vestigia Nulla Retrorsum*) (The History Collection / Alamy Stock Photo)

house, less than a ten-minute walk. They surely saw each other frequently enough, Mary Greer going so far as to speculate that they most likely met to discuss "their mutual interest in aspects of the spirit and in psychology."[8] As to the lack of any record of these encounters, we can easily imagine many reasons why Henri, for one, would have wanted to keep such associations private, if not completely secret, for the good of his budding philosophical and academic reputation. Perhaps Mina did, too, for both personal and ideological reasons. Yet, even if by some miracle they had never met alone and in person in this period, in what follows we shall show how they met, and continued to meet, in spirit.

* * *

Dennis Denisoff describes the public ceremonies of the Golden Dawn as "feminist ritual performance," and it is worth pausing to consider this point on a number of levels. First, it must be remembered that the Golden Dawn's primary concern was with knowledge as a means to emancipation and self-elevation. (It is telling that "Know Thyself" is the title of one of Mina Bergson's most important texts.) They were not interested in the use of magic for entertaining the curious or consoling the bereaved or gullible: there were no table turning (*"tables tournantes"*), rappings, levitations, flying objects, or ectoplasmic materializations to see here. Nicolas Tereshchenko enumerates the central practices of the Golden Dawn as follows:

1. The study of Qabalah, Alchemy, Astrology, the Tarot and the system of Magic called "Enochian";
2. Exercises in visualization, meditation, concentration, and other procedures such as divination;
3. The practice of rituals, either as a group in a properly furnished and consecrated Temple, or alone, in the privacy of one's own Temple or Oratory (which could be almost wholly imaginary, i.e. visualized, with the irreducible minimum of magical paraphernalia, such as a wand and a sword).[9]

The Golden Dawn, then, was an institute of sorts, involved in knowledge and learning, although its curriculum was esoteric in content. Even so, it had levels of achievement and awards (grades), and these were all open to all sexes. As Marco Pasi points out:

The exceptional status that women enjoyed in these occult organizations had several implications, which worked at different levels. On the one hand, groups such as the Theosophical Society or the Golden Dawn offered a space where not only men and women worked together, under conditions of equality, for a common goal, but also where women could experiment with positions of authority and power that were denied to them in society at large. On the other hand, an occult group such as the Golden Dawn could also function as a sort of educational institution. In fact, one should not forget that, at the time, women's access to universities was still very limited, if it was possible at all.[10]

Of course, this para-academic training, with its own entry requirements and graduating degrees, operated with a *secret* knowledge, a kind of gnosticism rather than publicly accessible research databases and outputs. This secrecy can doubtlessly be interpreted in terms of power, then, and through that, inequality. With access to higher, privileged grades of knowledge (gnosis) only coming through bizarre forms of ritual initiation (the rules of which were kept confidential) and a strict hierarchy of command maintained within the Order, from Zelator through to the various grades of Adept, it is easy to interpret its clandestine processes as a cover for various forms of obfuscation and control. Such tactics are familiar to anyone acquainted with modern-day cult movements, or at least their representation in mainstream media.[11]

However, even if one were to ignore the clear *disanalogies* between occult groups like the Golden Dawn and present-day prejudices about modern cult movements and their leaders, we are left with two other ponderable issues.[12] First, that knowledge, and access to knowledge, has always been connected to power (who would be so naïve to think otherwise?), and, though one might grant this fact while still maintaining that the difference of degree involved made these Hermetic societies that much more pernicious, it was nonetheless the Golden Dawn that actually practiced real equality in its admissions policy and paths to "promotion." Furthermore, a second thought concerns the question of secrecy directly. It is perfectly consistent that a group dedicated to self-improvement through education of the self, *self*-illumination in other words ("know thyself"), should employ methods involving first-person experience, privileged access to subjective states (and therewith states of the subject), and a knowledge that was less ineffable or incommunicable than bodily and performative (it had to be physically practiced to be achieved). That a prioritization of interiority, the private, and the personal informed its mission and structure should come as little surprise. Indeed, Pasi connects the primacy of embodiment in the rituals of the Golden Dawn positively to the question of power and equality:

> It could be argued that in occult groups such as the Golden Dawn, an attention for the body was already intrinsic to the kind of ritual work that was being practiced. Unlike mainstream freemasonry, in this case both men and women participated in the rituals. It is certainly no coincidence that several members of the Order were theater actors by profession, including one of the most prominent women among its membership, Florence Farr.[13]

Returning to the question of feminism, Mary Greer's study, *Women of the Golden Dawn*, points out that, as a group supporting radical social movements, the women members of the Golden Dawn—Mina Bergson and Florence Farr, as well as others like Annie Horniman, Maud Gonne, and Pamela Colman Smith—represented examples of the kind of "New Woman" appearing at the end of the nineteenth century. As she writes, in the late 1880s

> the public concept of a "New Woman" began to emerge. She could hold a job or have a vocation. She loved whom and where she chose. Although she continued to hold chastity as an ideal, she now considered the standard equally applicable to men.[14]

For the status quo, this was often regarded as a dangerous development:

> . . . for female members of a magical society known as the Hermetic Order of the Golden Dawn, who not only donned Egyptian robes and read books of magic but also divined the future with the cards of the Tarot, no other proof of their iniquity was required. In plays and novels, even those written sympathetically, the New Woman succumbs to hysteria or madness; she becomes physically ill or dies—often by her own hand; she *always* faces an unhappy end. Society is based upon order, which has no place for an independent, self-sufficient woman. In reality, these women existed, and they, in fact, changed society. As outcasts they were unacknowledged, but that very inability of society to see who they were and what they accomplished gave them a particular power that today we find incomprehensible.[15]

The Golden Dawn's heyday was in the 1890s. The first decade of the new century would belong more to Mina's brother, of course, especially following the publication of *Creative Evolution* in 1907. Yet Mina Bergson still had an imposing presence, and not only on account of her celebrated performances. The ideas embedded in these performances are not just "artistic in the extreme" (as we heard) but extremely thought-provoking as well. Notwithstanding ideas of, at best, "proximal authority" or, at worst, a supposed female "mind passivity" within occult Victorian circles, her spiritualist ideas and practices developed within the Golden Dawn remain fascinating on their own merits and worthy of comparison with other philosophies of the time.[16] That is not our only motive for examining them here, however. Though any influence she might have had on Henri's work (or he on hers) remains completely undocumented, she, like him, believed that a concordance was beginning to emerge between natural science and (mystic) spiritualism at the turn of the twentieth century. As she wrote in 1926:

> material science would appear to be spiritualizing itself and occult science to be materializing itself.... The Ancient Wisdom, the Sacred Books, taught that we cannot understand Matter without understanding Spirit, that we cannot understand Spirit without understanding Matter. That Matter and Spirit are only opposite poles of the same universal substance.[17]

Here, she has articulated almost verbatim a key tenet of the "new spiritualism" that had come to the fore in French philosophical circles near the start of the belle époque. Meanwhile, we know that Henri Bergson was always interested in philosophical spiritualism, psychical research (though somewhat furtively for the most part) and, latterly, religious mysticism.[18] Yet the sources for some of his own esoteric ideas remain largely uncharted, especially those appearing in the first and third chapters of *Matter and Memory*. Given that a nonstandard philosophy can be found in Mina Bergson's writings and mystical practices, this should give us pause. In her theorization of these performances, we go beyond aesthetics to find her use of costume, color, voice, movement, and forms of dance all playing a role as kinds of occult science, equal to any science of matter. Moreover, we will unearth ideas concerning time, process, and an "astral plane" that bear more than just a passing resemblance to one of Henri Bergson's most challenging concepts—that of the Virtual—which is his own, processual version of a "universal substance" that generates matter and spirit.

This brings me to another point of convergence, that around the Golden Dawn's feminist principles, Mina Bergson's "feminist ritual performance," and their analogue in what might be called "Bergsonian feminism." In the chapter of her book *The Philosophical Imaginary* entitled "Long Hair, Short Ideas," Michele Le Doeuff comments on a facet of the cult of (Henri) Bergson in the 1900s that struck many—its large female membership:

> We still smile at the court of women who flocked round Bergson, but we systematically forget to wonder whether this court was not in fact satisfying (or inspired by) Bergson's own desire. The fact that this court was composed of women who were following the Collège de France lectures in an amateur

capacity (without expecting qualifications, cashable university diplomas, from them) seems to me significant.[19]

The symmetry of women gaining entry to the academy, either through the public system of the Collège de France or the para-academy of the Golden Dawn (or, in some cases perhaps, both), reveals a parallel inventiveness needed by women in pursuit of knowledge at that time. Yet it also exposes a larger social issue. As Emily Herring asks in an essay on Henri Bergson's celebrity, "why, when Bergson was popular, was he *so* popular, and especially with women?"[20] Despite being given "derogatory nicknames such as *caillettes*" (a small bird signifying a "frivolous babbling woman"), or "*snobinettes*," as well as a simple prejudice that his female audience were "ignorant socialites more interested in being seen at a fashionable event than in learning about philosophy," Herring argues that there may have been something significant happening in this adulation.[21] On the one hand, it might have been that Henri Bergson's philosophy, being seen as "grounded in an unreliable and obscure mysticism that was "feminine" in nature," attracted many followers despite, or even on account of, this putative aspect.[22] This ascription was undoubtedly offered at the time as a slur, of course, hitting two targets at once (mysticism and presumptuous women). On the other hand, however, there may have been an intrinsic value to this association between Henri Bergson's philosophy and feminism—as Herring explains:

In 1913, the American author and feminist Marian Cox (born Mabel Marian Metcalfe) published the article "Bergson's Message to Feminism." She argued that humanity's quest for a better understanding of the Universe, both scientific and theological, had so far been entirely based on male, materialistically driven methods. Instinct and intuition, on the other hand, were in tune with the creativity of life and with the female mind. By placing instinct and intuition at the centre of his philosophical method, Bergson's outlook was therefore "an exposition and a plea for this female-method in the future quest of knowledge." Ultimately, said Cox, Bergson's philosophy would aid the liberation of women. Therefore, at a time when the idea that Bergsonism was inherently feminine was being used to diminish his authority as a philosopher, Cox argued that it was *because* Bergson's philosophy was feminine in nature that it should be taken seriously.

Certainly, this connection between Henri Bergson and the feminine can be unpacked further in a number of ways. On the question of mysticism, Marie Cariou was writing about Henri Bergson and mysticism in the 1970s in this very context: in the section titled "La Féminité" of her book *Bergson and le fait mystique*, she states how "the woman's gaze, we are told, is the prototype of the mystical gaze" ("*Le regard de la femme, nous dit-on, est la prototype du regard mystique*").[23] Though, of course, we must be alert to the presumption of a particular feminine essence supposedly found in mysticism (as if mysticism, alongside the feminine, were both givens that did not need to be historically reclaimed from patriarchal meanings and structures—as, for instance, Grace Jantzen attempted in her work),[24] Cariou's intervention reveals another curiosity in the history of Henri Bergson's philosophical legacy: its postwar domination by Francophone women. This will be hard to hear for some within the Anglophone reception of Bergson who, for various reasons (I'll say it—mostly ignorance), place the survival of Bergson's philosophy entirely at the feet of Gilles Deleuze and his 1966 book, *Le Bergsonisme*.[25] Yet the fact remains that the major commentators on Henri Bergson all through the 1950s, 1960s, and 1970s in France were mostly women: it was the works of Rose-Marie Mossé-Bastide, Madeleine Barthelemy-Madaule, Angèle Kremer-Marietti, Jeanne Delhomme, and Marie Cariou that kept the Bergson flame burning within the French academy for nearly forty years.[26] In the face of a Deleuzian consensus that has served as a gatekeeper to interpretations of Henri Bergson for many years now, their names and, in some cases, superior readings have all but been erased from the philosophical record, even in France. Small gesture though it is, we acknowledge their invaluable work here, for that record. In addition, the connections formed in this book between contemporary female philosophers of matter and Mina Bergson's spiritual practices and theories will also, we hope, be regarded as part of a historical revisioning of Bergsonism that works in a similarly unfashionable "fashion."

10° = 1° *Ipsissimus Covariant (Neophyte)*

There are many, many types of memory discussed in modern psychology—personal, semantic, perceptual, motor skill, cognitive skill, linguistic, episodic, procedural, explicit, implicit, intentional, incidental, and more—but collectively they underscore one thing: *the mystery of remembering*, the puzzle of how a living, present existence or state (such as a brain engram, for instance) can invoke an absence, the inexistent, the deceased past.[1] Why else would Henri Bergson have described, as we heard earlier, the reappearance of a memory as ghostly, as a "mysterious apparition"?[2] Historically, such a mysterious power was held in veneration. As Patrick McNamara reminds us, Mnemosyne, "the goddess of memory," was Zeus's wife and the mother of the Muses, those "goddesses of all of the arts and sciences." Though a minor deity, her status nonetheless reflected "the awe with which Memory was held in the ancient world."[3] In *Rewriting the Soul*, Ian Hacking describes how "no art was more carefully studied, or esteemed, from Plato until the Enlightenment, than the art of memory. Or perhaps we had better say the art of memorizing. This art was a collection of techniques or technologies of memory, variously called *De arte memorativa, memoria technica,* mnemonics."[4] Such mnemonics operated as a technique of storage and retrieval; that is, it relied on a model of memory as something *stored at a locality*, or, in terms that Plato and Aristotle would have understood, "placing." It only follows from this that a whole set of "architectural mnemonics" should arise, building on the idea of memory as storehouse, with ever more creative three-dimensional spaces, well-furnished houses, or even entire cities. Eventually, as we know today, the brain itself became the ultimate organ of storage—only now not as a mnemonic but a real place.

Yet for Henri Bergson the mystery and wonder of memory reside in something quite different from storage and recall, be they perfect or imperfect: it is less how we remember that needs to be explained and more why we *forget* that should meet with our astonishment. Moreover, as Trevor Perri notes,

Vestiges of a Philosophy. John Ó Maoilearca, Oxford University Press. © Oxford University Press 2023.
DOI: 10.1093/oso/9780197613917.003.0005

to suggest that there is a large but still limited number of forms of memory is to think of memory incorrectly in terms of "individual recollections" that are "fixed, static, and something ready-made (*tout fait*)."[5] Instead, for Henri Bergson "memory is a single dynamic process in and through which the past that is preserved in itself can be manifested in an infinite number of different ways."[6] As Henri Bergson writes in his 1904 course on the history of theories of memory, memory "is not a thing; it is progress; it is a movement."[7] The puzzle for him, therefore, was why this movement gets interrupted—why do we forget? Given the survival of the past through continuous movement, as in a speech act that might last a lifetime, the question becomes, why do we suffer any amnesia at all, why are we not all "hypermnesic"? The answer for Henri Bergson will also turn to the brain, but not as a mysterious organ of storage but one of selection, of exclusion. Turned toward life, the living must focus their attention on the practicalities of survival, on the future, leaving their past "elsewhere," so to speak, on the periphery of vision.[8] This is why the "mysterious apparition," the "ghost" of memory, only appears as such to those who do not experience the relevant continuity (as, of course, most of us are physiologically and cerebrally conditioned to do). Only some individuals have such a "weakness" in their futural, "forward" vision that it allows them to look backward as much as forward, to reverse the usual orientation of human experience. In this respect, it is significant that what struck Jean-Paul Sartre about Henri Bergson's theory of memory images was its supposed *magical* quality: they possessed "tendencies and powers as magical as the powers of attraction that Hume conferred on images." Yet, as we will explain later (in the "*Theoricus* Covariant"), this "magical" quality exists in the eye of each beholder, in a selective in/attention. Hence, what Sartre sees as the magical "force" belonging to memory that allows memory to "insert itself" mysteriously within present perception can also be seen, on another level, as a kind of continuity or covariance that has not been heeded.[9] The magic is natural, perhaps even material, but operating at a level such that some can only see it hyperbolically as preternatural (and even call "spiritual").

Let us stay with the issue of storage, though, and leave selection aside for now. Henri Bergson's key criticism of the theories of memory current in his era was that they thought that memory was a set of images stored in the brain. Today, we talk instead of "engrams" (from the Ancient Greek γράμμα, *grámma*, a "written character, letter, that which is drawn"), which are traces or pathways left from *repeated* cerebral activity—furrows for long-term memories. The brain as internal notepad. One of the earliest examples of memory localization is found in Plato's *Theaetetus*, which likens memory formation to impressions left in wax: "now I want you to suppose, for the sake of the argument, that we have in our souls a block of wax, larger in one person, smaller in another [. . .] We make impressions upon this of everything we wish to remember among the things we have seen or heard or thought of ourselves."[10] Even in these early days of thinking about memory, however, it was not long before the wax metaphor ran into trouble. Aristotle pointed out that this model is too fully present, whereas memory is an absence, being of what no longer exists, the past. Impressions or traces left in wax are, by contrast, too entirely present. As Paul Ricoeur wrote in his own work on memory and forgetting: "in the trace, there is no otherness, no absence. Everything is positivity and presence."[11] Leon ter Schure updates this wax metaphor in a helpful manner:

> The wax-metaphor has its modern equivalent in the "representationalist" (also called "instructionist") view that memory can be reduced to neurological traces in the brain. According to the representationalist view, the mind "stores" impressions from the environment, and uses these for its cognitive operations. Memory is thus a neurophysiological process that functions like a camera.[12]

The latest theories of memory localization now refer to specific regions of the brain ("hippocampi forming spatial maps") that function as sophisticated storage and retrieval mechanisms.[13] For some, that these regions are still fully present, existing in a "now" with no direct link with the past, does not pose a real problem (as Aristotle thought). Julian Barbour writes

> Everyone accepts that our memory (certainly our long-term memory) is somehow coded in the trillion or so connections between the several billion or so neurons in our brains. But this is a structure in one Now. It is a structure that contains mutually consistent records of what we call our past. Or brain is . . . [a] *time capsule*. It is a Now with such a special structure that, by itself, it suggests it is the outcome of a process that has taken place in time in accordance with definite laws.[14]

This "special structure" now carries the burden of the enigma of memory. Yet the problems for storage theories are only beginning. What traces also cannot do is convey how memory *feels*, or as ter Schure puts it, the "*historicity* of a memory, its historical feel that causes it to stand out distinct from the present."[15] Moreover, not only are impressions and traces unfaithful to the phenomenology of memory (which, in any case, could be discredited by self-styled eliminativists who regard *qualia* or "feels" like these as just so much deluded folk psychology), storage theories equally call into question the *veridicality* of memory. As Aristotle also asked: why should the perception of a trace be taken as a memory of something else rather than what it is—a perception? However, as ter Schure himself concludes, to escape this conundrum, we need to turn to Henri Bergson: his "radical answer" is found in his ultra-realism, the fact that "we know a memory from a perception because memory remains attached to the past by its deepest roots."[16]

Whereas for some philosophers, "realism" toward the past simply entails the belief that the past did once exist (that it was indeed once present), Henri Bergson's ultra-realism is the view that the past *still* exists. Opposed to both these positions is that of the "anti-realist," who would say that the past need not have existed, even as a previous present. It is perfectly logical to think of the past as an unreal fiction that is constantly *constructed* retrospectively within the present (which continually regenerates itself). This version of "now" really is special, and multiple. Bertrand Russell is probably the most renowned representative of such an extreme presentism toward the past, at least from the logical point of view:

> In investigating memory-beliefs, there are certain points that must be borne in mind. In the first place, everything constituting a memory-belief is happening now, not in that past time to which the belief is said to refer. It is not logically necessary to the existence of a memory-belief that the event remembered should have occurred, or even that the past should have existed at all. There is no logical impossibility in the hypothesis that the world sprang into being five minutes ago, exactly as it then was, with a population that "remembered" a wholly unreal past. There is no logically necessary connection between events at different times; therefore nothing that is happening now or will happen in the future can disprove the hypothesis that the world began five minutes ago. Hence the occurrences which are called knowledge of the past are logically independent of the past; they are wholly analysable into present contents, which might, theoretically, be just what they are even if no past had existed.[17]

In the face of such powerful logic, all is not lost for pastists, however. The Bergsonian response to the idea of an ever-renewed now turns on its already narrow, and question-begging, conception of the present. Henri Bergson's ultra-realism toward the past is based on his temporal holism: *it is the continuity or indivisibility of the past in the present that makes memory "real."* Indivisibility means that the present is always already partly "in" (what we call) "the past."[18] Hence, what Henri Bergson eventually calls "pure memory" is not a mental duplicate referring to the historical past (which can never genuinely prove its credentials as past), but rather *the past itself as it persists in the present*. Pure memory should not be confused with recollection, which always mixes memory images with present perceptions, which thereby also form corruptions and other inaccuracies in our faculty of recall. Whereas a recollection actualizes the past in an image, pure memory *is* this past. Indeed, any form of recollected memory, as habit, disposition, a picture, or whatever else, is simply one or other distortion of this purity of memory, which is, in truth, merely the reality of the past itself. The only way to prove the past is to show that it never left; or as *Matter and Memory* says, "the truth is that we shall never reach the past unless we frankly place ourselves within it."[19]

Admittedly, this stance is no less question-begging than that of an eternal Now, given that it assumes a uniform immanence of the past within the present, or rather, a shared extension of a present that continues into a so-called past. And yet we might recall the points made earlier about *qualia*, as well as the immanent experience of *durée*, "within the phenomenon": the fact is that different experiences of time qua *durée* are possible. This is not a relativism but an immanentism: different temporal experiences, or levels of attention, are equally real. It may well be that no one level of the distended present-past is shared by all; that Bertrand Russell, for instance, truly experiences (at times) an extremely narrow breadth of duration, though it may border on what is deemed "pathological" among humans (the parallels between philosophers and the insane need no rehearsal here). Naturally, as a Platonist of sorts, Russell would regard the logic of his argument as sui generis (having nothing to do with experiences *of* time), whereas, as empiricists, we would relate it to worldly matters—indeed, his logic simply *is one* kind or level of temporal experience. In the end, we should heed the advice of Ian Hacking, who cautions us against thinking that any opposition between a presentist, physicalist approach to memory (what he calls "memory as anatomy") and a more Proustian, phenomenological approach ("memory as narrative") is ever absolute: "memory-as-narrative is often part of an antiscientific ide-ology. Yet it should never be forgotten that memoro-politics emerges pre-cisely in the scientific context of positive psychology. It is part of the secular drive to replace the soul with something of which we have knowledge."[20]

Concomitantly, when a Bergsonian like Georges Mourélos writes in the 1960s against the physiological approach to memory in favor of a "spiritual space-time," the difference between the imagined positions may not be so great (a *Zelator* covariant connects them).[21] Indeed, the work of neurosci-entist Patrick McNamara, who is mostly sympathetic to Henri Bergson's views, suggests that the rejection of localization is not straightforwardly anti-scientific. The issue revolves around the question of what space is doing in these models:

> Memory images were not separated by spatial distances but by qualita-tive differences. If Bergson is correct about this claim, the consequences for memory theory could be immense. *If space was not essential to memories, then the storage metaphor collapses.* Similarly, if memories are "contained" in a nonspatial realm then communication of memory images between two personal consciousnesses should obey laws different from those of verbal communication. Finally if memory is nonspatial, then the identity, or iden-tities that memory supports should not be reducible to one particular or-ganized "container" like a brain.[22]

McNamara himself argues against the storage metaphor in favor of a *selectionist* model akin to the one forwarded in *Matter and Memory*. "we come equipped with a set of neuropsychological systems whose operations are compatible with the basic descriptive elements in Bergson's selectionist memory theory."[23] The brain does not *store* memories; it *selects* them: the correlation of brain events with mental-recall events (evidenced through imaging technologies, or cerebral pathology) would undoubtedly sustain both theses (storage *and* selection). But only the selectionist thesis avoids the problem of emergence (how does one mind-*substance* emerge from a qual-itatively different *substance*?). If the brain does not store memory but rather selects it, and if it is thereby only a record of something, if it traces something, it is of *types of selection*: hetero-continuous lines of selection.

So, allowing for a moment that correlation *could* prove causation, we would still not know *which* causation was at work, storage or selection. To support the first thesis, though, one must overlook the miracle of how ce-rebral matter can *be* both itself (grey matter) and our thoughts and feelings (short of eliminating the latter as illusions): the "hard problem" of mind-body interaction. In other words, causation is not identity. Though identity is less of a problem for the second thesis of selection, to support it one must make the leap to believing that memory is not stored anywhere at all (even "in" the past) but that the past survives as memory: "Bergson is at pains to point out that the selection-process involves a movement of the past toward the present rather than the present calling up the past. [. . .] The past is the active agent."[24] How the past can have agency, be an agent, is only one more puzzle emerging from this shift of paradigms in thinking about memory.

In addition, making matters even more complicated is the fact that memory itself must be understood in all its diversity, a finessing that works against the storage model in particular. Alongside episodic, procedural, explicit, implicit, voluntary, and involuntary memory (we know how the list goes on), McNamara cites "state-specific memories, sensory memories (as in phantom limb pain), emotional memories, olfactory memories, body memories, collective and cultural memories, dream related-memories, prospective memories, spontaneous memories. . . ."[25] Even stranger, memory frequently does not involve recollection, so that one can be influenced by the past yet still not experience "remembering." For instance, one can have a sense of familiarity in a moment, as in déjà vu, but still not "remember." Amnesiacs, likewise, can "refer to the past but cannot recollect the past. We can speak about the past with no accompanying remembering experience."[26] And so on: memory is myriad in variety. In fact, Henri Bergson would go even further. His theory of planes of memory entails, as he puts it himself, "a thousand repetitions of our psychical life" stretched between sensori-motor mechanisms and the "pure" memory that is the past itself in its virtual presence:

> between the plane of action—the plane in which our body has condensed its past into motor habits—and the plane of pure memory, where our mind retains in all its details the picture of our past life [*"le tableau de notre vie écoulée"*], we believe that we can discover thousands of different planes of consciousness, a thousand integral and yet diverse repetitions of the whole of the experience through which we have lived.[27]

Not one, two, or ten types, but thousands: thousands of levels or planes of memory. Memories from planes closer to the pole of action straddle all the different ways that a past can be enacted or embodied rather than simply "represented." As Stephen Kern puts it, "for Bergson every movement leaves traces that continue to affect all subsequent physical or mental processes. The past collects in the fibers of the body as it does in the mind and determines the way we walk and dance as well as the way we think."[28] Pure memories are not individuated pictures (Bergson's reference to "*le tableau de notre vie écoulée*" notwithstanding): they are more like embryos that "contain" the past as a "biological process" in waiting.[29] And even recollections that represent (or "think") that past do *not* picture it either: "to picture is not to remember," according to Bergson.[30] Recollection is not a static imaging, for every trace, be it localized or widely distributed, is a movement, the dynamic record of previous selections.[31]

Accordingly, this is not a quantitative multiplicity where memories differ only in an arithmetical scale of "rhythm," "complication," or "contraction," say, or of being more of less visually clear, or whatever else. It is a continuity of qualified variations that, of course, includes ideas of rhythm and contraction, but that are also as different from each other as a picture, a pain, a dance, a taste, a hallucination, or the passage of grief can be from each other. Henri Bergson is adamant that each plane is *completely different in nature* from the next: to put all memories on one plane would be to differentiate them only by "degree of complication" or "composition." The cone is a "solid" volume, as Bergson puts it in his lecture course on memory from 1904, and not simply a flat "surface."[32] And yet these qualitative differences are still in *continuity* because each plane is also the manifestation (in different modes) *of the same entire past*. Each plane is a different way in which the same surviving past— "*tout de la mémoire*"—reappears.[33]

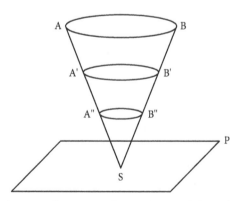

Figure 4 Bergson's Cone of Memory (first variation) (Reproduced from Bergson, *Matter and Memory*, 1911)

Henri Bergson's diagram of the Inverted Cone (see Figure 4) is crucially important as an illustration of this theory of memory. The apex of the cone S represents the point of insertion of memory as recollection into our actual perception of the world P. Above it are the thousands of virtual planes of memory AB, $A'B'$, $A''B''$, and so on (turtles all the way up, so to speak), awaiting the moment when they, too, might return to perception, like a reawakened ghost. In actuality, they are best seen as nonlinear continuities that may, or may not, find a covariant at another level. We will come back to this figure in the sixth part of this work on the "survival of images."

Returning to the image of the trace in these theories of localization and storage, Sarah Robins's essay on memory traces notes how pervasive this idea has been over a long time, featuring in nearly every account of memory since Ancient Greece, though often employing very different metaphors: "they appear as birds in Plato's aviaries and images in Locke's storeroom of ideas, as well as grooves in phonographic records, pictures in a gallery, and textual and digital archives in the vast library of the mind." They can also be "*static* or *dynamic*, *analogues* or *patterns*, *symbolic* or *connectionist*, *representations* or *dispositions*, *localized* or *distributed*."[34] More to the point, the ever-increasing evidence for "neural mechanisms of remembering" in contemporary science has led to an assumption that memory traces must exist to underpin how these mechanisms function:

> Memory scientists continue to assume that the functional description of memory traces . . . will serve as a guide to the cognitive and neural mechanisms that constitute the trace, or engram. [. . .] Memory scientists often take the discovery of the neural mechanisms involved in remembering as vindication of the assumed trace requirement. As more evidence regarding the neural mechanisms of remembering is accumulated, the question of whether there are memory traces recedes further into the distance. Within memory science, little attention is given to the justification of this commitment to memory traces. The question is not whether there are memory traces, but rather how they work.[35]

And yet, recalling Ian Hacking's warning not to see too great a divide between the anatomical and narrative approaches to memory, it is also noteworthy how "trace" can play a role in much more personal accounts of the past. In *Family Secrets: Acts of Memory and Imagination*, Annette Kuhn writes that "the past is gone forever. We cannot return to it, nor can we reclaim it now as it was. But that does not mean it is lost to us." In fact, for Kuhn the survival of the past comes only through its markers, its traces:

> The past is like the scene of a crime: if the deed itself is irrecoverable, its traces may still remain. From these traces, markers that point towards a past presence, to something that has happened in this place, a (re)construction, if not a simulacrum, of the event can be pieced together. Memory work has a great deal in common with forms of inquiry which—like detective work and archaeology, say—involve working backwards—searching for clues, deciphering signs and traces, making deductions, patching together reconstructions out of fragments of evidence.[36]

Significantly, because neither shares Henri Bergson's ultra-realism toward the past (that it survives), *both* Kuhn's biographical account and the neuroscientific version rely on traces being left behind by the past, either as markers on a "exterior" scene or as engrams within the interior body. For both, something *no longer existing* (the past) *caused* those traces. As Stephen Robbins describes it, if the past event and the present recollection "are separated by a temporal gap" (the past does not survive *à la* Henri Bergson), then only a *cause* can connect them because, quite simply, "action at a distance is impossible."[37] Whatever their make-up, personal, impersonal, objective, subjective—traces are intertwined with a "causal theory of memory" to justify themselves *as* traces. Robbins continues thus: "the only way for the past event to be the cause of the remembering is for there to be a memory trace—or series of memory traces—that form an uninterrupted causal chain between the two events. Causation must be gapless; hence memory causation requires memory traces."

* * *

The radical anti-realist—like Russell—places much more store on imagination as the creative agent in the process of remembering, present perception continually imaging a fictional wake trailing behind it. Even for less outlandish accounts, though, scientific evidence seems to support the view that "memory and imagination are profoundly intertwined."[38] As Kourken Michaelian, asks: ". . . the question for the theory of remembering becomes: What distinguishes episodic remembering from episodic imagining?"[39] Children, for example, are highly prone to embellishing their memories of an event with more detail and better organization than was ever contained within the original experience. As McNamara puts it, "the child's memory is creative. Each act of remembering is, for better or worse, a creative achievement."[40] Not only children participate in this fancy, however, and there is a huge literature dealing with "memory distortion" and "creative remembering" for all ages, young and old, *and* all states of mind, healthy and unhealthy. Medical cases of memory loss provide many examples of false memory, certain kinds of patient often filling in the gaps with fantastic or impossible accounts (of prior lives, how they arrived into hospital, what their current condition is, what the world beyond the hospital is like, and so on). These accounts are known as "confabulations." Yet these patients are not intentionally lying. McNamara describes the real tragedy of their situation thus: they believe they are reporting "true memories and one gets the feeling when witnessing an episode of confabulation that one is present at the birth of new memories."[41]

It is notable that such creative remembering poses a challenge for causal accounts of memory involving storage and localization (traces, markers, engrams, etc.) in as much as a major virtue of the causal account is that the *true* memory *is supposed to be real precisely because it was caused by real events.* If memories are now seen as fundamentally "intertwined" with imagination, *even in nonpathological cases,* what price now their basis in real causation by real events? "Simulationist" accounts, such as Kourken Michaelian's, renege on the need for a causal trace but also risk disconnection with any "representational content" (real events) as a result.[42]

Furthermore, what would follow were we to raise the stakes, and scale, of such (con)fabulations even higher, by returning to both the spiritualist and ultra-realist approach to memory and the past? Indeed, from the hermetic perspective, the opposition between memory and imagination is a false one. For practitioners within the Golden Dawn, for instance, imagination is not a faculty of the unreal, of the nonexistent—it has its own reality. As Tanya Luhrmann writes, the doctrine of the Golden Dawn explicitly stated that "imagination was a reality and that it could affect the material world. The different 'plane' that these magical writers present is not defined by different rules—that conception emerges somewhat later—but is rather composed of different materials, one apparently unsubstantial, the other substantive, but both ultimately interdependent."[43] Indeed, one of the Golden Dawn's teaching texts, or "Flying Rolls" (No. V, "Some Thoughts on the Imagination"), resolutely states:

The uninitiated interpret Imagination as something "imaginary," in the popular sense of the word; i.e. something unreal. But imagination is a reality. When a man imagines he actually creates a form on the Astral or even on some higher plane; and this form is as real and objective to intelligent beings on that plane, as our earthly surroundings are to us.[44]

Luhrmann helpfully expands on this claim by explaining how these practitioners "use a term like 'plane' to confer a separate but equal status upon this imaginative world. They also speak of the 'inner plane' and shorten the phrase to 'the inner.' 'Inner' is a disingenuous term, however. It does not mean 'merely' imaginative or emotional or internal."[45] Hence, the "visualization" of abstract shapes such as a hexagram, say, is a crucial initial phase of occult practices such as astral projection.[46] The inner, the imaginative, is fabulated *and* real: visualization (or any of the other sensory modes of creation) is not merely representation. This supernormalization of the imagination is one of the ways, according to Alison Butler, that the Golden Dawn revolutionized the Victorian practice of magic: it introduced the "dominance of the imagination and the will in the magical process." Moreover, the magic rituals were now controlled, not only by "the magician's will and imagination," but were so directed without intermediary.[47]

That said, it must be acknowledged that there is a long history to the "imagination-as-real" idea in Western esoteric thought. Figures including Alfred Sinnett and Rudolf Steiner, for instance, were making similar points to the Golden Dawn about images and the imagination at about this time, or even earlier. In 1881, for example, Sinnett wrote that "the human brain" has the power to "project into and materialize in the visible world the forms that his [the adept's] imagination has constructed out of inert cosmic matter in the invisible world."[48] He also wrote later that there were "conditions of being that, contemplated in imagination from the physical plane level, seem to represent different orders of creation," and that on the "astral plane under similar conditions, the things desired" can take on "objective reality" through this use of imagination.[49] In *An Outline of Occult Science* from 1910, Rudolf Steiner acknowledged that many see in imagination only the power of "invention," and yet, for occult science, what he calls the "imaginative" must be understood as a concept that stands for "that which is 'actual' in a higher sense than are the facts and beings common to physical sense-perception." The "imaginative" is called into being by the soul in its state of higher consciousness, the things perceived in this state of consciousness are spiritual facts, and spiritual beings, to which the senses have no access, and—since this condition of the soul is caused by meditating upon symbols, or "imaginations"—the sphere to which this condition of higher consciousness belongs may be termed the imaginative world, and the knowledge relating to it, imaginative knowledge.[50]

Contemporary research in Western esotericism has maintained this call to see in the psychology of imagination more than is allowed by an "overly rational bias." Wouter Hanegraaff, for instance, cites Gilles Fauconnier and Mark Turner, the pioneers of "blending" theory, stating that "the next step in the study of mind is the scientific study of the nature and mechanisms of the imagination." In a further turn toward scientific naturalism in this area, Egil Asprem has even analyzed Mina Bergson's descriptions of scrying and astral projection as a practice of extra-mundane imagination that was earnest in its methods of verification and error elimination. He shows in some detail how she used "test symbols" taken from a "vast system of correspondences" whereby a vision could be carefully checked for its authenticity, in particular against the possibility that it was "only taken from memory or constructed by one's own mental creativity."[51] (The tacit differentiation here between real imagination and merely imaginary imagination is telling.) Indeed, Asprem and others see strong potential for a *cognitivist* turn in esotericism research that would investigate "kataphatic," or image-based, practices of the Golden Dawn (like clairvoyance and astral travel, for example) in terms of "shifting attention to specific (internal and external) sensory cues," or as afterimage effects caused by the "physiology of the human eye combined with the brain's strategy for interpreting sense data."[52]

It is in Henri Bergson's realist theory of the memory image, however, that we possibly find the most potential for such naturalistic readings. In his Bergson-inspired neuroscientific study of "mind and variability," one of the primary objectives of Patrick McNamara is to demonstrate that selectionism is a compelling approach. In addition, he goes on to show how "imaginative activity and memory are indissolubly linked," and that what we call "personal identity might also be an imaginative creation," that "the act of recall or remembering really involves an experience of the self."[53] This second aim of his enterprise, however, leads to an odd moment in his reading of Henri Bergson, in as much as McNamara claims that "Bergson had little to say about identity" (and so instead turns to William James for this part of his enquiry).[54] Yet he does Henri Bergson a disservice on this front. Actually, at the very outset of *Matter and Memory*'s selectionist approach, it is not only the brain that is an instrument of selection (rather than localization), but my own identity, too, is intertwined with the selection among images. Among *"this aggregate of images which I call the universe,"* there is one of them, Henri Bergson says, "which is distinct from all the others, in that I do not know it only from without by perceptions, but from within by affections: it is my body."[55] One image stands out, is selected, through affect—the feeling of being embodied in the first person, as "my body."

It is worth lingering over this misreading, or omission, because it offers us a clear example of what Henri Bergson means by "continuous heterogeneity." His selectionist approach does not say that the self in irredeemably fragmented or fractured, but rather that it is multiple and unitary at the same time (this is also a major tenet of his 1903 essay, "Introduction to Metaphysics"). There is a continuity, but it is heterogeneous, even in oneself. Now, at one point in his study, McNamara puzzles over a "whole series" of autobiographical memory images: as someone who grew up in a family, went to school, met friends and developed these friendships, married, had children, parented those children, and so on. He then answers the subsequent question "Who am I?" as follows: "you are many."[56] In this dialectic of the one and many, McNamara also revisits a debate whose modern form was shaped by Joseph Butler's criticism of John Locke's theory of the self. When Locke based personal identity on memory ("the same thinking thing, in different times and places"), Butler pointed out that memory is an inherently *personal* selection. As such, memory presupposes personal identity and so cannot rest upon it.[57] In McNamara's updated version: "memory, therefore, presents to us a paradox": it can "constitute the basis for personal identity, since it preserves a record of the story of our lives," yet it also "imaginatively constructs multiple identities."[58] Continuity and discontinuity. One self and many selves. However, Bergsonian duration *also* allows for the same conjunction, the self as one and many, or a heterogeneous continuity of many selves, and indeed of many pasts. In fact, Henri Bergson devoted a good amount of his 1910/1911 course at the Collège de France to Morton Prince's pioneering psychological study of what we nowadays call "Dissociative Identity Disorder" (or previously, "multiple personality syndrome"). Prince's celebrated case of Sally Beauchamp particularly interested Henri Bergson, and he even likened the phenomenon of multiple personality to a series of *"possessions."*[59] Despite

McNamara's claim to the contrary, Henri Bergson does have a lot to say about identity, or at least its many varieties.

Integrated into Henri Bergson's own metaphysics of different levels of duration, one can only say that the self is one and many "at the same time," if this "sameness" is understood as covariance or invariance rather than simultaneity (which would be an abstract spatial rendering). As Leonard Lawlor writes,

> I may introspect and sympathize with my own duration; my duration may be the only one. But, if I make an effort, I sense in my duration a variety of shades. In other words, the intuition of duration puts me in contact with a whole continuity of durations, which I could, with effort, try to follow upwardly or downwardly, upward to spirit or downward to inert matter.[60]

In "selectionist" language, I am a selector (or my brain is), but I am also the product of another selection at another scale. Understood in a temporalized rendering, we might add that, in *my* contracted level of duration, when I *perceive* X, something else at a different level of duration, *remembers* X.[61] My *durée* is but one part of another *durée*.

In the Golden Dawn, the highest grade within the order, based on the Kabbalist system, is named "*Ipsissimus.*" *Ipsissimus* means the "superlative self," or "completely oneself." The likeness to Spinoza's definition of "Substance" or God as "what is in itself and is conceived through itself" hardly needs to be called to attention. It can also be likened to Henri Bergson's idea of the "whole of the self," as Vladimir Jankélévitch pointed out. And such wholes are open for Henri Bergson—they are not substances but processes. Consequently, given that wholes, too, endure and mutate, they can also be seen as incomplete *parts* selected by other wholes at other levels.[62] And so on (turtles, all the way). Each whole is also a part, each many is also a one. *Ipsissimus*, therefore, is also "*Neophyte*," the lowest grade or even the ungraded, the *incomplete* at a whole other level.

3

Hyper-Ritual

Even when compared to her brother's fickle celebrity, the ascent and descent of Mina's star was rapid. Other than a few cursory entries in biographies of Henri Bergson, Mina Bergson's name mostly survives through histories of the Golden Dawn and other occult societies. And apart from those histories, there are few references to her in contemporary culture.[1] Moreover, if we are to gain an impression of what Mina Bergson believed about spiritualism and the occult, she did not leave us much to go on. The available texts laying out her methods and ideas amount to four core documents (currently, at least): her 1926 preface to the second edition of Samuel Mathers's *Kabbalah Unveiled* (originally published 1898) and three teaching texts (or "Flying Rolls"): "No.21, Know Thyself"; "No.23, Tattwa Visions"; and "No.36, Of Skrying and Travelling in the Spirit-Vision."[2] Alongside these writings, and any historical documentation of her and Samuel's activities in Paris, we do, however, also have all of the ritualistic practices and paraphernalia from the Golden Dawn and Alpha et Omega grimoires (handbooks on magical practices): the copious phrases, symbols, languages, props, costumes, sets, mathematic equations, colors, choreographies, and stagings that were part of any member's initiation and ongoing training as they moved from neophyte through the higher grades within the Order.

Naturally, such a profusion of rituality brings with it a hierarchy of aptitude (*Neophyte, Practicus, Adeptus Major*, etc.) as well as hermeticity—but as we said, this does not necessarily imply inequalities within institutional power so much as advancements in aptitude. Henrik Bogdan describes its structures as follows:

> The initiatory system of the Golden Dawn is based on the kabbalistic Tree of Life. Each degree is attributed to a particular *sefira*, starting with the degree of Zelator which is attributed to *Malkuth*, and ending with Ipsissimus which in its turn is attributed to *Kether*. The degree of Neophyte is a preliminary degree and is considered to take place below *Malkuth*. The candidate

Vestiges of a Philosophy. John Ó Maoilearca, Oxford University Press. © Oxford University Press 2023.
DOI: 10.1093/oso/9780197613917.003.0006

thus symbolically ascends the Tree of Life through the rituals of initiation. At the initiations, he or she is instructed in the particular symbolism of the *sefira* that the degree is attributed to, as well as in the symbolism of the paths leading to the said *sefira*.[3]

These terms "*Malkuth*," "*Kether*," and so on will be explained shortly. The Tree of Life, as we know, is a hermetic adaptation from the Jewish mystic system of the Kabbalah.[4] The Tree and its arboreal system of *sefirot*, the ten "emanations" of the infinite (*Ein Sof*), was the foundation for the Golden Dawn's structure and practices, forming an extremely complicated symbolic system involving elements derived from Judaism, Christianity, astrology, and the Tarot.

Nonetheless, were we to suspend the ontological commitments behind these rituals to look at them instead as models of thinking and knowledge acquisition, we might begin to see them as ultra-performative *materializations*. They make spirit matter, both in the sense of making appear and, dare we say, rendering matter *as* spirit through performance.[5] The connections between ritual, performance, and "*as if*" behavior have been extensively discussed by theorists such as Victor Turner and Richard Schechner.[6] This is performance as an act of suspension of disbelief.[7] Such behavior can also be seen as a kind of attention training within a prepared environment, such as a Temple vault, and as such, one that forms a covariance with what is nominally "past" or "spiritual." (We will give a modern example of such a performance later in the *Practicus* covariant.)

We get one glimpse of the hyper-rituals and performativity of Mina Bergson's work in the dedication to her with which the poet and one-time Golden Dawn member W. B. Yeats began his 1925 book, *A Vision*:

> Perhaps this book has been written because a number of young men and women, you and I among the number, met nearly forty years ago in London and in Paris to discuss mystical philosophy. You with your beauty and your learning and your mysterious gifts were held by all in affection, and though, when the first draft of this dedication was written, I had not seen you for more than thirty years, nor knew where you were nor what you were doing, and though much had happened since we copied the Jewish Schemahamphorasch ["*the explicit name*"] with its seventy-two Names of God in Hebrew characters, it was plain that I must dedicate my book to you.[8]

The reinscription of seventy-two names[9]: such was the kind of painstaking spiritual labor undertaken at the Golden Dawn. Entries in Mina's work diary also show whole evenings given over to Tarot readings, many of them lasting four or more hours. Ritual here becomes hyper-ritual. And names and naming were a part of this excess. In fact, Mina Bergson had a penchant for collecting names. So far, we have only reported two (Mina Bergson/ Moina Mathers), but she also was known as "Bergie" (while an art student at the Slade), "*Vestigia Nulla Retrorsum*" (her Golden Dawn "magical name," meaning, among other things, "I Leave No Trace"), the shorter "*Vestigia*," the longer "the Very Honoured *Soror Vestigia Nulla Retrorsum*," the letters "VNR," the numbers "6° = 5°," and later "7° = 4°" (her varying Hermetic order grades), the titles "High Priestess Anari," and "Countess MacGregor of Glenstrae" (Samuel's influence), and finally, at least to her English niece in later years, "Auntie Mouse."[10]

The issue of multiple names will return, too, but what they all "denote" (if I may use that word) is a person behaving, not as an ascetic contemplative, but as a woman of action. Not only had she cofounded a temple and established a major occult Order, her performances were the public face of the Golden Dawn. As R. C. Grogin reports:

In 1899 Mina and the order caused something of a sensation in Paris when they staged a theatrical performance at La Bodinière Theatre, called the Rite of Isis. Jules Bois was on stage to explain the ancient cult to the fashionable audience. The Paris correspondent of the *Sunday Chronicle* reported that Mina achieved a great success. Rivalling her brother in popularity at least for the moment, she "completely won their sympathy by her graceful attitude and dignified manner. More than that, she is very handsome, she has a beautiful oval face with large black, mysterious eyes and beauty always tells in Paris." In gratitude for the performance the ladies offered bouquets of flowers and the gentlemen threw wheat on the altar.[11]

Such an engaged spiritualist might well remind us of the "heroes" and active models that Henri Bergson commended in his 1932 book, *The Two Sources of Morality and Religion*, as the great mystics within the Christian tradition.[12] Mina Bergson herself wrote that the mystic "should not retire from the world," that it is better to live among others and "influence them by our example."[13] In her preface to *Kabbalah Unveiled*, she adds that mysticism "is a system eminently suited to Western occultism, which a man can follow while living the ordinary life of the world, given that this is understood in its highest sense." So much for the "hermetic," the "enclosed." Here, the active mystic meets the ordinary human.

The need to restrain oneself from the usual stereotypes of mysticism, especially egocentricity and monomania, are also uppermost in Mina Bergson's descriptions. In Flying Roll No.21, "Know Thyself," she writes

> There is too much tendency to wish all to follow the Ideal of one—we are apt to forget that the Ideal of each will lead to the same Truth. We can help each other better, then, by helping each to rise according to his own ideas, rather than, as we often unwisely do, in advising him to rise to what is best in ourselves only. That error of wishing to make another as ourselves is another and a very hurtful form of most subtle egotism.[14]

Such a pluralism of approach was already hinted at in her more thematic concern with the relationship between science and spiritualism cited earlier. Indeed, *gnōthi seauton*, "know thyself," the Delphic maxim most famously associated with Socrates, was also connected with other Greek sages, not all of them philosophers in the modern sense but also scientists (Pythagoras, Thales), artists (Aeschylus), and of course mystics like Heraclitus. As we saw, Mina Bergson wrote as an ecumenist of sorts—endorsing an emergent monism of matter and spirit rather than the usual dualism associated with certain strains of occult thought: "Material science would appear to be spiritualizing itself and occult science to be materializing itself. [...] Matter and Spirit are only opposite poles of the same universal substance."[15] Of course, this duality of orientation over a dualism of substance is also highly reminiscent of the opening of Henri Bergson's *Matter and Memory*:

> We will assume for the moment that we know nothing of theories of matter and theories of spirit, nothing of the discussions as to the reality or ideality of the external world. Here I am *in the presence of images*, in the vaguest sense of the word, images perceived when my senses are opened to them, unperceived when they are closed.[16]

Instead of a dichotomized matter and spirit, for Henri Bergson, there is a unity within a universal imagery. And in 1907, when Henri Bergson begins the third chapter of *Creative Evolution* with an attempt to explain the seemingly mysterious correlations between intellect and materiality, he will propose that the two "are derived from a wider and higher form of existence" and that it must have been the one process that "cut out matter and the intellect, at the same time, from a stuff [*étoffe*] that contained both."[17] Mina Bergson's "universal substance" again, or perhaps what we will see her later call the "eternal attraction between ideas and matter": matter and ideas (or spirit) as "poles" within one spectra(l), continuous entity, which she then names "the secret of life."[18] Both of Henri's texts were written while Mina was in Paris, obviously, but it is especially *Matter and Memory* that stands out in this secret correlation—a book that has been variously described as his most "learned," "rich," "brilliant," and "difficult" works.[19] This is the book he published in that glorious decade of the 1890s, when Mina and Samuel, the "neo-pagan power couple," held court to great acclaim.

4

"O My Bergson, You Are a Magician"

In her 2015 doctoral dissertation at Northumbria University, Helen Green writes:

> The era's fascination with what Alex Owen in *The Place of Enchantment* calls, "a new esoteric spirituality" meant that, for some, the more mystical aspects of Bergson's thought were adopted and integrated into the outlooks of movements like Theosophy and the Order of the Golden Dawn. This connection, though unconfirmed by the philosopher, was for its disciples given credence by his acceptance of the presidency for the Society for Psychical Research (1913) and, furthermore, by public knowledge that he was the brother of leading occultist Moina Mathers (née Mina Bergson).[1]

Green then proposes that Mina Bergson herself must have felt sufficiently certain that her brother's ideas were in harmony with her own mystical beliefs to mention, again, how "material science would appear to be spiritualising itself" in her preface to *The Kabbalah Unveiled*. This is doubtless a crucial statement by Mina Bergson, of course. In point of fact, however, she did not name her brother in this connection at all, but rather the distinguished English physicist, and part-time psychical researcher, Sir Oliver Lodge (a figure Henri Bergson also admired, incidentally, and who had read the philosopher's work).[2] Indeed, Alex Owen's 2004 book, subtitled *British Occultism and the Culture of the Modern*, tempers this enthusiasm for the syncretic, especially on Henri Bergson's own part, by noting that when Yeats visited Mina Bergson in Paris in 1894, he was "aware that MacGregor Mathers was irritated by his inability to impress his brother-in-law with his magic." Owen goes on to add that "there is no indication that Bergson showed any interest in magic, but he was nonetheless involved with psychical research and deeply concerned with matters relating to spirit and consciousness."

Vestiges of a Philosophy. John Ó Maoilearca, Oxford University Press. © Oxford University Press 2023.
DOI: 10.1093/oso/9780197613917.003.0007

Owen's caution here raises an allied question: what was Henri Bergson's view of traditional religion? Though it has been argued elsewhere that Henri Bergson was a spiritualist even "from the start" of his philosophical career, and that the problem of God was central to all of his work, such interpretations of his ideas are outliers, to say the least.[3] As Vladimir Jankélévitch states in an essay on "Bergson and Judaism," the "pluralist immanentism of *Matter and Memory* and *Creative Evolution* doesn't lend itself well to the idea of a monotheistic transcendence." Indeed, it is difficult to see how a doctrine that is, as Jankélévitch says, "temporalist, continuationist, immanentist, and on top of all that pluralist [could] have anything in common with Hebrew monotheism."[4] All the same, Jankélévitch will also say that,

> over the absolute nothingness, Bergson would no doubt have preferred the mystical nothingness of the Kabbalah and Dionysius the Areopagite, because that nothingness is richness and plenitude, inexhaustible infinity (*En-Soph*) or, as Angelus Silesius says, "Super-Nothing"; that nothingness is not the void where the spectacular magic of creation is wrought in a coup de théâtre, but rather like the dynamic schema that is the germ of poetic improvisation: it is the unfathomable abyss and fertile night referred to in negative theology.[5]

It is fascinating to see Jankélévitch refer to *Ein Sof* and its emanations in this context. Moreover, if there is a perpetual theme of the Kabbalah, it is its understanding of the world as emanations within the divine, and the idea that knowledge of this process of emanation only comes through learned techniques designed to retrace the path of this emanation, by returning to the original infinite. Compare this retroactivity, then, with Henri Bergson's own exhortations in *Matter and Memory* to "seek experience at its source, or rather above that decisive turn where . . . it becomes properly human experience." Before this "turn of experience," he continues, there remains to be "reconstituted, with the infinitely small elements which we thus perceive of the real curve, the curve itself stretching out into the darkness behind them."[6] The "darkness behind them" is not an empty nothing, however, but a "Super-Nothing," rich and inexhaustible.

Such a reorientation within experience does offer a strong echo of this Kabbalist movement of involution. Likewise, the need to "*reverse the normal direction of the workings of thought*" as described in "Introduction to Metaphysics," the obligation to "think backwards" as one commentator put it, provides a similar covariant.[7] For Kabbalists, then, it is clear that one must retrace the emanations in order to progress through the *sefira*. As Grogin notes,

> the Bergsonian and Kabbalistic views of man, so popular in the late nineteenth century, proceed from the same assumptions: that man lives a highly routinized, mechanical life, mundanely bound by the rhythms of his body and by habits of reaction and perception. He is a man who blindly seeks pleasure and avoids pain, and it is only the rare man who, through the proper instruction, can overcome this, break the outer crust of habit and enter into a higher spiritual awareness.[8]

And the "proper instruction" is to move in reverse. Admittedly, these retrograde movements might appear odd at first, when seen coming from a Bergsonian perspective. Normally, duration only moves forward in Henri Bergson's rendering (though without any fixed direction) and so is irreversible. True, but how we falsely yet habitually conceptualize real time itself precisely as *reversible*, and so actually expendable or unreal as passage, *needs itself to be put in reverse* according to the philosopher. *This is a double reversal, therefore, one that, like the negation of the negation, reorients us toward positive, creative movement* (going backward in order to go forward, so to speak).

Returning to the God question, in "Existentialists and Mystics," Iris Murdoch may have put her finger on something closer to what really connects Henri and Mina Bergson on the matter of religion—even more so than certain movements within thought and technique (philosophical and Kabbalistic). In that text she writes that mystics inhabit "a spiritual world unconsoled by familiar religious imagery." Rather, she claims, mystics should be thought of as "artists" who "invent their own imagery."[9] Certainly, the biography of Mina Bergson fits that profile very well. With respect to religion and the Golden Dawn more broadly, it has even been suggested that calling it a religion, even a "syncretic" one, is a misnomer. As Ronald Hutton shows, the Golden Dawn's practices were not about worshipping God but empowering the practitioner:

> . . . the ceremonies of the order were not acts of worship; their focus was the celebrant. It was far from obvious, in the performance of the Qabbalistic Cross, whether the kingdom, the power, and the glory belonged to God or

were being promised to the human carrying out the ritual; this ambiguity no doubt made it acceptable to people with a wide range of beliefs.[10]

Wouter Hanegraaf reports that such an emphasis on the individual rather than the collective, one that is concerned more with cultivating personal experience through praxis rather than doctrinal belief, might be best summed up by the term "spirituality" rather than "religion."[11] *Qua* spiritual practice, then, the Golden Dawn was radically heterodox when compared with institutional religion. This heterodoxy, sometimes termed "Victorian and Edwardian immanentism," is explained by J. Jeffrey Franklin as follows:

> The heterodox responses, as in Theosophy and the Golden Dawn, were cosmotheistic and therefore more than prepared to exchange revealed monotheism for immanence, scripture for nature. Rather than defending Jesus's revealed divinity, they embraced Osirian mythology, even celebrating Jesus's membership in that lineage, and also reinstated the divine feminine.[12]

Such avowed heterodoxy can be seen in the approach of Mina's brother, too. Recalling Henri Bergson's adage that one can only understand "what one can in some measure reinvent," we must also note that *both* brother and sister were lapsed or secularized Jews, with each eventually inventing his or her own means to engage with the most abstract questions of existence. Significantly, Henri Bergson's definition of the "amateur" as opposed to the professional in philosophy completely upends our usual understanding: it is the former who approaches problems entirely using the ready-made techniques and terminology set by others, by the "tradition"; the professional approach is instead to invent one's own route through the problem.[13] In place of doctrinal belief, we have an immanent, almost artistic practice.

Contrary to Yeats's account, moreover, we know that Henri Bergson *was* actually interested in magic, at least as a field for academic study, and this concern culminated in the publication of *The Two Sources* in 1932. Hence, it should not be so surprising to Owen, as it seems to be, that "in a *striking parallel* with occult thought, he argued that matter and spirit are not opposites but part of a whole."[14] Our book's primary concern is precisely with this striking parallel. Owen even notes how the great historian of mystic thought, Evelyn Underhill, attended Henri Bergson's London lectures of 1913 in the wake of her own recent success with the book *Mysticism* and reported back that she was "drunk with Bergson."[15] Significantly, much of the historical re-search underpinning Henri Bergson's own theories in *The Two Sources* did in fact come from her work. In a note in *The Two Sources*, he acknowledges a mutual influence with Underhill: "similar ideas will be found in the remark-able works of Evelyn Underhill. . . . The latter author connects certain of her views with those we expressed in *L'Evolution Creatrice*, and which we have taken up again, to carry them further, in the present chapter."[16]

I said "significantly" earlier because, for a number of years in the mid-1900s, Evelyn Underhill was also a member of the Golden Dawn. Indeed, Underhill even wrote "a defence of magic" in 1907.[17] Now, I opened this sec-tion with an irreverent use of William James's famous note to Henri Bergson, dispatched after he had first read *Creative Evolution*, "O my Bergson, you are a magician and your book is a marvel."[18] Taken literally (other than as fawning praise or a lazy slur), Henri Bergson was no magician to be sure, but he was philosophically interested in the topic. He was clearly aware of mediumship where "the magician sometimes works through the medium of spirits" and the notion of occult forces.[19] That a magician might even believe she is able to influence events and material objects at a distance is described in *The Two Sources* as "a logic of the body, an extension of desire, which comes into play long before intelligence has found a conceptual form for it."[20] Rage against an absent enemy, for instance, can so magically transform the world as to make our gestures of attack (pouncing, throttling) bring the image of our opponent within our grasp.[21] Expressed bodily, it is a "logic"; taken conceptually, it is a force, though one with many names:

> Words such as *mana*, *wakonda*, etc., express this force, and at the same time the prestige surrounding it. You will not find the same precise meaning for all of them, if you are looking for precise meanings, but they all correspond to the same vague idea. They express that which causes things to lend them-selves to the operations of magic. As to these operations themselves, we have just determined their nature. They begin the act which man cannot finish. They go through the motions which alone could not produce the desired effect, but which will achieve it, if the man concerned knows how to prevail upon the goodwill of things.[22]

Henri Bergson's descriptions of this force were based on research by contem-porary anthropologists (some of which is regarded as dubious today), but his conclusion, which immediately follows the passage earlier, was not. He declares that magical thinking is *not* the preserve of the so-called primitive mind or the magician, but that "magic is then innate in man." Indeed, it is in all men and women. He continues:

> Let there be no talk, then, of an era of magic followed by an era of science. Let us say that science and magic are both natural, that they have always co-existed. . . . Driven back by science, the inclination towards magic still survives, and bides its time.[23]

Ahead of his time, Henri Bergson has no truck here with the idea of a teleological *progress* from "primitive" mentality toward the modern rational (usually Western) mind. He offers an *evolutionary* view, without a doubt, but he does not confer moral or intellectual value on its later "stages" such that the modern psyche leaves the earlier ones behind in its inevitable advance. Each phase lives on in all minds.

Henri Bergson's own discussion of "fabulation" in *The Two Sources* is itself an examination of one such natural tendency toward magical thinking, namely our inclination to anthropomorphize certain physical processes as "Events." Some processes are deemed to possess *intent*, especially ones with deadly effects (natural and man-made disasters). An earthquake, say, seems to be deliberately trying to kill me. It is as if there was some malign purpose from the outset: hence, the disparate processes (which is "all" an earthquake actually is—a set of natural processes) are combined into one Event, the "Earthquake," with its own intentionality. The reason we fabulate the event like this is in order to give ourselves the possibility, overwhelmed as we are, to thwart the will of this larger being: though we may appear physically doomed, if it has an intent, then we may be able to outwit it.[24] This is the peculiar kind of innate magical thinking, that is, for Henri Bergson, latent within each of us. As a tendency, it "bides its time" and emerges only *in extremis*, with processes involving death or serious injury in accidents or disasters. So basic is it that it would be wrong to think of fabulation as "only" a form of imagination, according to Henri Bergson, still less a form of play, artistry, simulation, or pretense: it is far more elementary than each of these and lies not only at their source but also at the source of much religious belief—animatism, animism, polytheism, and so on. If imagination is only imaginary for Henri Bergson, then it seems that fabulation is, at least at some level, more than imaginary.

Moreover—*and this point will become ever more crucial in what follows*—given that in *Creative Evolution* Henri Bergson attributes consciousness and memory to life at all levels of the real, and even to matter (understood as a relatively distended duration), it is not a little ironic that the magical fabulation of life and mind within physical processes is *not* actually philosophically baseless for him.[25] Such fabulations are simply operating at the wrong scale, one where human intervention deludes itself as to its own power over matter. Our "magical" beliefs are never thrown away by the so-called modern mind, nor should they be. Matter *itself* is "magical," so to speak (a panpsychism runs through Bergson, as we will soon see), but it would be wrong to think that it must respond to *our* interventions. Such an illusion is simply thought, logic, or desire, projecting itself at what is an inappropriate level for it. Counterfactually, then, we might say that magical thinking *might be right* to behave *as if* ritual, incantation, or performance could conquer space, time, and the standard laws of physics and biology, were it not for the case that:

1. It projects itself at an improper level (it is not necessarily operative at our scale); and
2. It thinks of its causal powers as voluntarily (even though they are not in our power to control); and
3. It thinks of the source of magic as a substance (when it is, rather, a movement, a process).

Whether or not these "errors" of judgement, of scale, are irredeemable is another matter. Perhaps we can fashion the conditions for an involuntary event, or at least increase its likelihood, if only to some infinitesimally small degree (when that one infinite monkey succeeds at typing the complete works of Shakespeare). And, as with fabulation's own fashioning of hope in the face of certain death, it may be this chance, however small, that spurs us on to attempt the act, no matter how improbable in the long run.[26]

Tellingly for our present concern, when Henri Bergson elsewhere writes about a "panoramic vision of the past" in its totality, it is in the context of near-death perception: the "sudden *disinterestedness in life* born of the sudden conviction that the moment is the moment of death." At such a final realization of the *inescapability* of one's death, there is a total recall of the past rather than the fabulation of life talked of in *The Two Sources*.[27] Our orientation from future to past is put into reverse as at least part of what was keeping our entire past from flooding our present is breached. Henri Bergson talks about this "panoramic vision" in 1913 during his address, as its new president, to the Society for Psychical Research (which was founded by Frederic

Myers, by the way). In fact, beyond this discussion of magic, his ongoing engagement in psychical research has already been noted, even though it was not always made public.[28] Long before this Presidential Address, his interest in the paranormal was clear, as Howard Caygill has discussed in his essay "Hyperaesthesia and the Virtual." This essay deals with an early report by Henri Bergson, published in the *Revue philosophique* in 1886. In "*De la simulation inconsciente dans l'état d'hypnotisme*," he records his participation (with his assistant, "Robinet") in the case of a boy who had been credited with powers of telepathy while hypnotized. This boy was supposedly able to read the mind of a man who was reading a book unseen to him (the boy would report back the words the man was silently reading). In this case, though, Henri Bergson demonstrated his skepticism. He was able to disprove telepathy by discerning instead an extraordinary degree of sensitivity of vision (hyperaesthesia) under hypnotic suggestion (the man reading was also the hypnotist). The boy could read the book's text, reflected (back to front) *in the cornea of the reader's eyes*. Here is Caygill citing Henri Bergson's account:

> For Bergson and Robinet it was as if the hypnotised subject "read everything correctly, but as if read in a mirror where they had perceived symmetrical images of real objects." From this the investigators drew the startling conclusion that the reading took place "on the cornea of the hypnotist, playing the role of a convex mirror. Without doubt the reflected image must have been extremely small, given that the numbers or letters must have been hardly 3 millimetres in height. Taking into account the radius of the cornea at 7 to 8 mm, a simple calculation shows that this cornea, working as a convex mirror, would reflect an image of the numbers and letters a little less than 0.1 mm." This extraordinary deduction pointed to the existence of *hyperaesthesia*, or the ability to perceive way beyond the limits of normal perception.[29]

The solution to the case was both more ordinary than telepathy and yet extraordinary, too. Seeing in miniature, in a biological crystal ball so to speak, only hugely reduced in scale. Smallism. Here is a good example of supernormalization—extracting the supernatural by natural means: the boy is not telepathic—he is only seeing things, albeit seeing things extraordinarily well—hyperacuity. This is less a deflation (of the psychical, the paranormal, spiritualism, or magic) and more a case of the ordinary being elevated from within—hyperaesthetic conditions going unnoticed (because they are natural, innate) in Frederic Myers's sense of the supernormal. Where we would extend Myers's version of supernormalization, via Bergsonism, in this context would be by showing that even normal levels of *any* visual acuity are only normalized after the fact. The "magic" of all vision is the "always already" of an immanent bond with reality: the visual image that is part of the real-whole, which is itself, according to *Matter and Memory*, a set of images. Our vision of the world is not a constructed representation (in a Kantian-style duality between mind and reality), but what remains, a selection, from a reality made of images. Hyperacuity is simply a different selection. As a comparison, even normal, rather than telepathic, intersubjective communication can often appear to employ a "power of divination" between individuals, according to Henri Bergson.[30] Hence, the need to insert a mysterious "theory of mind" (or, in miniature, "mirror neurons") to explain intersubjectivity. This insertion comes retrospectively in a rationalist reconstruction or reverse engineering. In point of fact, it is simply that individuals (minds, images, thoughts) are not fully individuated, being the product of a partial *dissociation* (a set of images refracting themselves) rather than an *association* (one image representing another). Or if you prefer, our mental separation was never a given, solid *factum*, but follows a much waterier logic.

Incidentally, while we know that Henri Bergson read Myers's work (they even corresponded in 1886), and that he had this early interest in psychical research, we also know that his 1886 report on telepathy would be the last time for many years that he would engage with such research, or anything else close to the paranormal and spiritual, at least publicly.[31] It is no coincidence, then, to learn that Henri Bergson was admonished for showing this interest by one of his own supporters, Alphonse Darlu (1849–1921). Darlu was a professor of philosophy and would eventually become the Inspector General of Higher Education from 1901 until his retirement in 1919. Even earlier than that, however, he was a mentor to many young philosophers within the French education system (he even founded the journal *Revue de métaphysique et de morale* in 1893 with some of his students).[32] Darlu would have known, therefore, that dabbling with such fringe experiments in telepathy could easily harm the early career of any academic perceived as deviating from the orthodoxies of the day, which were still highly positivist and materialist.

Nearly thirty years later by 1913, however, Bergson's career, and reputation, was unimpeachable. The title of his address to the Society for Psychical Research was "Phantasms of the Living and Psychical Research," and here, finally, he was free to discuss another case of apparent telepathy. It concerns a woman who claimed to *perceive* (not merely sense) in every detail the death of her husband, a military officer, who was killed on a battlefield a great distance away: "at the very moment when the husband fell, the wife had the vision of the scene, a clear vision, in all points conformable to the reality."[33] What is really fascinating is that Henri Bergson sidesteps the debate between whether this was a case of telepathy or clairvoyance on her part as follows: "if the picture was the reproduction of a real scene, it must, by every necessity, be because *she perceived that scene* or was in communication with a consciousness that perceived it."[34] Significantly, it is still a matter of *perception* here for Bergson because of the concrete details in her record of the death scene, even though it was operating through some form of "*communication*" (this is not mind-reading). Henri Bergson refers to this case as explicitly offering "... the possibility of perceiving objects and events which our senses, with all the aid which instruments can bring them, are incapable of attaining."[35] This will sound odd to many: how can we perceive without sensing, how can there be, as he then puts it, a "veridical hallucination" such as this?

Normally, we might entertain the idea that we can sense things without noticing them, without perceiving them ("subliminally" shall we say). Yet Henri Bergson has got it the other way around: perception is wider than sensation, for sensation is a narrowing or restriction of perception. One might conclude that he is simply referring to *extra*-sensory perception here, were it not that his philosophy has never been one that wishes to transcend the body and its powers (as many philosophers frequently do), but rather enhance them (and expand attention, too). Instead of an attempt to escape perception, Henri Bergson elsewhere speculates on what might result were we to "return to perception, getting it to expand and extend." Perhaps, he suggests,

> instead of trying to rise above our perception of things we were to plunge into it for the purpose of deepening and widening it. Suppose that we were to insert our will into it, and that this will, expanding, were to expand our vision of things.[36]

And, in fact, *Matter and Memory* offers a model of such perception which is only different from sensation *by degree*, as part is to whole. Moreover, it is not that perception is built upon the priority of the senses but that the senses are a posterior narrowing of, or selection from, this "pure" perception.

A perception that is more powerful than our senses—or a percept that is more than a sense: this is the hypothesis that the first chapter of *Matter and Memory* calls "pure perception"—a kind of Leibnizian, monadic perception that mirrors the entire universe with varying degrees of attentiveness. Attention again. For his part, Caygill concludes his essay on the 1886 telepathy case by quoting from *The Two Sources*'s final words and finding a similarly cosmic meaning there:

> Bergson intimates that the life of action and utility preserved by the "attention to life" of consciousness can be succeeded by a new attention to life appropriate to hyperaesthesis and the virtual, an "attention to life" to which he gives the name "joy." Such an attention to life, one of hyperaesthesia, would free us from the limits of action and survival and would bring the "refractory earth" back in line "with the essential function of the universe, which is a machine for making gods."[37]

We will speculate later on what the idea of "making gods" might entail (Henri Bergson does not expand), especially as regards the Egyptian mysteries performed by Mina Bergson. In the meantime, the "striking parallels" Alex Owen spoke of between the investigations of brother and sister will only continue to mount, be they in terms of magic or the psychical. For it may well have already struck those readers with an interest in psychic phenomena that Henri Bergson's analysis of the case of the dying officer above is neither one of standard telepathic nor clairvoyant power: when Henri Bergson says that "*she* perceived that scene," it advances the prospect of something far more occult—that this was a case of spontaneous *astral projection*, what we will hear Mina Bergson describe as "travelling in spirit vision."[38]

Before we turn in more detail to Mina Bergson's own oeuvre, however, a word about terminology. Owen recounts how "Bergson's ideas resonated with Kabbalistic and other occult notions of the crucial conjunction of words and images in creating a timeless moment of spiritual illumination."[39] In similarly imagistic vein, we just heard Howard Caygill make reference to "hyperaesthesis and the *virtual*." In the context of discussing perception and images, however, I have long argued that Henri Bergson's notion of the virtual must be taken in all of its optical specificity. Alas, the Deleuzian effect on many readers of Henri Bergson has resulted in my protests often falling on deaf ears, with some exceptions. Perhaps we will have a better hearing from

Mina Bergson. The following comes from her introduction to the *Kabbalah Unveiled*:

> Take the astral plane in its varied divisions, where some of the adventures
> described by the seer take place. This plane may be described as a hall
> panelled with *mirrors*, where one is confronted with bewildering reflexes.
> Manifesting therein *are numerous and varying entities*.[40]

As explained in Mina Bergson's own discussions of "scrying" (a type of
spiritual seeing), or demonstrated in her practice of "Tattwa visions," the
importance of imagery ("thought-pictures") to astral projection, astral clairvoyance, or travelling in "spirit vision," is obvious.[41] *These images are fundamentally actual and specific in form. Tattva* is a Sanskrit word meaning
"thatness," "principle," "reality," or "truth." It is to hermetic spiritualism what
both "*logos*" (word, form, logic) and "*haecceity*" (thisness) are to Western
philosophy.

The language of "planes" in the Golden Dawn's theorization of astral projection is obviously reminiscent of *Matter and Memory*'s discussion of the
"different planes of consciousness" strung between a "plane of action" or pure
perception, where images are in their most concentrated form, and a "plane
of dream" or pure memory, where they exist in their most relaxed state.[42]
Most important, though, is the detailed, concrete existence of those images
on Henri Bergson's plane of pure perception, which I have speculated could
be his version of astral projection. Throughout his argument for a real perception in the story of the dying officer, he bases his case *on detail*—on "an
infinity of details all independent of one another." For Henri Bergson, individual specificity is all: "one blade of grass does not resemble another blade of
grass any more than a Raphael resembles a Rembrandt," as he says in his essay
on "The Possible and the Real."[43] And this is no less true for Mina Bergson,
for whom there is not "a single grain of sand to which an idea is not attached,
the idea which formed it."[44] A real perception of a man dying on a battlefield
would involve numerous details, of faces, uniforms, weaponry, movements,
light, and landscape: were this vision a mere coincidence, therefore, to "see"
each of these details accurately in their real specificity would involve a count-
less number of further intersecting coincidences, giving us a degree of improbability far outweighing that posed to common sense by the existence
of such a psychic phenomenon. So, when *Matter and Memory* opens with
the statement, "here I am in the presence of images, in the vaguest sense of

the word," the vagueness of the word belies the individuality of its sense. For Henri Bergson, the *individuality* of movement and image simply *is* its *metaphysical* status—that is how what he calls a "true empiricism" merges with a "real metaphysics," for there is no such thing as movement "in general" (or anything else "general" for that matter).[45] Any "principle of individuation" exists immanently within real, actual movement *rather* than a "metaphysical"—meaning immaterial—substrate of "prime matter," as Aristotle might have it. For Bergson, matter is already individuated by its own movement, rather than being merely an instrument of individuation.

5

On Watery Logic, or Magical Thinking

In their 1900 joint interview with Frederic Lees, Mina and Samuel, performing as High Priestess Anari and Hierophant Rameses, discussed their
personae and what was occurring on stage in their performances. Samuel/
Rameses first:

> we are not monotheists, and for that reason we have sometimes been called
> idolators. But is not the universe, God manifest in matter, a great eidolon?
> We are pantheists; we believe that each force of the universe is regulated
> by a god. Gods are, therefore, innumerable and infinite. . . . Nothing that
> you can see here is without its meaning, nothing is without its purpose. For
> instance, here is a sistrum [an ancient Egyptian musical instrument like
> a rattle] which is shaken during our ceremonies. One side of the wooden
> body of this instrument represents the Beginning, the Alpha; the other side
> the End, the Omega; the metal part symbolises the Arch of Heaven; the four
> metal bars are the four elements. You will notice that on each of these bars
> are five rings, which, being shaken, represent the shaking of the forces of
> nature by or through the influence of the divine spirit of life. It is the same
> with our dress. . . .[1]

And so on. Leaving aside the language of representation for a moment (x
"symbolizes" y), what strikes the reader most here is the exactitude of detail in their use of images ("eidolon") and instruments—"nothing is without
its purpose." The hyper-ritualized use of objects is both the invention of the
Golden Dawn and a continuation of sorts: after all, these paraphernalia and
their spiritualized roles were fabricated from hybrid sources—established
religions, occult texts, and other mystical traditions. In the expanded sense
of the performance (performer plus object plus stage . . .) this is also a type of
continuity, but one with change, mutation, built in.

In the interview, Lees then turns to Mina/Anari, and we hear her take a
step back from this specific performance to make a more general, philosophical point. In particular, she argues for the need to think the divine through

Vestiges of a Philosophy. John Ó Maoilearca, Oxford University Press. © Oxford University Press 2023.
DOI: 10.1093/oso/9780197613917.003.0008

the female principle. Why, she asks, do we so often neglect the feminine as that part of the divine

which represents at one and the same time the faculty of receiving and that of giving—that is to say, love itself in its highest form—love the symbol of universal sympathy? That is where the magical power of woman is found. She finds her force in her alliance with the sympathetic energies of Nature. And what is Nature if it is not an assemblage of thoughts clothed with matter and ideas which seek to materialize themselves? What is this eternal attraction between ideas and matter? It is the secret of life. Have you ever realized that there does not exist a single flame without a special intelligence which animates it, or a single grain of sand to which an idea is not attached, the idea that formed it? It is these intelligent ideas which are the elementals, or spirits of Nature.[2]

One could easily interpret these descriptions in hylomorphic terms—passive matter informed by ideas—but Mina Bergson is no Aristotelian. There is an agency to matter, too, in this "eternal attraction between ideas and matter," which is also the "secret of life." Of course, much of what she also says about this female element will strike us now as banal romanticism, but we must not forget that such ideas were radical in their time, formative for much that would come later, and resonant with ideas that, in her brother's more acceptable idiom, were once deemed ground-breaking. Seven years later in *Creative Evolution*, Henri Bergson would write:

We have this sudden illumination before certain forms of maternal love, so striking, and in most animals so touching, observable even in the solicitude of the plant for its seed. This love, in which some have seen the great mystery of life, may possibly deliver us life's secret. It shows us each generation leaning over the generation that shall follow. It allows us a glimpse of the fact that the living being is above all a thoroughfare, and that the essence of life is in the movement by which life is transmitted.[3]

Life and its secret(s). Love, attraction, and "sympathy," too—the last, a key term in Bergson's theory of intuition but also a word with strong mystical significance—form a set of images shared between Mina and Henri.

In respect to "secrets" in particular, the language of cloaks, films, and veils (removed, as in *Kabbalah Unveiled*, or not), is also concurrent between the two. In his 1911 lecture "Philosophical Intuition," Henri Bergson talks about "films," "screens," and other veil-like structures in a thought-provoking manner in so far as he does so while directly addressing the *use* of conceptual imagery itself. Discussing how a philosopher might use images to think through philosophical concepts such as, for example, Berkeley's subjective idealism, he writes that

> It seems to me that Berkeley perceives matter as a *thin transparent film* [*mince pellicule transparente*] situated between man and God. It remains transparent as long as the philosophers leave it alone, and in that case God reveals Himself through it. But let the metaphysicians meddle with it, or even common sense in so far as it deals in metaphysics: immediately the film becomes dull, thick and opaque, and forms a screen because such words as Substance, Force, abstract Extension, etc. slip behind it, settle there like a layer of dust, and hinder us from seeing God through the transparency. The image is scarcely indicated by Berkeley himself though he has said in so many words "that we first raise a dust and then complain we cannot see."[4]

Such a heuristic image is both troubling and evanescent. In that it is also, he claims, "a receding and vanishing image," it "*haunts*, unperceived perhaps, the mind of the philosopher."[5] Such veil-like images are then contrasted with another type of imagery, that of language:

> according to this, matter is a language which God speaks to us. That being so, the metaphysics of matter thickening each one of the syllables, marking it off, setting it up as an independent entity, turns our attention away from the meaning to the sound and hinders us from following the divine word.[6]

Crucially, however, for Henri Bergson all such images are actually *superior* to philosophical concepts because, when aggregated in number, they suggest *a movement that straddles time*. The very same philosophy could operate "in other times," only not through concepts. If Berkeley's thought survives it will be as a meaningful image that "is less a thing thought than a movement of thought, less a movement than a direction."[7] This is what survives from Berkeley or continues through a Berkeleyan movement in thought: what we have called covariance.[8]

One exceptionally prominent image throughout Henri Bergson's *own* writings is that of water. Given his metaphysics of transformation, that images of fluidity, liquidity, flow, and water itself are so prevalent is not surprising. As Camille Riquier points out, Henri Bergson uses the material image of water (and, to a lesser extent, air and fire) "in order to suggest, through the image, the moving reality in which his new metaphysics is installed." Hence, we get a thoroughly liquid metaphysics propounded through such images as "the 'jet of vapor,' the 'fluid,' the 'ocean of life,' the 'sheaf,' the 'immense wave' [onde], the 'wave' [vague], the 'flow' . . . and the 'fluent.'" Riquier argues that this "mediating image of his [Bergson's] own thought" operates by suggestion. These images "*suggest* what escapes" the concept, what the concept "cannot absorb and which continues to be felt as the properly active moment of being: its mobility, its moving [mouvance], its duration."[9] Indeed, Riquier goes so far as to say that, "if water is a privileged image it is because Henri Bergson himself cannot do without it. It runs through all his writing as the new element *into which he wants to install philosophy*. It is the mediating image of his own thought and from which no intuition, even his own, can be deprived."[10] That is why we can say, without exaggeration, that Bergsonism is not simply a philosophy *of* flow and the fluid, but that it is a fluid philosophy built upon, as Henri Bergson himself demands, "almost fluid representations."[11] Of course, less tangibly material images can also be found in his work, such as those taken from music, but nonetheless, Riquier still asks, whether we "have to wonder if it is not the fluidity of water, air or fire and the continuity of their passage into each other (fluidification of boiling, condensation, freezing, fusion) that then provides Bergsonian imagery with its *evocative* power."[12] (Parenthetically, we could contrast Riquier's use of evocation, wherein a continuity of passage is suggested through a flowing medium, with Mina Bergson's use of invocation, wherein the continuity is embodied through the medium herself. And the apparent pun on "medium" here is intended, though not in jest.)

This primacy of water imagery even extends to Henri Bergson's discussion of the origins of religion in *The Two Sources*. The evolution of religious thought, he argues, follows a path whereby matter was originally "fabulated" as a living being through a process he likens to a "partial anthropomorphism." In fact, there are at least three forms of fabulation (animatism, animism, and theism) in his account of religion that can also be seen as three forms of mediating imagery. The intentionalization and vitalization of matter begin with diffused, impersonal forces (animatism) before concentrating those forces into spirits localized in particular places (animism), followed by the attribution of increasingly more human personality to those spirits that at the same time detaches them from the world, until we have a full-blown theism with a divinity that transcends its creation, including a material world now deemed spiritless and inert.[13] Despite the clear teleology here, each "stage" is an end in itself and retained as a fundamental perceptual faculty. Two features of fabulation stand out, however: first, that it more or less mirrors Bergson's own philosophical progress, *only in reverse*—his first book *Time and Free Will* (1889) confining *durée*, and with that life, memory, and consciousness, to the human mind, before *Matter and Memory* (1896) and then *Creative Evolution* (1907) extend this durational being to all life and even matter. In that sense, Bergsonian metaphysics reascends the slope that the "modern" mind has come down (or in Kabbalist terms, it retraces the path of emanation). Second, the image of water—itself full of metaphysical purpose in Henri Bergson's iconography—is central to his discussion of animism. He argues that "water spirits," for example, began as "vague entities dwelling, for instance, in springs, rivers and fountains." Once given a name, they acquire their "own particular shape," a "clearly defined personality," and even later become a "minor deity." Yet, before these religious reifications occur (substantializing and immobilizing in one), there was the *fabulation of the water spirit directly*:

> the spirit of the spring must have been the spring itself, as possessing a beneficent virtue for man. To put it more clearly, that beneficent action, in its ever-present aspect, was the spirit. It would be an error in such a case to regard as an abstract idea, I mean an idea extracted from things by an intellectual effort, the representation of the act and of its continuation. It is a datum provided directly by the senses. Our philosophy and our language first posit the substance and surround it with attributes, and then make such and such acts arise therefrom like *emanations*. But we cannot too often repeat that the action may be forthcoming first and be self-sufficient, especially in cases where man is particularly concerned. Such is the act of pouring us a drink [*nous verser à boire*]: it can be localized in a thing, and then in a person; but it has its own independent existence.[14]

"It has its own independent existence." The spirit of the spring *is* its "drink-pouring", so to speak, *is* its gift-offering. Despite further and further anthropomorphism (further down the slope of "emanations"), the original fabulation of life is basic: such early spirits, "in the elemental form which they first possess . . . fulfil so natural a need that we must not be surprised to find the belief in spirits underlying all ancient religions."[15]

Water is also central to Mina Bergson's self-understanding of her practice, as can be seen in the "Tattwa Visions" Flying Roll. The Flying Rolls, remember, were types of lecture—teaching texts—that were also instruction manuals for members of the Golden Dawn. The date of "Tattwa Visions" is uncertain but it must predate *The Two Sources* (which appeared in 1932, four years after Mina's death). In it, she describes a vision of one of the "elementals," the "spirit of water" or "Akas of Apas." It begins thus:

> A wide expanse of water with many reflections of bright light, and occasionally glimpses of rainbow colours appearing (perhaps symbolising the beginning of formation in Water). When divine and other names were pronounced, elementals of the mermaid and merman type appear, but few of other elemental forms. These water forms are extremely changeable, one moment appearing as solid mermaids and mermen, the next melting into foam.[16]

It continues in this fashion of strongly figural anthropomorphism ("mermaids and mermen") mixed with abstract elemental properties (light, color, solidity, melting). Whereas the image of *Isis* mixes spiritual abstraction (she is the goddess of life) with personifying traits (she is the all-encompassing mother, nourisher, the healer of her brother Osiris) in a manner allied to Henri Bergson's "spirit of the spring" that fabulates an intention directly from an action (of offering, of pouring), these "elementals" of Mina Bergson are both more and less individuated as persons: they are equally figural and processual—"water forms" that appear as mythical sea-beasts *and* flowing matter ("foam"), yet without mental attributes.

This Flying Roll, and other works by Mina Bergson, are found in the Golden Dawn handbook compiled and edited by Israel Regardie in the late 1930s. Other entries on the "Apas" Tattwa instruct the user to "imagine something of the shape and brightness of the half moon, putting down heat and thirst, and that he is immersed in the ocean of water." He or she should also "at that time repeat the word Vam" (a syllable denoting "body, speech, mind, and gnosis").[17] Mina Bergson herself talks about both images and also "vibrating the names of Water," before concluding that "these operative *forces* are represented by Angels, each with their respective office in the world of moisture. These forces working in Yetsirah, when descending and mingling with the Kether of Assiah, are initiating the force of that which we as human beings call Moisture."[18] Prolix though this appears, it is clearly a technique of image and sound manipulation employed to attune our perception within a watery logic.[19] Seen through the assortment of New Age formulae that have accumulated around similar practices since (opening the "doors of perception," drawing back the "veil," "altering" or "raising" our state of consciousness, etc.), this will doubtless seem both far too *outré* and equally old-hat to be refracted into anything useful for us. *Alternatively*, we could regard them as epistemic models or technologies: structural placeholders within nonstandard techniques for thinking that involve images and sounds, body practices, and ritualized movements (a "magical thinking" rehabilitated for thought). In Henri Bergson's language, if the embodied brain is a filter, then varying that body-brain by whatever means—art, philosophy, mysticism, diet, self-harm, injury, disease—must also alter the filter, our *attention*, for good or ill (no drugs required).[20] Performed knowledge—or what others might call the need to "think *in* duration" (not *about* it).[21]

In the (relatively) respectable direction of this very same thought, we see Henri Bergson writing, for example, about Socrates as a philosophical exemplar who operates more as a *posture* or contagious *emotion* than a set of ideas. His thought is described as "alive" (*vivant*), a "living thing" that conveys an "attitude" (from *attitudine*, "fitness," "posture"). When later philosophers adopt that attitude, one of dialogical critique with others, with society, then "Socrates is there, Socrates alive." These successors do not follow an archetype so much as a Socratic movement, which is a *form* of living. The Socratic is also called a "creative emotion."[22] Others might be tempted to call it an affective "meme," or "block of affect."[23] Yet the continuities at issue here are *remakes or translations* rather than "replicators"—they mutate in each act of copying or emulation (a hetero-continuity).[24] So, when we wrote earlier that, for Henri Bergson, the *individuality* of movement was both its lived, empirical truth and its metaphysical reality, we might now take this further: movement is personalized (being general and individual at once).[25] We can therefore ask, which is more insane: invoking "spirits" through ritualized bodily behavior, or continuing a life as movement, as attitude? Continuing the Socratic movement or, indeed, George Berkeley's philosophical thought (the Berkeleyan movement) through the manipulation of images; or *expanding* one's spirit-vision through objects, practices, and sound?

Don't answer that question just yet. In a peculiar concurrence, George Santayana produced a scathing critique of Henri Bergson in 1913 that would certainly imply that committal papers were needed for both brother and sister. It is sufficiently entertaining and illuminating, however, that it is worth quoting at some length:

> There is a deeper mystification still in this passage, where a writer [Bergson] is said to "plant himself in the very heart of the subject." The general tenor of M. Bergson's philosophy warrants us in taking this quite literally to mean that the field from which inspiration draws its materials is not the man's present memory nor even his past experience, but the subject itself which that experience and this memory regard: in other words, what we write about and our latent knowledge are the same thing. When Shakespeare was composing his *Antony and Cleopatra*, for instance, *he planted himself in the very heart of Rome and of Egypt, and in the very heart of the Queen of Egypt herself*; what he had gathered from Plutarch and from elsewhere was, according to M. Bergson's view, *a sort of glimpse of the remote reality itself*, as if by telepathy he had been made to witness some part of it; or rather as if the scope of his consciousness had been suddenly extended in one direction, *so as to embrace and contain bodily a bit of that outlying experience.*[26]

Bravo! Mina Bergson would certainly not see a problem here—invocation is a sound method. Though perhaps a little embarrassed, Henri Bergson, too, would have to concur with Santayana's following conclusion: "so perception, for him, lies where its object does, and is some part of it; memory is the past experience itself, somehow shining through into the present. . . ."[27] Again, spot on! Furthermore, "*in the universe at large* the whole past is preserved bodily in the present; duration is real and space is only imagined; all is motion, and there is nothing substantial that moves; times are incommensurable; men, birds, and waves are nothing but the images of them (our perceptions, like their spirits, being some compendium of these images)." Images, yes, which are moving. So, if the "Queen of Egypt" is understood as a complexity of movements (posture, attitude, at micro- and macro-scales), then it is, of course, possible *in principle* to place oneself into her "very heart"—to become her, by invoking covarying movements. And this might involve, ridiculous though this will sound, the literal cells and organelles of a heart *qua* biological organ, and every other part materially implicated in what was unique about Cleopatra, what her movement embodied. Movement is all that survives.

Of course, this was all intended as a reproach: for Santayana—the "melancholy Platonist," according to George Steiner—Henri Bergson offers us "nothing but the images" of real things, and that will not do.[28] Bergson's opening renunciation in *Matter and Memory* of both idealism and realism is but a sham, Santayana says: Bergsonism is merely a "terrified idealism," a philosophy where "appearance is all."[29] Yet "appearance" is taken by Santayana to mean *idea* at best, and an image at worst. And for him an image is only a picture (when it is far more than that for Henri Bergson). Moreover, Santayana is also a dualist, and so for him it follows that there can be no middle ground between realism or idealism. This part of his attack concerns *Matter and Memory* when Henri Bergson says that he is using the word "image" *universally* to designate "a certain existence which is more than that which the idealist calls a *representation*, but less than that which the realist [*read* 'materialist'] calls a *thing*—an existence placed halfway between the 'thing' and the 'representation.'"[30]

Admittedly, the word "image" would seem to be a very poor starting point for a philosophy that purports to be *neutral* as regards idealism and materialism, at least if image is to act as some form of "neutral monism" (to use Bertrand Russell's term).[31] So why did Henri Bergson choose the term "image"? Images are also affective and moving, according to *Matter and Memory's* first chapter, so their visuality may well be *synaesthetic*—as pure perceptions, the individuated modalities of the senses would emerge only latterly, once these images have been refracted.[32] The neutral, therefore, may be less semantic impartiality than simple *equalizing*, a flattening within a *dynamic monism of movements*. This is an *equalizing* along a continuum or spectrum made of *time—images of/as time*. There would still be differentiation by degree—so mind and world are not identical: again, my memory is a (real) part of the past—but it would not be *spatial* ("remote," as Santayana puts it). When Santayana speaks of the scope of consciousness being "extended in one direction, *so as to embrace and contain bodily a bit of that outlying experience*," he is not that far off the mark. Mina Bergson's spiritualization of matter and materialization of spirit is not a neutral monism either, but another way of demonstrating a watery, mind-world intermingling (a "halfway" existence) that operates temporally through movement (when understood as both general and individual).

2° = 9° *Theoricus Covariant*

Possibly the most emblematic of the new materialisms to have emerged is the "vital materialism" of political theorist Jane Bennett. A good deal of her contribution to the movement revolves around what she sees as a misunderstanding of matter as something inert or passive, devoid of all vitality. Reversing this attitude is her primary objective. As we heard John Zammito describe before, "spirit" has always posed a problem for new materialism. And this problem also provides the theoretical context for Bennett's own materialism in the following manner:

> One of the essentially contested issues surrounding the new materialism is how to conceive the relation of "spirit" to the natural. Should the project be to divest even the human of the last vestiges of "spirit," thus completing the "disenchantment of the world," or should the project be to read "spirit," traditionally taken to be exclusively human, as more widely and essentially distributed in nature itself? [...] Two stances have emerged: "reenchantment of the world" as "vibrant matter," celebrated by Jane Bennett and others; and "visceral" materialism, heaping scorn upon any residue of the "ghost in the machine."[1]

We will see, however, that Bennett would actually contest any connection between her vibrant matter and "spirit." In her materialism, it is matter alone that has both real agency and life. So far, so old vitalism perhaps, but this rough similarity to older vitalisms conceals a real advance on them in her view. For example, she rejects Aristotle's hylomorphic dualism of a "passive," "raw, brute, or inert" matter that, like some sleeping beauty, awaits a suitor to wake it into apparent life. This dualist view sees "vibrant life" as what arrives from an *outside* to insert itself into a "dull" material (*hyle*), give it form (*morphé*), and make it flower into a semblance of its own life.[2] Though she admits that the hylomorphic model is "a kind of vitalism, positing some

Vestiges of a Philosophy. John Ó Maoilearca, Oxford University Press. © Oxford University Press 2023.
DOI: 10.1093/oso/9780197613917.003.0009

nonmaterial supplement with the power to transform mere matter into embodied life," the fact remains that, in its approach, "any "formative" power must be external to a brute, mechanical matter."[3] For Bennett, though, matter is not like this at all: against a dualist *and* mechanist tradition going back to Descartes, her matter is not comprised of "merely mechanical operations."[4] It has real agency. Nor is matter a separate world within a world (that also contains spirit, life, or mind): rather, "everything is made of the *same* substance" (matter), which comprises all "things" and "events," human and nonhuman.[5] Fundamentally, then, matter is "vibrant, dangerously vibrant," and comes *already* "formed" as active bodies that, much as Spinoza would have thought, "strive to enhance their power of activity by forming alliances with other bodies."[6]

Certainly, then, matter is not mechanical in this approach: this is a nonreductive materialism. Following Bruno Latour's actor-network theory of "actants," Bennett defines *vitality* as "the capacity of things—edibles, commodities, storms, metals—not only to impede or block the will and designs of humans but also to act as quasi-agents or forces with trajectories, propensities, or tendencies of their own."[7] This stance will allow her, she claims, to "theorize events (a blackout, a meal, an imprisonment in chains, an experience of litter) as encounters between ontologically diverse actants, some human, some not, though all thoroughly material."[8] Such "vital materialism" in Bennett's eyes is a true ontological equality. And, despite any appearance of anthropocentrism and anthropomorphism (the second of which Bennett does not find off-putting anyway), this is a political equality, too, of sorts: a material democracy in action. Bennett's thesis is, after all, not only a philosophical one: it is also "a political ecology of things"—a vital materialist theory of democracy.[9]

Two additional features of Bennett's materialism is its focus on *things*, "thing-power," and the *networks* which they comprise (again following Latour but also Deleuze and Guattari's "assemblage theory"). Being already formed, matter is never amorphous and always "thingly."[10] She is interested in the "materiality of the glove, the rat, the pollen, the bottle cap," as well as "fire, electricity, berries, metal." These are all things, that is, vivid entities not wholly reducible to the "contexts in which (human) subjects set them, never entirely exhausted by their semiotics." These entities possess "thing-power," a phenomenon, she says, that "gestures toward the strange ability of ordinary, man-made items to exceed their status as objects and to manifest traces of independence or aliveness."[11] Importantly, these things act within a "human nonhuman assemblage," a "federation of actants."[12] As Isabella van Elferen points out, in a Latourian actor-network, action "is continuously distributed between actors, always overtaken or "other-taken" by other actors." Action is always interaction with others, and this is the case irrespective of whether or not "these others are human or non-human."[13]

This wide distribution of action, of "doing," among participants allows Bennett to sidestep subject-centered questions of intentionality: Did the garbage disposal unit *decide* to break down? Does the temperature gauge *know* how hot it is? These seem like reasonable examples of *reductio ad absurdum*. Yet mental attitudes alone do not an action make. Instead, Bennett asks such thingly questions as the following:

> Did the typical American diet play any role in engendering the widespread susceptibility to the propaganda leading up to the invasion of Iraq? Do sand storms make a difference to the spread of so-called sectarian violence? Does mercury help enact autism? In what ways does the effect on sensibility of a video game exceed the intentions of its designers and users?[14]

In this celebration of thing-power and material vitality, Spinoza, Latour, and Deleuze are frequently invoked by Bennett as allies. So, what of Henri Bergson and his vitalist philosophy? Here, Bennett is more circumspect. On the one hand, she opens her research with the clear acknowledgment that if a "vital materiality can start to take shape," one must awaken what Henri Bergson described as "a latent belief in the spontaneity of nature."[15] On the other hand, however, Henri Bergson's own vitalism is still too dualistic for her, being "based on the distinction between life and matter" that leaves matter as "unfree, mechanistic, and deterministic."[16] Though she shares with Henri Bergson a "common foe in mechanistic or deterministic materialism," and even accepts that for him life and matter are not separate substances but "tendencies," or "strivings that exist only in conjunction and competition with each other," or even just "nascent changes of direction," still and all, even Henri Bergson is tarred with the same brush of participating in "the tradition of imagining matter as inert."[17]

This is an inaccurate reading, or rather, it is inattentive. Yes, across an entire philosophy spanning over forty years of work, one can dig out phrases from Henri Bergson that sound dualistic and traditionally ungenerous in their attitude toward matter. Nonetheless, the vast majority of his core ideas do not treat matter as mechanistic, inert, and passive. *Space*, however, understood as a projection made upon matter, is indeed a tool, a pure means, by which organized matter (life) seizes other things around it. But matter for Henri Bergson has its own duration, and therewith a vitality and even consciousness of its own (at a certain level). *Matter and Memory* states it clearly: "matter thus resolves itself into numberless vibrations, all linked together in uninterrupted continuity, all bound up with each other, and traveling in every direction like shivers through an immense body."[18] Summing up his philosophy in 1920, Henri Bergson even invoked the notion of "World Soul" as prefiguring what can only be called a "vital materialism":

> The ancients had imagined a World Soul supposed to assure the continuity of existence of the material universe. Stripping this conception of its mythical element, I should say that the inorganic world is a series of infinitely rapid repetitions or quasi-repetitions which, when totalled, constitute visible and previsible changes. I should compare them to the swinging of the pendulum of a clock: the swingings of the pendulum are coupled to the continuous unwinding of a spring linking them together and whose unwinding they mark; the repetitions of the inorganic world constitute rhythm in the life of conscious beings and measure *their duration*. Thus the living being essentially has duration; it has duration precisely because it is continuously elaborating what is new and because there is no elaboration without searching, no searching without groping. Time is this very hesitation, or it is nothing. Suppress the conscious and the living (and you can do this only through an artificial effort of abstraction, for the material world once again implies perhaps the necessary presence of consciousness and of life), you obtain in fact a universe whose successive states are in theory calculable in advance, like the images placed side by side along the cinematographic film, prior to its unrolling. Why, then, the unrolling? Why does reality unfurl? Why is it not spread out? What good is time?[19]

Of course, Henri Bergson is talking here about atomic and subatomic levels of matter rather than at Bennett's more thingly scale, but his point still stands: that time exists at all, that the whole is never given but always unrolling, always unfurling—this is *the* central question. In fact, the importance of real time (its ineliminability) in Henri Bergson's philosophy is such that the answer to the question—what good is time?—shows *why* the material universe must be regarded as living. Even *predictable* processes (such as the clock mechanism he describes above), given that they, too, are processes and so rhythmic and temporal, indicates for Bergsonism the presence of life in the material realm. As Camille Riquier comments, taking color vibrations as his example, and all the while interpolating Henri Bergson's own words:

> Red is, at one level, a light that "accomplishes 400 trillion successive vibrations," at another level, a sensation of color for a perception that has contracted it "in a duration too narrow to capture the moments." Body and soul, matter and perception, "flow posed on a flow," the "difference in tension" between their rhythms "explains their duality and their coexistence." At the same time as consciousness intensifies in perception, its own rhythm is thwarted and delayed by the rhythm of matter.[20]

It is a "*difference in tension*" *between their rhythms that* "*explains their duality and their coexistence.*" So, yes, Henri Bergson incorporates the appearance of duality into his explanation rather than brushing it aside as a misunderstanding. But "body and soul" have rhythm, vibrate, and so are alive, albeit at different levels. There is even a moral case to be made that Henri Bergson actually sees matter as *unfairly* deprived on its own *durée* by other levels—those that regard only themselves uniquely as forms of life. This vitalist chauvinism condenses the *durée* that belongs to matter and with that, an indeterminate realm is transformed into a determinate one:

> one might ask . . . if it is not precisely to pour matter into this determinism . . . that our perception stops at a certain particular degree of condensation of elementary events. In a more general sense, the activity of the living being leans upon and is measured by the necessity supporting things, by a condensation of their duration.[21]

A "condensation of *their duration*." Matter clearly belongs to the same stuff as life, even while being different. It may have no agency in the Bennett-Latour sense of the term (which is already an anthropomorphism, as Bennett will happily admit), but it is not "mechanistic," not "passive," and not "inert."

Why, then, does Bennett not see this? Why does she not give Henri Bergson the same benefit of, if not doubt, then at least the partial ambiguity that she accords to others? Spinoza, for instance, is still regarded as a "touchstone" for her work, despite his theism and the foundational nature of God in his philosophy.[22] Riquier's reference to "body and soul" earlier ("*corps et âme*") may hold the solution. I believe that the answer to Bennett's selective vision comes down to the word "spirit," a term still associated with Bergsonism, despite Deleuze's "monstrous" reading that downplayed its role to that of a bit part.[23] To participate in Bennett's version of a new materialism, all notions of spirit must be exorcized. As she puts it, there can be no "spiritual supplement" added to matter.[24] "The vibrancy I posit in matter," she writes, can never be "attributed to a nonmaterial source, to an animating spirit or 'soul.' "[25] The "temptation" of pervious vitalisms, including Henri Bergson's but also Hans Driesch's, is always to "spiritualize the vital agent"—and this must be avoided in any new vital materialism that she could support.[26]

Admittedly, Bennett is honest about some of the extra-philosophical motives in her animosity toward spiritualism, taking a considerable time-out to familiarize the reader with specifically American trends in political culture. In particular, there is what she calls the "soul vitalism" of Christian evangelists (promoted by ex-President George W. Bush while in office between 2000 and 2008). Caught up with the politics of embryo rights and women's rights, these Christians interpret "vital force" as "a divine spirit that animates the matter of the embryo."[27] And, though Bennett is careful to distinguish the vitalism of Henri Bergson and Hans Driesch from this soul vitalism, one still suspects that there remains some guilt by association nonetheless, a good deal of the problem resting on the term "soul" and its connections with "spirit." Yet, as we know, not all spiritualisms are alike, and we should be careful to distinguish "spiritism" from *philosophical* spiritualism.

Indeed, the term "spiritualist" belongs with a whole constellation of other titles that can be ascribed to Henri Bergson equally. As Mark Sinclair proposes: "Bergson is an animist, a spiritualist, and a panpsychist" (ironically, only "vitalist" is missing from his list here).[28] Marie Cariou would add "pantheism" to that list, though it would be unlike any form that went before: "if Bergson rejects traditional pantheism and monism it is on the ground of a new pantheism and a new monism: an open pantheism and monism where the union of God with nature is not confusion, where the unicity of the *élan vital* is not reductive but where one cannot deny, without contrivance, that the all is in the same and the same in all."[29] "Dynamic monism," "dualist and unitary," "dualism of tendency"—these descriptions, and others, can be taken as synonymous, or at any rate as alternative images for the "heterogeneous continuity" we have been defending throughout these pages.[30] They certainly do not denote reductive, mechanical conceptions of matter.

Panpsychism, for instance, though not a term Bennett uses in *Vibrant Matter* at least, should not be so neglected and can be taken as an approach allied to vital materialism (assuming that any version in question does not simply replicate a hylomorphic duality in micro). Certainly, Bruno Latour is not allergic to the term, especially given his admiration of A. N. Whitehead's philosophy. More to the point, though, attributing psyche to all being, which is a recurrent reading of Bergson, must surely dispel the impression of anti-matter tendencies in his thought. From Henri Hude ("panpsychist theses are constant in Bergson. It is a Leibnizian heritage"), through Mark Sinclair as cited above, to Yasushi Hirai's recent work on this very topic, categorizing Henri Bergson as panpsychist is hardly controversial.[31] Hirai also cites Barry Dainton on the issue, an analytical philosopher who commends Henri Bergson's version of panpsychism as "an attractive position in the contemporary analytical context." Dainton himself says that

> Bergson's solution to the problem of consciousness is not solely of historical interest. For anyone interested in a unified, monistic, world-view, one where the mental and the physical are not fundamentally different in kind, then the approach pioneered by Bergson—a novel combination of direct realism and panpsychism—is well worth considering.[32]

The quotation from Henri Bergson that we used earlier to introduce his own vital materialism (and panpsychism) referred to the ancient conception of a "World Soul," an idea he then stripped of its "mythical element" in order to offer us his metaphysical variation on the same theme. Oddly enough, for all Bennett's aversion to "soul vitalism" in favor of something more non-human, we know that she is not against all forms of anthropomorphism in principle. A "touch of anthropomorphism" she says, can "catalyze" our sensibilities: "revealing similarities across categorical divides and lighting up structural parallels between material forms in "nature" and those in "culture," anthropomorphism can reveal isomorphisms."[33] Furthermore, Bennett goes so far as to liken vibrant matter to that sense of the word "nature" that historically "signaled generativity, fecundity," and was anthropomorphically named "Isis or Aphrodite."[34] (We will return to Isis, or rather she to us, later.)

Such anthropomorphizing may even be "worth running the risks associated" with it, Bennett concedes, namely "superstition, the divinization of nature, romanticism"—in other words, the mythic language of souls.[35] Again, her charity of interpretation does seem rather one-way. For the fact is, it only takes a little first-hand knowledge of Henri Bergson's texts to move beyond the stereotypical interpretation of Bergsonian vitalism as a notion regarding some mysterious substance or force animating all living matter in a hylomorphic fashion. The theory of the *élan vital* has little of the *anima sensitiva*, *archeus*, *entelechy*, or vital fluid of classical vitalisms. This is a *critical* vitalism focused on life as a thesis concerning time (life as continuous change and innovation) as well as an explanatory principle in general for all the life sciences. When asked directly about the meaning of his vitalism, Bergson was adamant: "all that is positive in my *vital impetus* is motion."[36]

This hermeneutical aspect of Bergson's vitalism should give us pause. It is part and parcel of his own nonreductive, anti-mechanistic approach that cautions against excessive objectivism in biology. Indeed, even *Creative Evolution* describes vitalism simply as "a sort of label affixed to our ignorance [as to the true cause of evolution], so as to remind us of this occasionally." He then adds that it is the mechanistic (neo-Darwinian) interpretation of the development of life that "invites us to ignore that ignorance."[37] Going further, among the various meanings of Henri Bergson's *élan*, one that stands out comes from *The Two Sources* as a principle of *unknowing*, an obstacle to totalizing explanation. The *élan* here again stands for the intractability of any complete "physico-chemical explanation of life," for the "inadequacy of Darwinism," the "mysterious character of the operation of life," and finally for "what is still unknown" in our philosophy of life.[38] Can it be doubted, then, that Henri Bergson's *élan* is also an *epistemological* corrective? Indeed, Richard Green goes further still, citing the *élan* as an idea that was never intended "to explain anything; he [Bergson] merely wanted this poetic expression to mark that about living things which could not be understood in mechanistic (or in finalistic) terms."[39] From this perspective, it could be argued that Henri Bergson's vitalism has transformed in his last monograph from what was misunderstood as an inexplicable and inexpressible *force* into a principle of *conceptual insufficiency* when faced with vital phenomena. More than merely an epistemic principle of "negative capability," however, this notion goes well beyond representation, true or false.

Valorizing the unknown is not mystery mongering for the sake of it. Bennett herself writes that "a careful course of anthropomorphization can help reveal that vitality, even though it resists full translation and exceeds my comprehensive grasp."[40] Well, the question of what "exceeds my comprehensive grasp" is central to Henri Bergson's *élan*, too, but without gratuitous mystification. Going beyond supposedly clear concepts when discussing life, the vibrant, or vitality, and instead embracing "merely" *suggestive* imagery is not the second-best option in his view, but the only way to think of life consistently, or rather covariantly. Admittedly, Henri Bergson's use of highly imagistic language for the *élan* won him as many enemies as it did friends. Yet it has to be said that Bennett's own work is also strewn with images (or "modifiers" as she calls them) of life's movement: there is a "pulsing" dimension to agency, things are "aquiver" with virtual force, matter is "vibrant, vital, energetic, lively, quivering, vibratory, evanescent, and effluescent."[41] Bennett is not at all ashamed of her ornate language, of course, and it comes atop of her well-informed discussions of stem cell biology or metallurgy that certainly offer up much more fine-grained empirical evidence than is found in the work of many other post-Deleuzian theorists. The ornament is neither for show nor (however) heuristic purpose. It just is. For Henri Bergson, though, "vague" imagery is actually the most precise means available when it comes to durational phenomena, the best way to suggest its intuition when a "clear" concept is not only lacking but also unwanted (and harmful). The *élan*, and the images that instantiate it, suggest a movement when we cannot know it conceptually. Nevertheless, any possible turn to the unknown as a *positive* reality like this is not entertained by Bennett in the way that Henri Bergson believes necessary.

Placing such heavy value in the unknown, on what remains below our fullest "sensibility" and conceptualization, is not, incidentally, forwarded here as a kind of "God of the gaps," or rather, "vitalism of the gaps" (the "gaps" in question would need specification in any case—would these be spatial gaps or temporal ones, and at what scale?). Of course, one can praise *uncertainty* as a virtue, but it can also be a crutch. Perhaps it is its religious connotations that make many resist embracing such an under-knowing, believing adamantly that only dogmatic credulity will follow from it. Nonetheless, unknowing can itself be positive, an immanent force worth cultivating as a movement first rather than only as misrepresentation. Unknowing in this context is not an epistemic state—qua lack in knowledge, a privation or failure in *accessing* the Real—but a countervailing force, orientation, or movement already *within* the Real.[42] The *occult*—from the Latin *occultus*, "hidden from sight, secret, esoteric"—need not be a cult (of power). *Occultus* comes from the past participle of *occulere* "to hide from view, conceal" (which itself goes back to Indo-European **kel-* meaning "cover, conceal"). The *Theoricus* grade, however, means "beholder, spectator" (just as "theory" does). In this context, we might say that Bennett beholds just as much as she disregards. This is not a fault to be corrected through a rectification in thinking from the outside. She cannot see value in spirit because she beholds, and theorizes, matter in another way. The *Theoricus* covariant. To see spirit differently, not as immaterial substance but as multiple movements shared equally between both things deemed "material" and those things deemed their opposite, would be a reorientation, a shift in attention, and, perhaps, a further democratizing gesture in thought and vision.

When all movement is mysterious (not just God's), then preserving the "mystery as mystery" (as Martin Heidegger put it) is neither obfuscation nor epistemic failure—it is vital. Why, after all, was becoming or change so mysterious to ancient philosophers that Parmenides would deny its reality? Why was movement also so mysterious (or "paradoxical") to Zeno of Elea subsequently? These were not just thought experiments in the modern sense, but real experiences of unknowing, some things being seen and understood, others not. According to Henri Bergson, real time, understood as qualitative change, the constant upsurge of novelty, or movement, is something which we "cannot think"—but we can feel it: "all this we can feel within ourselves and also divine, by sympathy, outside ourselves, but we cannot think it, in the strict sense of the word, nor express it in terms of pure understanding."[43] To the "pure understanding" or conceptual mind, real time, change, or movement is not only unfathomable, it is unseen or unattended. Significantly, the etymology of "mystery" is shared with that of "mystic." Both come from the Greek *mustikos* and *mustés*—meaning an "initiated person," but they also hark back to *muo* and *muein*, meaning to "close the eyes or mouth."

In every variation there are unknown, unseen variables. *Theoricus*, to behold. *Occultus*, to conceal. Two sides of one dyad. When we turn to Karen Barad's "agential realism" and its use of Neils Bohr's atomic theory, we will see a different balance of insight and blindness to that of Jane Bennett's vital materialism. None of these occlusions should be seen as epistemic failures but rather as the ocular dynamics of thought, the necessity of selective in/attention. Moreover, we will soon propose that there are unknown or hidden variables that are real-as-unknown. Following David Bohm's alternative interpretation of the mysterious phenomena of nonlocality seen in the operations of quantum mechanics, we will argue that the unknown is not essentially unknowable *in any one location* (localization again) but functions in a radically *holistic* manner that makes their "hidden" status ontological rather than epistemological: the whole is itself open, indeterminate, and indefinite, not just our knowledge of it.

6

Of the Survival of Images

Modern theories concerning the relationship between images and magic run from examples like André Bazin through Stanley Cavell to Vilém Flusser, each emphasizing in their own fashion how images operate very differently when set within the context of magic. As Flusser writes, "in the historical world, sunrise is the cause of the cock's crowing; in the magical one, sunrise signifies crowing and crowing signifies sunrise."[1] He extends this reciprocity of meaning further when discussing color images:

> If one compares the colour of our own world with that of the Middle Ages or of non-European cultures, one is faced with the difference that the colours of the Middle Ages and those of "exotic" cultures are magic symbols signifying mythical elements, whereas for us they are mythical symbols at work on a theoretical level, elements of programs. For example, "red" in the Middle Ages signified the danger of being swallowed up by Hell. Similarly, for us "red" at traffic lights still signifies "danger," but programmed in such a way that we automatically put our foot on the brake without at the same time engaging our consciousness.[2]

Within the Hermetic context, the power of the image, and the making of images through special use of the imagination, gains even more power, taking the image well beyond any unreal representational interpretation. Recall the guidance from the Flying Roll on "Some Thoughts on the Imagination" stipulating that the creation of images is a very real act: the imagination is not "imaginary"—it forms a reality.[3] Imagination, "the faculty of building an image" as Mina Bergson puts it, is a creative tool that the occult practitioner uses with trained skill.[4] When she discusses Tattwa cards revealing the "spirit of water," or "Akas of Apas," the images of each are no mere pictures alone—they are implements as well. The image for "Akas" is a black or indigo egg, and for "Apas" a silver crescent (see Figure 5).

Vestiges of a Philosophy. John Ó Maoilearca, Oxford University Press. © Oxford University Press 2023.
DOI: 10.1093/oso/9780197613917.003.0010

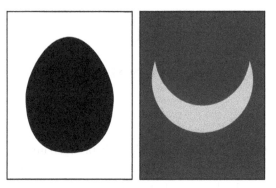

Figure 5 "Akas of Apas" Tattwa Cards

These images or thought-pictures, produced on Tattwa cards, could be used for a number of occult practices. As Joscelyn Godwin explains in "Esoteric Theories of Color," the use of flashing colors such as on Tattwa cards employed "a physiological phenomenon, in which the eye projects a color that is not there, to create an imaginal situation. The purpose is to enter a realm where vision operates without a physical substratum. Such things happen in dream and drug experiences, but the object of the Golden Dawn's, as of most initiatic training, was to enter such states voluntarily and to control them."[5]

In "Of Skrying," Mina Bergson herself writes "in both skrying and astral projection, then, the key to success would appear to be, alternately, to employ intuition and reason, firstly by permitting each thought-picture to impress itself on the brain in the manner comprehended generally by the word 'inspiration,' followed by the reason applying its knowledge . . . to an affirmation or correction of the same."[6] Whereas astral projection—a form of self-hypnosis through concentration upon a symbol (a self-induced pure consciousness event perhaps)—can begin with figurative images, scrying more often than not begins with *real or quasi-reflective surfaces*. Hence, the Tattwa card acts a *kind* of mirror, allowing the practitioner to perceive

some scene in the universe reflected in the symbol which you hold, this latter being to you as a mirror which shall reflect to you some scenes not within your range of sight. And secondly, you can continue the operation by using the same symbol, and by passing through it project yourself to the scene in question, which before you had only perceived as a reflection.[7]

In other words, the Tattwa vision is a form of virtual image. She continues: "you must be prepared to receive impressions of scenes, forms, and sounds as vivid thought forms." Such "thought forms" are not only visual, though, but involve complete "experiences," that is, "things heard, things felt, as well as things seen, which would prove that the qualities that we are here using are really the sublimated senses." This material "crystallizes the astral plane and completes it."[8]

The image is not "imaginary," remember, and there is almost a quasi-synesthesia of images being employed here, one that defragments our separate sensory modalities in order to remount the slope of emanation from the infinite *Ein Sof*. When neuroscience argues that synesthesia could be an example of "human vestigiality" (reflecting a phase of brain development prior to its evolution into specialized sensory functions), then synesthetes themselves become vestiges of our neurological past—living embodiments of the "spiritual in art" (as Wassily Kandinsky put it) or the art in spiritualism (seen in members of the Golden Dawn and their practices).[9] A "spiritual synesthesia" might even be something nonsynesthetes could acquire through the Golden Dawn's training methods: operating on the plasticity of mind and brain to reintegrate separate images into a more holistic, continuous perception.

Indeed, in what could almost be Mina Bergson's own invocation of Leibniz's notion that each monad's perception is a more or less confused image of the entire universe (a reference Henri Bergson was fond of making), she adds that these "insignia and implements" embody "a perfect representation of the universe."[10] The ritual implement is a monad, no less than each image of the universe in *Matter and Memory*'s first chapter is also a monad. And when writing about travelling on the astral plane, Mina Bergson goes further still:

> Having succeeded in obtaining the thought vision of the symbol, continue vibrating the divine names with the idea well fixed in your mind of calling before you on the card a brain picture of some scene or landscape. This, when it first appears, will probably be vague, but continue to realize it more and more of whatever nature (imagination or memory, etc.), you may believe it to be— remembering that this is a passive state of the mind, and not yet is the time to test or reason. Only when the thought picture shall have become sufficiently tangible and vivid, and you find that you are beginning to lose the sense of confusion and vagueness, should you begin to apply tests.[11]

We earlier heard Egil Asprem talking about this testing phase of occult travel in the imagination as a method of verification and error elimination with quasi-scientific rigor. Mina Bergson herself finally notes that the return to this world from the Astral Plane can also be challenging:

> Some students, I believe, have great difficulty in returning. In such a case one can do so gradually by first flying into space, thinking of this planet, fixing the thoughts on the particular country, then on the particular spot therein, then on the house, and lastly on the room and entering therein. But in most cases this would be unnecessarily complicated.[12]

We need no reminder that *Matter and Memory* begins with images "in the *vaguest* sense of the word"—a vagueness that is not by chance and is not a lack. Again, Henri Bergson's position was that his seemingly vague (and ornate) language was the *clearest* way to depict *durée*.[13] In an interview with Lydie Adophe, he responded curtly to the suggestion that his ideas were sometimes metaphorical: "I rarely make metaphors, interrupted Bergson sharply. These are images."[14] Indeed, when it comes to the "spiritual world," for Henri Bergson it is the suggestive power of the image that may allow us a "direct vision."[15] Here is my point: vagueness also operates in Henri Bergson's travels, not on the Astral Plane, but on his own virtual one of pure memory, where the past/my past exists. In one passage from *Matter and Memory*, he offers us instructions on how to "actualize" a recollection from this virtual plane of pure memory (so beloved of Deleuzian readers):

> . . . we detach ourselves from the present in order to replace ourselves, first, in the past in general, then, in a certain region of the past—a work of adjustment, something like the focusing of a camera. But our recollection still remains virtual; we simply prepare ourselves to receive it by adopting the appropriate attitude. Little by little it comes into view like a condensing cloud; from the virtual state it passes into the actual; and as its outlines become more distinct and its surface takes on color, it tends to imitate perception. But it remains attached to the past by its deepest roots, and if, when once realized, it did not retain something of its original virtuality, if, being a present state, it were not also something which stands out distinct from the present, we should never know it for a memory.[16]

Gilles Deleuze, and Deleuzian readers of Bergson, ontologize this plane of pure memory, making it absolutely *non*psychological. In doing so, they ignore the fact that Henri Bergson never opposed *psyche* to matter or being. Everything endures to some degree: even the absolute endures (be it taken as

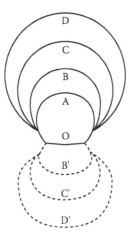

Figure 6 Bergson's Circles of Expanded Memory (Reproduced from Bergson, *Matter and Memory*, 1911)

Divine Being or Being as such)—it is never complete, but open, becoming, or indefinite. Yet, irrespective of whether the ontology of the virtual is really a (cosmic) psychology, the parallels between entering and leaving the virtual and astral planes, as described by Henri and Mina respectively, are conspicuous. Both use images that are vague and wide in scope at the outset, becoming sharper in detail, more concrete and particular as we progress, falling back either to earth or the world of actual perception.

I have frequently stated that *Matter and Memory* is Henri Bergson's strangest book. It is also his most graphical, being by far the most illustrated with diagrammatic images. The most famous diagrams from it are the Circles of Expanded Memory, the Cone of Memory, and the Line of Pure Memory to Perception.

The diagram above (Figure 6) is of the "circles of (expanded) memory" (A, B, C . . .), reflected in the "deeper strata of reality" (A,' B,' C' . . .). We have already seen the inverted cone image (see Figure 4 on page 50), one of two variants appearing in *Matter and Memory's* third chapter titled, "Of the Survival of Images." As we know, the base of the inverted cone, A, B, represents the virtual plane of pure memory, understood as the persisting past itself. Memory operates first through a relocation upward, moving away from the apex and toward the summit, A, B, before then redescending down toward the point S. The summit is also the "place" where images survive—as if images could live, die, and return.[17] In truth, they do not die so much as fall into a disregard. The next image (Figure 7) shows our entire "psychical life" rendered as a line straddling pure memory and perception.[18]

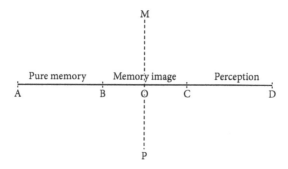

Figure 7 Bergson's Line of Pure Memory to Perception (Reproduced from Bergson, *Matter and Memory*, 1911)

The diagrams found in the handbook of the Golden Dawn are clearly embedded within a very different network of mystical references and practices. Nonetheless, though they do not offer us a stand-alone philosophy (unless we take their practices *as* philosophy), they do evoke many continuities with Henri Bergson's diagrams in *Matter and Memory*.[19]

The image on the next page (Figure 8) is the "Connection Between the Worlds" of *Malkuth* and *Kether*. *Malkuth* (מלכות), drawn top, is the most "material" emanation from *Ein Sof* (אין סוף). *Kether* (כֶּתֶר), shown bottom, is the closest or most direct to *Ein Sof* of any order of manifestation. Note that its orientation is inverse to the Tree of Life, where *Malkuth* is at the base, *Kether* at the summit. The Tree of Life itself (see Figure 1 on page 19), leaves even less to the comparative imagination. It is composed of ten spheres ("*Sephiroth*"), with each sphere (*Sephirah*) denoting a divine or universal quality, an emanation of God, but also possessing specific attributes of angels, angelic orders, or astrological correlates. They are arrayed according to these orders, ranked in terms of immediacy to the highest divine quality, with *Kether* utmost at the top. Every aspect of an adept's training is to allow him or her to progress from the base to the summit. The final image (Figure 9) is titled "Directions of Force in Enochian Pyramids."[20] What echoes here are the lines of force of each of the elements, which are similarly centripetal and placed along two perpendicular axes in the diagram, similar to Henri Bergson's "psychical life" drawing (Figure 7).

Particularly redolent, however, are the conic images and the movements they outline, there even being a clear though indirect influence between Henri Bergson's usage and the Golden Dawn's via W. B. Yeats. The famed images of "widening" gyres, cones, and vortices strewn throughout Yeats's poetry, but especially in his book *A Vision* (that he dedicated to Mina Bergson), stem from

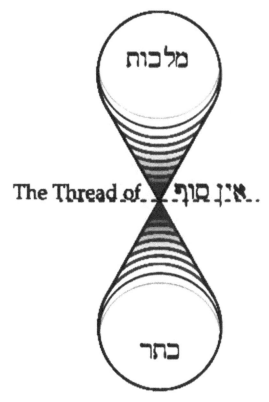

The Thread of אֵין סוֹף

Figure 8 Connection between the Worlds (Reproduced from Israel Regardie, *The Golden Dawn*, 1937)

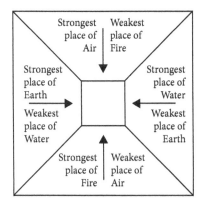

Figure 9 Directions of Force in Enochian Pyramids (Reproduced from Israel Regardie, *The Golden Dawn*, 1937)

the "experiments and thinking" he took away from his time with the Golden Dawn. Furthermore, according to Meghan McGuire, Yeats was also influenced by Henri Bergson directly after his Golden Dawn period, and those very same gyres correlate heavily with "the diagrams of cones and gyres scattered throughout Yeats's copy of *Matter and Memory*."[21] Naturally, however, such figures do not establish any sure lineage—they are just lines after all—and so they do not prove influence (be that proof through logical argument or empirical evidence). But this display is not about influence. What it does demonstrate (show) are visual echoes, covarying images, that, circumstantial though they are, help to complete a picture in our imagination.

The diagrammatic and rich, colorful use of Tattwa symbols is also part of this image-building practice. I already introduced some of the Tattwa visions for Akas and Apas earlier. The most significant others are reproduced here in full (Figure 10).

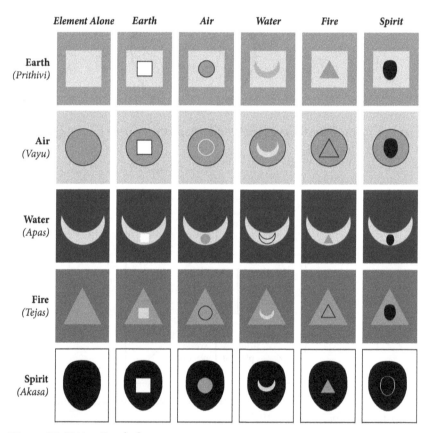

Figure 10 Tattwa Symbols

Even more complex are the myriad diagrammatic drawings found within the grimoires of Golden Dawn members, each one devoutly copied out by hand. Several pages, from the copy held at the Free Masons' United Grand Lodge in London, are reproduced here (Figures 11a–c).[22]

Of course, though seldom mentioned thus far, the contribution of the Tarot—or divination cards—to the graphical toolkit of the Order is extremely important, too. In fact, Mina Bergson designed her own set specifically for the Golden Dawn—as did each member, irrespective of his or her artistic talent.[23] We should consider, though, that Mina Bergson was also the most accomplished visual artist in the Golden Dawn (see Figure 12),[24] and this left her responsible for illustrating various manuscripts as well as much of the visual design and decoration of the Ahathoor Temple in Paris, including its contents—the props, implements, and other paraphernalia of ceremony.

Indeed, Mina Bergson's artistic skill and training were eventually dedicated to spiritual practices alone, such that when she writes to Yeats about conducting "various experiments with colour," this should be understood as more than simply an aesthetic development—it must have been an occult experiment, too.[25] As Charlotte de Mille notes, Mina Bergson "may have mostly stopped painting oil on canvas, but she did not stop creating. And in accordance with the beliefs of the GD, she regarded her work in ritual as a means of manifesting a truer, more insightful consciousness in the individual, and by that individual, in society at large—the noblest endeavor possible in a lifetime."[26]

The stage design for the Ahathoor Temple must be included in this spiritualized art practice. A computer graphic of a temple Vault and its layout for one ceremony ("Adeptus Minor Temple, Third Point") is reproduced here (see Figure 13). The stage design and "directions," so to speak, are conspicuous.

The ceremonial vault is clearly both a sealed room and one species of Proustian space, a prepared chamber with choreographed movements interwoven with a configured area that is both highly decorated and populated with various apparatuses. Like all such ceremonial vaults, it was based on descriptions of the tomb of Christian Rosenkreuz, the mythical fifteenth-century founder of the Rosicrucians, from which the Golden Dawn claimed ancestry in their system of beliefs and practices. A continuity of movements, but with a semifictional origin—confabulation again.

A helpful idea in the context of interior design comes from Jane Bennett and her own re-enchantment of space. She employs the traditional Chinese concept of *shi*, which involves "the style, energy, propensity, trajectory, or

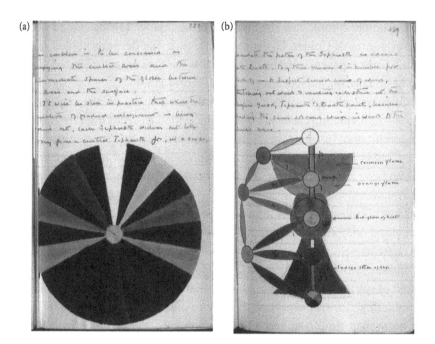

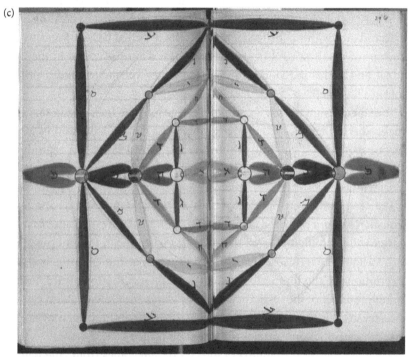

Figure 11 Three Images from the Golden Dawn Grimoire (Courtesy of the Library at the Grand Lodge, Holborn, London)

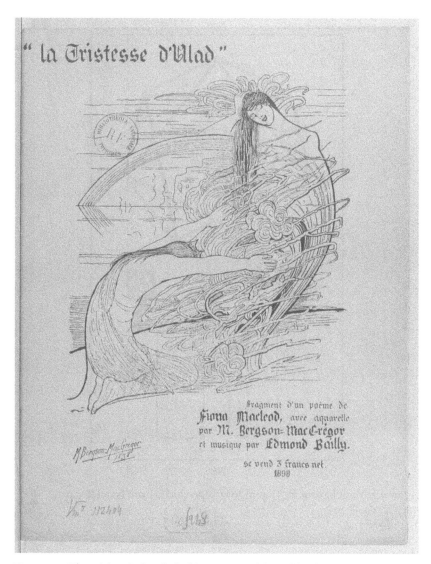

Figure 12 The Melancholy of Ulad (Courtesy of the Bibliothèque nationale de France)

élan inherent to a specific arrangement of things." It is another example of a "vibratory" notion:

> The *shi* of a milieu can be obvious or subtle. It can operate at the very threshold of human perception or more violently. A coffee house or a

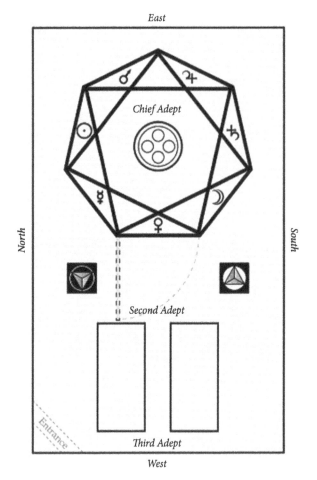

Figure 13 Vault Layout for Ceremony (Reproduced from Israel Regardie, *The Golden Dawn*, 1937)

school house is a mobile configuration of people, insects, odors, ink, electrical flows, air currents, caffeine, tables, chairs, fluids, and sounds.[27]

Not that the *shi* itself is static (a container)—it is a continuity that includes change: "it is the mood or style of an open whole in which both the membership changes over time and the members themselves undergo internal alteration." Intertwined with the agency of human celebrants, the prepared space of the Golden Dawn's temple can consequently be seen to have its own agency in how it both remembers/continues its past arrangements while innovating novel forms out of them through emerging practices. Such a space is never static. Its own movements are a memory, too, that is, a type of continuity keeping the "present" specious and the "past" immanent.[28]

Alongside this "montage-collision" of visual images that we have staged here, we must not forget sound: "thought forms," remember, are "things heard, things felt, as well as things seen," according to Mina Bergson. For every clairvoyant, there is also a clairaudient. Mina Bergson was both. The vibratory method—sounds produced by the practitioner—is key to this.[29] After all, "chanting," the rhythmic repetition of voice, shares its etymology with "enchantment" (from *cantare*, to sing) wherein the world is brought under the influence of magic. Instructions for the "correct pronunciation and vibration" of divine names (often from the Enochian "angelic" language)—for *water*, say—appear repeatedly in Mina Bergson's texts.[30] Pronunciation is a careful *material sounding* that must be performed correctly if it is to be effective. And the vibratory mode is even more corporeal: according to Samuel Mathers's script, it starts with inhalation and a vivid picturing of the letters to be vibrated, followed by exhalation and slowly pronouncing "the Letters so that the sound vibrates within you. . . . Imagine that the breath, while quitting the body, swells you so as to fill up space. Pronounce the Name as if you were vibrating it through the whole Universe, and as if it did not stop until it reached the further limits."[31]

Setting aside this last cosmic aspect for now (the parallels with techniques in certain forms of transcendental meditation are clear), we can also find a counterpart to this "vibratory mode" of thought in Henri Bergson. This is another aspect of his own philosophical strangeness emerging from those passages in his writing that emphasize the form and rhythm of sound as a tool for communicating meaning. Here he is in the 1912 lecture "The Soul and the Body":

> Consider thinking itself; you will find directions rather than states, and you will see that thinking is essentially a continual and continuous change of inward direction, incessantly tending to translate itself by changes of outward direction, I mean by actions and gestures capable of outlining in space and of expressing metaphorically, as it were, the comings and goings of the mind. Of these movements, sketched out or even simply prepared, we are most often unaware, because we have no interest in knowing them; but we have to notice them when we try to seize hold of our thought in order to grasp it all living and make it pass, still living, into the soul of another. The words may then have been well chosen, but they will not convey the whole of what we wish to make them say if we do not succeed by the rhythm,

by the punctuation, by the relative lengths of the sentences and part of the sentences, by a particular dancing of the sentence, in making the reader's mind, continually guided by a series of nascent movements, describe a curve of thought and feeling analogous to that we ourselves described. [...] The rhythm of speech has here, then, no other object than that of choosing the rhythm of the thought: and what can the rhythm of the thought be but the rhythm of the scarcely conscious nascent movements which accompany it?[32]

The "rhythm of the thought"—from *rhuthmos*, which originally meant simply "to flow," *rhein*. And the oddness does not end there. In Henri Bergson's 1922 introduction to *La pensée et le mouvant* (*Thought and the Moving*), he writes that "before intellection properly so-called, there is the perception of structure and movement; there is, on the page one reads, punctuation and rhythm." To understand a writer, one "must fall into step with him [the author] by adopting his gestures, his attitudes, his gait" (this is another reason that I emphasize the corporeal reading of "attitude" in Henri Bergson's use of the term).[33] Where we might normally talk about communication as information transfer, Henri Bergson talks about the need to "seize hold of our thought in order to grasp it all living and make it pass [or flow], still living, into the soul of another." What seems so ordinary in our language as to verge on the banal, its sound (be it written or vocalized), is made strange by this emphasis on rhythm and structured movement as the bedrock of communication. Where Mina Bergson and the Golden Dawn used vocal repetition (chanting) to enchant the voice (making it a divine communication), Henri Bergson made it normal again, but only by supernormalizing the ordinary communications of one soul with another. Both, nonetheless, saw in the "vibratory mode" something that is usually missed in our understanding of how images (in this case sonic ones) are transported, or survive, across space and time.

7

On the Meta-Spiritual

Are we being credulous in these spiritualizations of the real, believing too much too easily? Yes, this is a kind of thought experiment, a hypothesis in nonstandard philosophy and knowledge, but is it also excessive to ask the reader to suspend her disbelief for this long? Why am I doing this anyway? Why look so hard for correspondences between one seemingly half-crazed philosopher and another half-rational occultist? Two drunks, managing to stay upright by leaning into each other's fall, might look impressive, but they are falling nonetheless. So, yes, again, perhaps some parallels of imagery, "mystico-metaphysical" theory, and metatheoretical approach (balancing intellect with intuition) can be found between an allegedly estranged brother and sister, both celebrated in varying degrees, and both living and working in Paris at the same historical moment. Some restorative justice is surely involved, too, not as regards any influence that was denied (to either party), but in terms of "her-storical" interest: Mina Bergson should be "remembered" more than she is, and given more due for her work on spiritualization (even *if* she never wanted to leave any traces or "vestiges" in history).[1] And, of course, this is indeed an exercise in nonstandard philosophy that strives to expand what we understand by philosophical thinking by taking occult spiritualism as a model for thought. As an equalizing and pluralizing gesture in philosophy, however, it will attract as many (yay democracy!) as it will repulse (New Age baloney).

Yet this spiritualist turn is not to be confused with a simple inversion of dominance within a matter-spirit binary that does nothing to alter either of its terms. What is needed, and called for, is a non-Platonist model of spirit: *spirit brought back down to earth*, so to speak. So, a demotion of sorts, but one that does not entail such incompatible categories as the immaterial or the disembodied, but instead something like a degree of hyperaesthesia operating unnoticed and wholly naturally in our ordinary perception. Would this not be the natural sibling to an "inflated" matter? Such alternative and radical concepts of spirit might then be seen as complements—or even alter egos—to new materialism and its notions of vibration, entanglement,

Vestiges of a Philosophy. John Ó Maoilearca, Oxford University Press. © Oxford University Press 2023.
DOI: 10.1093/oso/9780197613917.003.0011

and plasticity. Only when polarized as incompatible substances would spirit and matter enter a duel of antagonistic opposites, caricatures of themselves in fixed states: lumpen bodies versus unearthly specters. On this alternative view, spirit would not *name* one insubstantial substance opposed to another, substantial one: it would name one aspect of a changing relation (a *heterogeneous* continuity), or the features of a changing relation, both of whose relata are mutating, too.

Likewise, the "meta-" of metaphysics should no longer name that which leaves or transcends the physical world (metaphysics as crypto-physics, "spooky physics"), but rather that *in* the world which changes, change or becoming. As Zeno of Elea might contend, even the most pedestrian movement is a metaphysical gesture of sorts (though a false and mysterious one for him). Henri Bergson's solution to Zeno's "Achilles Paradox" is perfectly ordinary: Achilles's steps were "overtaking-steps"—and that is how he overtook the tortoise: "I take a first step, then a second and so on: finally, after a certain number of steps, I take a last one by which I skip ahead of the tortoise."[2] Such banality belies the fact that gesture is complex. As Pasi Valiaho describes Bergson's usage, "gesture is not simply bodily movement but "'a manner of carrying the body.' . . . It is a corporeal rhythm that has become expressive, a rhythm of quality. [. . .] For Bergson, 'my body' organizes the world into meaningful patterns through gestures with function and purpose."[3] Like G. E. Moore's proof of an external world (he holds up his two hands, gestures with each hand to the other while saying, "here is one hand . . . and here is another"), the ordinary bodily gesture carries a (non-Platonist) metaphysics within it.[4]

As regards the primacy of matter, commentators Christopher Gamble, Joshua Hanan, and Thomas Nail rightly argue that "it is not enough merely to say that everything is matter. This amounts to saying everything that is is. For us, there is 'nothing but matter,' but unlike old materialisms this is not a reductionistic claim because matter is not a substance that everything can be reduced to. Matter, for us, is a fundamentally indeterminate performance or process-in-motion."[5] Yet again, however, just as we saw (with Meillassoux and Boutroux) that radical contingency can evidence one definition of materialism just as equally as another of spiritualism, so, too, indeterminate "process-in-motion" can cut both ways: in *Creative Evolution* this is precisely how Bergson describes the latter: "we understand by spirituality a progress to ever new creations, to conclusions incommensurable with the premises and indeterminable by relation to them."[6] Neither Mina Bergson's "universal substance" nor Henri Bergson's "wider and higher form of existence" name fixed things or states, only tendencies: spirit as becoming, force, creativity, and certainly process-in-motion (vibrating, entangled, plastic, even).

Spirit, consequently, can act as a structural placeholder—or "meta-spirit": whatever falls outside of, and resists, a reduction to nothing. Such a meta-spirit can have a multitude of names, one of which might even be "matter," or, understood as a tendency, the "meta-material."[7] The objective is to naturalize spirit, and even matter (as supernormal) in the ordinary Real—not with *only* one name ("plasticity" or "vibrancy" or even "duration") but with multiple names, equally pronounced—all the names of all the practices of the Real. Hence, while Mina Bergson's "thought-forms" can be regarded as materializing spirit in the manner that she depicted, Bennett's "thing power" or "vibrant matter" can, as we saw, *equally* be seen as "spiritualizing" matter, despite her disavowals. As Henri Bergson says on a related issue, "if telepathy be real, it is natural": all we need to know is *which* "nature," and whose naturalism, is in question.[8]

Supernormalization is not, therefore, the decision that all and any "spooky," "meta-psychical," or paranormal phenomena are real, but rather the hypothesis, the thought experiment, that asks, *if* such phenomena were real, how would we naturalize them, how would we integrate or reverse-engineer them into (one knowledge of) nature? *If* X be real, X is natural—but what would this integration into *our* view of nature look like? What we need, to use a Wittgensteinian strategy, are redescriptions that leave "everything as it is": we see things, attend to them, and theorize them, differently, *within* the Real rather than outside of it in some impossible view from nowhere. The *Theoricus* covariant does not *re-enchant* phenomena; it restores them within the Real—one might say that it merely *de-impoverishes* them. Hence, for example, *if* ghosts were real, we can ask what they might be like, naturally. What part of the ordinary might they continue, in some degree? Would they look like . . . memories, for example? We already heard Henri Bergson describe how the reappearance of a memory in consciousness "produces on us the effect of a ghost." It is most likely a coincidence, then, but still interesting to learn that Maurice Maeterlinck, who thought of Henri Bergson as "the greatest thinker in the world" (and who was also one of Henri Bergson's favorite writers), should employ memory in his 1908 play *The Blue Bird* as a faculty of *resurrection*: as the awakened spirit of Granny Tyl tells her grandchild, "every time you think of us, we wake up and see you again."[9]

Naturalization need not entail reduction, however. For example, one supernormal interpretation of time travel (or at least one of its more feasible versions) leaves it hidden within the status quo: if time travel is possible, then it will have already happened. And if such be the case, then *we in our world* might already be a "future" being visited by its relative past or vice versa: if the anomalous phenomenon is real, it is natural.[10] In other words, to the proposal that all memories are ghosts, we might add that some ghosts might be time travelers, too.

On this issue of seemingly anomalous phenomena, Ian Hacking offers a helpful insight on the related topic of "marvels":

> scientific curiosities are topics whose existence is acknowledged by scientists, but about which they can do nothing. The Brownian motion of molecules was a curiosity for a century. It was well known. When it was fashionable for nineteenth-century country houses to keep microscopes, one showed one's guests the latest insect from the Amazon—and the Brownian motion. The photoelectric effect was a more recherché curiosity for eighty years. These effects were scientific because they could be observed with a certain amount of instrumentation; they were curiosities because they were isolated phenomena that fit no vision of the world. [. . .] One way to silence a topic of research is to treat it as a curiosity or turn it into a marvel. Science abhors a marvel, not because marvels are vacuous, empty of meaning, but because they are too full of meaning. . . .[11]

On this account, ghosts could be similarly "natural" even without *complete* inter-theoretical integration into other naturalistic discourses: they would coexist as "marvels" *alongside*, if not *within*, networks of more mundane meaning. The marvel is both seen and unseen: an observable, but one of such excess that it does not fit any standard vision of the world. Here is another instance of such excess meaning: when Ernest Rutherford and Frederick Soddy discovered that radioactive thorium could transform into an inert gas, Soddy could not suppress his joy and exclaimed to Rutherford that they were looking at "transmutation," only to be cautioned straightaway by Rutherford in no uncertain terms: "don't call it transmutation. They'll have our heads off as alchemists." In fact, as Mark Morrison observes, "the newly emerging science of radioactivity routinely generated comparisons to alchemy."[12] And, of course, radiation (X-rays) was invoked by psychic researchers, too (though less so spiritualists) as a model by which to understand parapsychological phenomena. Until its effect had been completely integrated within extant discourses of science, it was a "marvel" that could feed into various esoteric systems of thought or "visions of the world."[13] Even the mystical "astral plane," though it had its roots in medieval thought, could be mundanized as a fourth spatial dimension in the late nineteenth and early twentieth centuries. *Zelator* covariance again.

The repetition of a supposedly supernatural phenomenon, which is not the same as its repeatability (it may still recur spontaneously and unpredictably), is one route to such naturalizations. Images stemming from popular entertainments are a prime site for such everyday miracles. For example, the banalization of even the dead returning to life is a favorite trope of science-fiction television (*Les Revenants*, 2012–15; *Dr Who*'s "Army of Ghosts," 2006), film drama (Jonathan Glazer's *Birth*, 2004), every ghost film ever seen, and the entire zombie horror genre. Fictional biological processes, mind manipulation, or time slips may be some of the mechanisms deployed to support such bizarre events. Resurrection or reincarnation would be religious variants of such para-explanations, too, of course.

Alternatively, were one to clarify properly the *immaterialist* version of spiritual return or survival after death, so as to ask, "What would it be for a spirit, *qua* purely immaterial entity, to return in all its unembodied phenomenality?," the subsequent answer might be surprising. What would *pure* spirit look like, divested of all matter? This would be a thought experiment akin to Henri Bergson's purifying method in *Matter and Memory*, which attempts to separate out completely what we understand as the *substantial* difference(s) between matter and spirit, perception and memory, in the most rigorous sense of their opposition. The results are what he calls pure perception and pure memory, two virtual forms of normal perception and memory, only completely dissociated in terms of any spatial properties. He pursues this purification so that we might be better able to discern the immaterial in both its difference and its continuity with matter, that is, in its difference of tendency, of orientation, within a continuity. Here is a kind of "dualization"—not to be confused with a dualism of substance, for this concerns a process—a dualization of different kinds of movement in order to found a new monism of movement.[14] This dualizing would be in contrast to the fudge between bodilessness and nonbodilessness found in literalist approaches, be they in the Christian tradition (with the conundrums that follow from the resurrection of all bodies: are they clothed or unclothed, old or young, cremated, amputated, etc.?), the phantasmagoria of ghostly tales, or the pseudoscience of science-fiction and zombie horror.

More sophisticated versions of these hybrid conceits do exist, however, such as in Philip K. Dick's novel *Counter-Clock World*, which, as James Burton tells us, can be read as a gnostic text in rendering "resurrection commonplace due to a cosmic event that reverses certain biological and temporal processes, and yet having it result neither in salvation nor in everlasting life."[15] Again, setting the clunky mechanism aside (biological reversal), there is something of value in this naturalism nonetheless, as Burton demonstrates. In such a flattened approach, we can begin to understand how "gnostic Christians saw the Resurrection as a spiritual truth rather than an actual event, a symbolic expression of the possibility that anyone might be 'resurrected from the dead' at any time, to become spiritually alive." Quoting one gnostic text from the Nag Hammadi Library, Burton explains how ordinary resurrection comes to stand for "the transformation of things, and a transition into newness."[16] Those "biological and temporal processes" notwithstanding (should they merit close examination), the mundanization of resurrection as *renewal* is another means by which the supernatural refracts into the supernormal.

Hollywood cinema remains, however, stubbornly confused about the supernatural, mixing ordinary material properties with supposedly "immaterial" ones (that are, in truth, simply other forms of matter) in order to achieve the extraordinary as so-called spirit. With respect to ghost films, for example, from a Bergsonian perspective their spirits are never ghostly enough, never sufficiently *insubstantial*, and are always a confusing mix of matter and spirit interpreted as two kinds of incompatible substance (ghosts who cannot speak, cannot move objects, yet who can still see, stand on firm ground, and so on).[17] However, this is not the place to repeat scholastic debates on the possible existence of beings that have no mass and yet can still move and act (following Aquinas on angels). Nor will we take the Derridean route of affirming the spectral *on account of its aporia*, by insisting on the ghost consisting entirely of "mutually exclusive states, oscillating unpredictably between life and death, visibility and invisibility, materiality and immateriality, as well as the past, present, and future."[18] Rather, it is the specter's conflation of temporal tenses (past, present, and future) that should give us pause, especially as regards cinema itself (irrespective of its ghost-story genres). More useful for us, then, would be Edgar Morin's view that "cinema itself has become a world of spirits where phantoms manifest themselves like a great number of the archaic mythologies: an ethereal world filled with omnipresent spirits." I turn to Morin here because he then adds that this cinema is where we see "past, present and future oscillate as in a state of osmosis just as in the human brain, memories, the imaginary future and the experienced moment merge. This Bergsonean [sic] duration, the perceivable indefinite, it is the cinema that defines it."[19] Cinema is composed of images that fuse time and haunt us—memories that are ghosts and ghosts that are time travelers. Yet, as images, these specters are *equally* material *and* spiritual in the Bergsonian rendering of these terms as *temporal* (rather than in Hollywood's confused dualities of substance).

In fact, it is the very same sub-Cartesian dualism that still dominates contemporary philosophy of mind and transhumanist culture (where mind is seen as an intelligence separable from any one physical "platform"), that equally reigns on the silver screen through ghost films, body-swap comedies, reincarnation stories, and other genres where spirit is simply a form of faux substance, a transferable energy, or quasi-thing (basically, fanciful equivalents to the telegraphy, X-rays, and higher-dimensional planes that so impressed certain nineteenth-century spiritualists). For Henri Bergson, these are confused dualities that require proper separation in order to be reunited *temporally* (not in space). As he puts it in *Matter and Memory*: "questions relating to subject and object, to their distinction and their union, should be put in terms of time rather than of space."[20]

All the same, if we also strip away *everything substantial* from spirit (extended space, inert body, mechanism, efficient cause and effect), with what are we left? Movement. According to Henri Bergson, movement is alteration or qualitative becoming (not spatial transition). Something truly ordinary is "hiding" in *plain* sight (nothing is hidden, or "virtual," to *everyone*): a something that might also survive at some level, then, that might straddle those things we call "past" and "present." Only that "thing" is not a thing but a partial continuity, a movement, a specific becoming in person (there is no "becoming in general").[21] Spirit, purified in this way as a kind of movement, is, oddly enough, visible everywhere, restored to space, bodies, and even causation. But this is not a hylomorphic reinsertion of "spookiness." I think I can see why Jane Bennett only sees such restorations as dualistic: because they are viewed in terms of a substantialized space—*res extensa* and "*res inextensa*" (extended and unextended things)—rather than in terms of time. A logic of separated, solid bodies, rather than a watery, temporalized logic. The Bergsonian restoration or reintegration is only the *temporalizing* redescription or revisioning that leaves everything as it is, while also uniting difference "*in terms of time rather than of space*." Nonetheless, what results is at best a marvel to some, or an unseen variation to others. What is unseen, or unknown, though, can itself be a force, an *élan* in thought.

The standard Hollywood version of the supernatural is simply what it projects as the inconsistent hyperbolic of the natural, an outsider or "qualitative" emergent, rather than what it is—the "merely" quantitative, the difference of degree. It is the difference within the one and many *durées* understood as heterogeneous continuity. For we have said it often enough: there are only differences of degree. But a "degree of what?" one might ask. In fact, how can there be *degrees* or even levels and planes in duration, in creative change? Isn't that simply another form of spatialization? This question requires the mereological response—the "part" or degree being of a whole that is open, incomplete, enduring, or *not*-whole. As a part, it is "smaller" and contained or foliated (if one must speak now in terms of size and scale), and yet it is not strictly quantifiable, measurable, or reducible to being a mere component: its participation concerns temporality or movement, a covariance that is shared, continued, and not owned by any part, large or small.

At an even more metatheoretical level (without this "meta-" implying a logic of higher-order representation, by the way), we can say that matter is simply *this*, and spirit *that*—too gestural demonstratives, literally and figuratively. These gestures, or "poles," in Mina Bergson's language, are the minimal dyad (be it of substance, property, or even direction of process), and all that "matters" is that they be mutually irreducible. This irreducibility explains why the Real does *not* appear *as just one thing*, even if only in virtue of the illusion or hallucination of at least two things (because then we have the illusion *and* nonillusion—two things): "spirit" and "matter," "manifest" and "scientific," "living" and "dead," or just "illusion" and "reality." There is always the dual aspect, the double life. The names are unimportant, but the demonstrability is (showing "this" and "that" by giving each a name). Naturalisms are rarely naturalistic enough, then, and need to be *hyper*-correlational, *hyper*-parallel, with psycho-physical parallels going all the way "up" and "down," "in" and "out." So, to say that everything is X (an old or modern *arché*), that everything is matter, or everything is spirit, or difference, or *durée*, is ultimately vacuous, for there is always the real *illusion of at least two*. (You could say that this illusion is itself an illusion, but I wouldn't if I were you.)[22]

Conversely, for a pluralism that says, "Everything is many," its own formula, too, must be sufficiently recursive if it is to avoid a substantial monism, a static nomination: it must continually and indefinitely reperform itself anew with novel formulations and names. To speak like a gnostic, it must perpetually resurrect itself. As we will see next, this performance of new names (and new ways of naming, many of them nonlinguistic) simply is the ramification or bifurcation of types (kinds, levels, planes, or degrees), at once both logical and cosmological, that emanate from the paradoxes of reflexivity. In what follows, a *Philosophus* covariant will be visible at work in the plasticity and epigenetics of Catherine Malabou's thought—one that tackles this same aporia of reflexivity and asks: must a philosophy of change, change, too?

4° = 7° *Philosophus Covariant*

It is time to speak more about scales and scalarity, a topic that has dogged our discussion from the moment we first referred to levels, parts, or degrees in space, time, and memory. In "Philosophical Intuition" (1911), Henri Bergson says this: "the matter and life which fill the world are equally within us, the forces which work in all things we feel within ourselves; whatever may be the inner essence of what is and what is done, we are of that essence."[1] Mina Bergson, in "Know Thyself," states as follows: "*the God of the Macrocosm only reflects Himself to Man through the God of Man's Microcosm.* [. . .] hence the great assistance given to us in the teachings of our Order which insist on a careful study of the Kingdoms of the Macrocosm and the Microcosm side by side with our Spiritual Development, one study helping the other; in fact the two are almost inseparable."[2] Microcosm and macrocosm. One of the key principles of Hermeticism is that of "as above, so below." This is the idea that earthly events reflect those occurring on an astral plane by means of correspondences and attunements. In "Of Skrying," Mina Bergson describes how

> imagination (*eidolon*) means the faculty of building an image. The imagination of the artist must lie in the power, which he possesses more or less in proportion to his sincerity, and his intuition, of perceiving forces in the macrocosm, and allying or attuning himself thereto, his talents naturally and his artificial training permitting him to formulate images which shall express those forces.[3]

Once again, we see the importance for the Golden Dawn of a nonimaginary use of imagination—here as the ability to "build" an image attuned to the macrocosm. (We should also remind ourselves that the Kabbalistic "Tree of Life" was also called the *Minutum Mundum*—the "little world or universe.") As regards levels, in Wouter Hanegraaff's analysis of the systematic "correlations between the macrocosm and the microcosm," he describes how the occultist was able to explore "the various dimensions of the astral plane

Vestiges of a Philosophy. John Ó Maoilearca, Oxford University Press. © Oxford University Press 2023.
DOI: 10.1093/oso/9780197613917.003.0012

so as to change his or her own inner structure and to enable him or her to mediate divine influences to the world."[4] The divine is immanent to the human. Obviously, this can be turned on its head, as Ludwig Feuerbach does by reducing God to a human projection of our species' perfection ("as below, so above," as it were). Beyond the religionist or anti-religionist commitments of theism or atheism, however, in secular terms we can say that the occultist's spatial model removes the need to transcend oneself in unity with the "above" because each human can already ally or attune him or herself with the Real in the "below." The self is remolded, not annihilated.

Sometimes the esoteric homologies between macroscopic and microscopic employed obvious anthropomorphism (the sun and moon as eyes, the moon as breast, the sun as face, and so on).[5] Yet, as Joscelyn Godwin notes, these doctrines of correspondences, complements, or analogies were not just between polarities of large and small, human and divine—they also existed between elemental colors and sound, colors and elements, or colors, letters, and shapes.[6] And indeed, Mina Bergson's own "allying and attuning" would seem to denote quasi-physical images of connection: an "alliance" is a *binding* (from *alligare*, "to bind"), while an attunement is a tension or stretching (from *teinein*, "to stretch").[7] In each image, a material connection, binding and tensile, is formed between micro- and macro-levels, a physico-spiritual amalgam that is both unifying and multilayered. Writing about the *Corpus Hermeticum*, Joshua Ramey explains its teaching that "materiality and spirituality are profoundly united," with life itself being a process in which "the nature of the divine is both discovered and produced in an unfolding of personal and cosmic, evolutionary and historical time. This is the meaning of 'as above, so below': the process of natural life as a 'manifestation of encosmic divinity.' "[8]

We might say that the center is "decentered" through a proliferation of centers: in Bergsonian terms, a kind of "complete relativism" is installed, a flattened ontology with no unsurpassable hierarchy of macro over micro (at least in principle)—there is movement between levels. We have noted, however, that with the fabulation of minds beyond our own, such proliferations should be treated cautiously: attributing powers at the wrong scale, irrespective of the equalities of macrocosm and microcosm, can lead to delusions of voluntarism and control (what cognitivists call "hyperactive agency detection"). Moreover, this type of Renaissance "episteme," one governed by a relation of *analogy* between every level of nature, above and below, need not be seen simplistically as *only* spatial, despite the language used to describe it. Scale is not always a set of nesting Russian dolls, of quantities containing quantities. Many authors agree on this. For Bruno Latour, the notion of continuous, transitive scales needs to be dismantled entirely, such that switching dimensions is never a smooth "zoom" in or out, but a disorientation that is "as much temporal as spatial."[9] Likewise for Karen Barad, scale is "much more complex than simply a "nesting relationship," being instead "a property of spatial phenomena intra-actively produced, contested, and reproduced."[10] Even Gilles Deleuze and Félix Guattari's idea of the "molar" and "molecular" must be seen, they say, as systems of reference or relation rather than as spatial scales.[11]

Indeed, even *quantitative* scales themselves can be *qualified*, too, as being more than quantity, more than the ability for one magnitude to *contain* another.[12] Size, too, can resist quantification. Writing about "bigness" within the theoretical humanities, David Wittenberg points out that

> Size change is a confrontation with the hyperfactical density and opacity of *the body* itself: the body is constantly in the way, inhibiting conventional views and viewpoints, and often directly terrifying. To be big, or rather to be too big—or to be compelled to confront what is too big—is to reanimate a primal physical relationship with objects that the acquisition of correct scale sublimates or distills away. [. . .] Bigness is not something we accomplish by rescaling. Bigness comes *before* scale, maybe strictly speaking *before size*. And therefore, all the more, it precedes any analytic of magnitude or of the sublime.[13]

Bigness is a quality, no less than oneness or twoness are not quantities in the first instance either, but qualities, *qualia* even (at least for mathematical intuitionists like L. E. J. Brouwer or Henri Bergson).[14]

Admittedly, a top-down mereology, regarding the part from the perspective of the whole, might seem to be an impossible task if one is actually the part in question. How can the small transcend its partial point of view? And yet Spinzoa starts from God, or Substance, just as Deleuze and Guattari write, it is said, from the point of view of the Earth on itself as a giant molecule.[15] The era of "Big data" is one empirically anodyne way in which patterns of change, rhythms, and continuities might reveal themselves to their own participants. Big data can be seen as a temporal resampling, time-lapse geo-anthropology operating at higher degrees of tension. Such bigger pictures might reveal who knows what was happening when we were collectively doing "X," even though we each thought at the time that we were operating individually doing "Y."[16] Hence, as Bennett suggested earlier, American food may have facilitated the invasion of Iraq, and sandstorms may be involved in the spread of violence. As we see, the part-whole relations in play in these examples are not at all scalar in any quantitative sense of containment. The principle of "as above, so below," of the "micro" reflecting the "macro," can also be translated into a number of other, more contemporary vocabularies, such as general systems theory, complex systems, Deleuzian assemblage theory (giant molecules *and* "microbrains"), or David Bohm's radical holism (which we will address later), to name just a few more ordinary renderings. Each of these translations brings its own difficulties with it, no doubt.

Much of the puzzling nature of scale and composition can be tempered, however, when we think of it in terms of time. The relations between parts and wholes, mereology in other words, must be thoroughly *temporalized*.[17] For example, we can also qualify a scale by temporalizing it in terms of rhythm, say, or in the language of memory. We can follow the second route by comparing Henri Bergson's ideas with those of Carl Jung (no stranger to esoteric ideas either in his own psychology). Pete Gunter does exactly this when he writes about Jung's "collective unconscious" alongside *Creative Evolution's* theory of a "biological memory" contained within each animal, "dormant potentialities, 'memories' of a common past which it shares with all other living creatures."[18] Examples given by Henri Bergson himself include the Ammophila wasp, which seems to have a magical knowledge of the physiognomy of its traditional prey, a caterpillar, allowing it to apply just enough venom to paralyze but not kill it (mummifying it alive for later consumption).[19] In what could be seen as an animal prefiguring of Arthur C. Clarke's "third law"—that "any sufficiently advanced technology is indistinguishable from magic"—for Henri Bergson, any sufficiently evolved "instinct" will appear to reason as magical knowledge. Yet this miracle is only apparent: what is real is the *continuity* formed by the coevolutionary movement of two apparently separate entities—wasp and caterpillar—in one relation. These biological forms are really two sides of a continuous process—a process that is itself composed from other, interpenetrating processes. Instinct appears miraculous only when we do not think of it in terms of continuous evolutionary movements at the correct scale, movements that are "reciprocally determining" (in Deleuzian language), "entangled" (Barad), or, in Henri Bergson's idiom, "interpenetrating" each other. Though this biological account from *Creative Evolution* would need updating, its essentials remain the same, as

Patrick McNamara explains: "each organism, therefore, carries within itself a 'replica' of the local environment, as well as the collective memory of its species. [. . .] The 'memory' of each person, therefore, supports the paradoxical experience of infinite depth and personal intimacy."[20]

Henri Bergson's acknowledged influence on Jung, of course, led to this biological memory being thought of as a *collective unconscious*, one where, as Gunter describes it, a "mystic or an artist is 'seized by an archetype' [. . .] grasped by fundamental energies which it is his task to express in novel forms."[21] This collectivization of memory is also to be found in the practices of the Golden Dawn. As Charlotte de Mille tells us: "Golden Dawn members relate episodes of collective dreaming, whereby multiple consciousnesses could permeate one another to create shared experience. Moreover, they believed that this activity opened access to a universal 'Great Memory.'"[22] W. B. Yeats himself, de Mille then reminds us, wrote on essay on "Magic" in 1901 that described individual memories as "part of one great memory, the memory of Nature herself." Yeats even recounts a particular vision of a past life, a moment when participating in a Golden Dawn ritual, which exemplifies precisely this collective. In this vision, Samuel Mathers

> held a wooden mace in his hand, and turning to a tablet of many-coloured squares, with a number on each of the squares, that stood near him on a chair, he repeated a form of words. Almost at once my imagination began to move of itself and to bring before me vivid images that, though never too vivid to be imagination, as I had always understood it, had yet a motion of their own, a life I could not change or shape.[23]

What is strange about this account—and why it might be deemed proof of a "Great Memory"—is that the recollected scene was not Yeats's vision, *but that of another member of the Golden Dawn.* And yet he recalls it, not so much as his own memory than as a shared one, a collective memory. In fact, for Yeats, these experiences were proof "of the power of many minds to become one, . . . till they have become a single intense, unhesitating energy. . . . all the minds gave a little, creating or revealing for a moment what I must call a supernatural artist."[24]

This nonspatial "upscaling" of memory through mystical means has ties with other thinkers than just Henri Bergson and Jung. Joshua Ramey's research on the hermetic tradition's influence on Deleuze's thought demonstrates effectively the connection between the mystical perspective and Deleuze's notion of a "cosmic Memory." In Deleuze's own words, this Memory is one that actualizes "all the levels at the same time, that liberates man from the plane or the level that is proper to him, in order to make him a creator, adequate to the whole movement of creation."[25] Unsurprisingly, those words are from Deleuze's 1966 monograph *Bergsonism*, as Ramey well knows when he also connects Bergson directly to the hermetic tradition: "mysticism is thus, for Bergson—and one might add, retrospectively, for Renaissance hermeticism—not so much an ability to distance oneself from time and circumstance through identification with God, but an intensification of cosmic memory, an involution in the past of a universe. . . ."[26]

Moreover, upscaling memory in this fashion is only one form of temporalized mereology, where the small regard themselves as composing the Big through collective experience, through shared "memory." The direction or orientation of this upscaling can be inverted by looking at rhythm or tension. Comparing Henri Bergson's work to Whitehead's theory of structured societies, Leonard Eslick argues that the latter is perfectly "analogous to Bergson's hierarchy of durational rhythms."[27] The aggregate can now be seen working top-down rather than bottom-up. In both these cases, however, it is a matter of rhythm. In *Matter and Memory*, Henri Bergson words this top-down assembly as a "higher degree of tension":

> would not the whole of history be contained in a very short time for a consciousness at a higher degree of tension than our own, which should watch the development of humanity while contracting it, so to speak, into the great phases of its evolution? In short, then, to perceive consists in condensing enormous periods of an infinitely diluted existence into a few more differentiated moments of an intenser life, and in thus summing up a very long history. To perceive means to immobilize.[28]

These "higher degrees" are also rendered as "planes" in Henri Bergson's work, of course. We have already examined the resemblances evoked between the plane of pure memory (or virtual) and the Golden Dawn's astral plane as extensions of our optico-perceptual apparatus (the latter once described by Mina Bergson as a "hall panelled with mirrors"). But they share a distribution or scalarity in how they work as well. *Matter and Memory* tells of a "scale of being" along which diverse rhythms of duration are arrayed. For Henri Bergson, "there is no one rhythm of duration; it is possible to imagine many different rhythms which, slower or faster, measure the degree of tension or relaxation of different kinds of consciousness and thereby fix their respective places in the scale of being."[29] Yet the scale is temporal, not spatial or hierarchical in value (at least at face value, for they all belong equally to *durée*). The same might even be said for Mina Bergson, for when she writes of the "Three Planes of Being" traveled in "psychic experiment," though these grades are ranked ontologically, they all belong to *Ein Sof* nonetheless. *Ein Sof* is indeed distributed differently, but still *immanently* in its ten emanations.[30]

* * *

A final discussion of levels, of above and below, must now involve philosophy itself, the *Philosophus* covariant. In her essay "Before and Above: Spinoza and Symbolic Necessity," the philosopher Catherine Malabou ordinarizes the "sacred" in her own particular manner through what she calls "an *experience of overreading*." For Spinoza, she writes, the mind

> has a *natural tendency to overinterpret—and such is the origin, the very possibility of the sacred.* [. . .] For Spinoza, to overread or overinterpret means to confer semantic content on a word or phrase by inflating its (absence of) referent. This overinflating is fundamentally both spatial and temporal. Spatial: God is understood as a central power, coming from above, a highness (hence all the superpowers attributed to a God conceived as a legislator: jealousy, arbitrariness, love, and others). *Above*, in Spinoza, is the most acute example of the spatial overreading of the sacred. It implies an overarching and overlooking position proceeding from a hidden and unreachable power. Temporal: in its temporal sense, *above* means "before." All prophets have seen, have heard somebody or something that was there before, already, waiting to be seen or heard. *Above* and *before* are the two main structures or patterns of sacralization. . . . In these two structures, we recognize the very economy of *superstition*.[31]

The "over" can be understood as excess but also, in its excess, as a fabulation of the *spatial* in terms of superstition—the God or gods operating above us. However, just as Henri Bergson's theory of animist fabulation found that its error rested only in its animating the natural world *at an improper level*, so Malabou argues that superstition can be redeemed within a theory of interpretation. And this also operates on superstition of the past, the Before, alongside the Above. Citing Emile Benveniste's work in linguistics, she reports: "*superstitio* is the gift of second sight which enables a person to know the past as if he or she had been present, *superstes*. This is how *superstitiosus* denotes the gift of second sight, which is attributed to 'seers,' that of being a 'witness' of events at which he has not been present."[32] For Benveniste and Malabou, then, as a tendency to overread, superstition is not "bad per se":

> On the contrary, it marks the origin of the symbolic, and in that sense it cannot be totally separated from ideality. [. . .] what he showed is that the origin of interpretation resides in overinterpretation. . . . No need, for Spinoza, to refer to any transcendence in the message. Overinterpretation is, in a certain sense, *immanent* to the message.[33]

There is much to discuss in this passage: superstition as both belief and action (or presence) at a distance; or sacralization as equally temporal and spatial ("before and above"). But we will focus first on Malabou's theory of interpretation in this regard, and especially on how it impacts on the question of language and the evolution of theory—how philosophy mutates into different forms from itself. For the fact is that the excess or overinterpretation that Malabou sees within the "sacred" message can also be applied to her own work as a new materialist. Her text *Morphing Intelligence* can be (overly?) read as immanent to the evolution of her project's ambition to keep Continental philosophy informed by the latest research emerging from the brain sciences. In maintaining this acquaintance with the empirical, she has found that her own renowned thesis concerning the "plasticity" of our brain requires reformation.[34] In her book *What Should We Do with Our Brain?*, she originally argued that the concept of neurological plasticity, the idea that our brains change throughout the course of our lives as they adapt to evolving circumstances, brings with it the promise of a new kind of human freedom. It opens up the possibility that we can intervene in our brain's evolution by changing those circumstances: we are not biologically *determined* bottom up, but can change our fates, top down, working in tandem with this biological flexibility.

   And yet, in the preface to *Morphing Intelligence* she offers a new account that mitigates, among other things, the voluntarism of her earlier view. She admits that "for a long time I believed that neuronal plasticity proscribed any comparison between the "natural" brain and machines, especially computers. However, the latest advances in artificial intelligence, especially the development of 'synaptic' chips, have mounted a serious challenge to this position."[35] The need to develop her concepts and languages—in particular, replacing the centrality of plasticity with that of "epigenesis"—can be regarded as both a drawback for *any* philosophy trying to maintain its currency through an ever-evolving scientific materialism but also as the virtue of a thought like hers that is attempting to materialize its own performance through these co-variant mutations. Epigenesis is the theory that the embryo develops progressively from an undifferentiated egg cell. That life follows a program of sorts, going through a predictable sequence of events, lessens both the plasticity of biological forms as well as, at least in Malabou's view, any clear distance being kept between the organic and the artificial. She charts her conversion from plasticity to epigenesis as follows:

> For years, I explored the concept of plasticity, viewing it as the potential starting point for a new conception of freedom that would no longer be separated from the biological definition of thought and action. Isn't brain plasticity exactly this vitality of intelligence—the one that tests, measurements, and factors will never identify? [. . .] Unfortunately, however—or is it fortunately?—recent developments in artificial intelligence shook me out of my nondogmatic slumber. I came to see that the conclusions I presented in *What Should We Do with Our Brain?* were, to put it bluntly, wrongheaded. Shortly after that book came out, it became apparent to me that it needed revising, if not a complete rewrite. This suspicion dawned on me upon reading an article about recent computational architectures, especially IBM's creation of an entirely new type of chip, a "neuro-synaptic processor" that dramatically increases processing abilities while minimizing the energy required for computation. But the title of the article, "IBM's Neuro-Synaptic Chip Mimics Human Brain," was misleading. In fact, this chip is not capable of "imitating" synaptic functioning: it functions de facto as a synaptic connection. It *is* a synapse.[36]

With a certain zeal of the new convert, the philosopher pushes further than the science, proclaiming a real *identity* over a correlated function. More than that, however, Malabou's own thesis has "morphed:" as a bio-philosophical hybrid of deconstructive thought and brain science, it has deconstructed itself, rendered plasticity plastic by tempering its own freedom with epigenetic predictability, programmability. As such, she asks, "how could we not conclude that plasticity is programmable, since it is becoming the fundamental program of cybernetics? But is a programmable and programmed plasticity still plasticity? Not that plasticity is the opposite of the concept of program on principle. Epigenetic mechanisms are programmed genetically."[37]

Such a renewal in language-thought no doubt reflects in part a desire to seek out the new and extraordinary within science in order to maintain a philosophical distance from the ordinary (empirical evidence quickly dating itself and the philosopher's reliance on it). However, there is the counter-vailing need to renew language simply in order to *think in duration*. This is part of the price paid by any "scientific philosophy," in the truest sense of the term. In *Time Reborn*, physicist Lee Smolin writes with great relevance to this point: "Scientists think in time when we conceive of our task as the invention of novel ideas to describe newly discovered phenomena, and of novel mathe-matical structures to express them. If we think outside time, we believe these ideas somehow existed before we invented them. If we think in time, we see no reason to presume that."[38] And this is exactly what Henri Bergson meant by the requirement of philosophy to "think in duration"—the need for it to use "flexible, mobile, almost fluid representations" in order to stay true to the "mobility of the real."[39]

Like Malabou, Henri Bergson formed much of his philosophical research around the empirical sciences, *Matter and Memory* focusing on studies of the brain in particular. Yet, as Paul Atkinson explains, Henri Bergson was looking to place "the brain within an ontology of perception rather than deriving a theory of perception from the operation of the brain."[40] And that ontology was processual and immanentist. In terms of methodology, therefore, he insisted on the inevitability for any serious philosophical terminology—and he includes his own language of "*durée*," "multiplicity," and "differentiation" here—to lose its purchase on real process unless it, too, continually mutated.[41] Every new idea is eventually stripped of its suggestive power as it slowly absorbs the more mundane thoughts linked to it by associ-ation. Philosophy must renew its language and imagery if it is to remain vital. A theory of change must itself change. Or, as Malabou would say, intelligence morphs.

Even *our* attempt here to reintegrate the paranormal within the normal (as "supernormal") is also, for now, a renewal of language that must eventually lose its way, not by coming to the end of its line, but by being replaced with other lines of continuity. Following Henri Bergson's lead and Malabou's re-cent example, *philosophy must overinterpret itself*. This need not be achieved only through scientific fluency (though that could be part of it, too): what is needed is the ability to create new philosophical concepts and images using whatever materials come to hand. Changing names once or twice is not sufficient either: the real is not comprehended simply "by giving it a name." On the contrary, because reality and logic, too, are essentially processual (or *inessential*) for Henri Bergson, philosophy must *keep* creating the right expression to fit new realities. *Names need to keep multiplying, like images.*

Such mutation or morphing could even act reflexively as the recursive metamorphosis of "meta-physics" itself, so it would be understood now as an ever-expanding perception rather than an intellectual grasp of some eternal truth—an empirical metaphysics *sub specie durationis*, as Henri Bergson put it, over Spinoza's *sub specie aeternitatis*. Yet such ramifications would not proceed within a disembodied logical regress of *types* or *orders of representation*, so much as a *real* progress within cosmological tiers, levels, or planes.[42] And this is why *overinterpretation*—a multiplication of names—is not the *representation* of this one level, but the invented effects of many levels constructively interfering with each other.[43] Out of the paradoxes of "reflexivity" (does a theory of change, change?) stem not only different, ramifying *logical* types, but different *cosmological* levels, generated through a material-spiritual autopoetic agency, or what we will hear Thomas Nail call "bifurcation." As above, so below, micro and macro, super and sub: heterogeneous kinds of continuity operating "vertically" and "horizontally" on different scales, temporal and spatial.

And so also, before and after. An expanded perception (or "second sight") for Bergson means that a "past" is brought back to presence by distending, or stretching, this present if only momentarily. *Superstitio.* For Mina Bergson's "superstition," one becomes a "seer" of the "before," a witness of events at which one was never present, but which continue in lines of movement that can be recreated. And that recreation also involves renaming conventions—all the names of the divine, and more.

8

Vestigia Nulla Retrorsum

"Leave No Trace"

Dennis Denisoff's essay on Parisian occulture in the *Belle Epoque*, "Performing the Spirit: Theatre, the Occult, and the Ceremony of Isis," discusses Mina's and Samuel's celebrity in the context of performance art. A contemporary account from the time might explain why. In 1900, journalist André Gaucher attended one of these Rites and reported back to his journal *L'Echo des merveilleux* as follows:

> When the rite began the priest and priestess knelt at the foot of the statue [of Osiris] to light a diffuser of perfume, and the sanctuary was filled with the scent of benzoin and incense. Then they sprinkled grains of wheat and flowers on the floor and on the worshippers. [. . .]
>
> The white veils and garlands along the walls fell with an ominous shiver and the walls were revealed to be covered in black. At the same time the torches were extinguished, as if by an invisible wind. The drapes at the rear of the hall then tore apart with a sinister rustling. In the distance a shapeless, chaotic mass was slowly emerging from the blackness. The worshippers sat up, rigid, motionless, then cried out, three times: "Osiris! Osiris! Osiris!" [. . .]
>
> All around were sighs and convulsive cries. Bodies rolling on the ground, in the darkness, prey to terrible nervous spasms. Others stood up, straight and rigid, their faces drained of blood, their eyes haggard. A reddish glow lit the depths of the sanctuary with an infernal light, from behind the gigantic statue which seemed to be locked in a terrible grin. At the foot of the statue appeared a fantastic circle of superhuman beings: the hawk's head of the god Horus, the jackal's muzzle of Anubis, the bull's head of the god Thor.[1]

At some point soon after, Gaucher admits to losing consciousness. *Quelle performance!* Osiris, Horus, Anubis, Anari, even Thor. Theater as ritual/ritual as theater—Antonin Artaud should have been so fortunate to achieve similar

Vestiges of a Philosophy. John Ó Maoilearca, Oxford University Press. © Oxford University Press 2023.
DOI: 10.1093/oso/9780197613917.003.0013

effects in his Theater of Cruelty thirty years later. In his essay, Denisoff is most interested in the ephemerality of such a performance, its transience as an event, which he connects with Peggy Phelan's idea of the "unmarked": "the transience of performance—its amorphous function across the private and the public—was recognized as a source of power and is what drew Golden Dawn initiates to it."[2] For Phelan herself the "power of impermanence" is real: "there is real power," she contends, "in remaining unmarked; and there are serious limitations to visual representation as a political goal."[3] Hence, Denisoff for his part continues thus: "the evanescence of the supernatural is one with that of performance; while the latter can be recorded, it is nevertheless itself impermanent. This agency of the unaccountable, I argue, occult practitioners recognized as a magical power."[4] The unmarked, the evanescent, the traceless—these terms can indicate lack, absence, or what stands hyperbolically beyond the fullness of nature as supernature; but they can also signify something quite ordinary—the plenitude of movement.

Of Mina Bergson's numerous names, possibly the most telling is her chosen Golden Dawn magical name, *Vestigia Nulla Retrorsum* (often abbreviated in manuscripts to VNR). A condensation of a phrase from Horace's *Epistles*, I, i, 75, meaning "the past leaves no traces," it can also be variously translated as: "I Leave No Traces Behind," "No Stepping Back," or, most suggestively, "Leave No Trace."[5] Given that these chosen names were often aspirational, we might ask what it might have signified in Mina's case. The past as ephemeral? Or a traceless existence in which "there is real power"? Or a desire to be untraceable, to be unmarked in some way? Mina Bergson certainly did her best to have it so. Mary Greer notes that, at the end of her life, having rejected all friendly offers of support, she essentially starved herself to death. All of the original temple furniture from Alpha et Omega and all of her remaining papers were subsequently burned (following instructions from the highest order of the "Secret Chiefs").[6]

In terms of Phelan's thesis of performance as unmarked, and Mina's invocation of spirits as an *occult* performance, we might say that what is *not* left behind is also what *can* be brought to "presence" in such performance: a movement, a bodily gesture, projected colors, vibrated sounds—but no solid residues, no "permanent" things. Not representing (picturing) the past but performing it, even with images. And no spooky *substances* either, no *confusion* of matter and spirit as opposed things—only traceless ghosts. Indeed, the very idea of séance or ectoplasm was anathema to both the Golden Dawn and the Alpha et Omega which followed it—they did not practice *that* kind of "magic." The spiritualization of matter is not its *transubstantiation* (the insertion of a ghost into another substance), but its *ephemeralization*—seeing matter as moving, traceless, evanescent, and thereby real. One such material was Mina's performing body: in the words of Rebecca Schneider on "theatrical re-enactment": "this body, given to performance, is here engaged with disappearance chiasmically—not only disappearing but resiliently eruptive, remaining through performance like so many ghosts at the door marked 'disappeared.'"[7]

Recall how, for Henri Bergson, memory is not a set of images stored in the brain. Talk of "engrams" as traces left in the brain from repeated cerebral activity raises as many questions as it supposedly answers. Why *those* traces, why those repetitions, if not because they were made by what *I* was interested in, by *my* attention? Deflation to a purportedly mechanical brain, but followed by an inflation of that brain re-envisioned as the brain in all its own individuality, not even Catherine Malabou's "*our* brain," but *my* brain: the brain as an individual assemblage of selective movements, intersecting lines of continuity.[8] For Henri Bergson, there are no general, that is, *mechanical* laws of mental association, only personal ones, "plastic" ones. When looked at closely enough, the brain reveals itself to be more than an impersonal, predictable mechanism, but a set of such individuated movements. Perhaps then, and so to listen to Mina Bergson again, the memories that recur (the special ones, the evocative-involuntary, Proustian ones) are connected to the ritual memories or experiences that are *attempting to repeat, to return, to survive* at another level—what we heard Malabou earlier describe as "something that was there before, already, waiting to be seen or heard." These "somethings" (Gaucher's "shapeless, chaotic mass" perhaps?) only need a ceremony, performance, or rite as their conduit, their interrupted continuation. The ritual—bodies in motion, instruments, staged space, sounds and light included—as macro-brain and collective memory. Smallism *and* "largism"; or, to proliferate the hermetic principle as follows: "as below, so above, as above, so below. . . ."

In this regard, a peculiar significance can be found in some of Henri Bergson's previously unpublished lectures at the Collège de France. The lecture scripts from 1903 and 1904 have recently appeared and throw a slightly different light on this "something" that tries to return.[9] Furthermore, in the midst of these "new" texts, a famous image does return: the renowned diagram of the cone in *Matter and Memory* that we discussed earlier. Only, in the 1904 lecture on memory, the cone here comes back in a new guise, with a different shape and different symbols that actually connect with ideas of ephemera (the untraced), performance, and the spiritualization of matter (see Figure 14).[10]

The topmost plane of the cone, marked by *RR"*, is the "plane of dream" ("*plan du rêve*"). Note, however, the way that the lines of the cone now pass upward beyond *RR"*. Indeed, they do so indefinitely because the human dream state never *defined* pure memory for Henri Bergson—it merely indicated ("figuratively," as he says) the direction of those planes approaching pure memory "above" more closely than those "below" nearer to living perception.[11] As he explained in these lectures, there are memories that, the closer to *RR"* they approach, the more personal, virtual, and really past they are ("in" a past that is real). Memories that come closer to a perception at the point of the cone *M* gather together through various "dynamic schemata" (marked *SS"*) rather than simply falling chaotically into our present perceptions (at least while we are awake and not dreaming).[12]

M symbolizes a "plane of movement" (sometimes also called a "plane of action") at this point of the cone.[13] But it is how Henri Bergson newly describes the way in which memories move down from *RR"* to *M* that is truly revealing. *Matter and Memory* described how a memory produces on us the effect of a "ghost," but eight years later, his language has amplified: now, he says, "there are ghosts," of a sort. Though the memories located at *RR"* are still "obscure," he claims that they nonetheless exert "a kind of thrust" that might help them "return . . . to full light." "In a way," he continues, they are "ghosts who would like to materialize themselves." The analogy proceeds as follows:

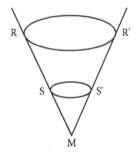

Figure 14 Bergson's Cone of Memory (second variation) (Reproduced from Bergson's notes, 1904)

At the top of the cone, at point M, there is movement, there is, one might say, life; there is the flesh and blood that make life; but on the plane RR", there are ghosts. These ghosts would like to borrow from point M the blood and flesh found there to become living beings. [. . .] Which . . . amongst all these ghosts, will be the ones who succeed in materializing themselves? Those who have the strongest relationship with the present perception, those best able to insert themselves, those also who exist better than others in the movement that we are sketching. . . . [14]

Thus, we see the significance of calling the point of the cone *M*, the "plane of movement." To return, a ghost must fit into a movement that (we might add) calls it, invokes it, and so allows it to materialize (materializing "spirits" by spiritualizing matter with a particular movement, so to speak).

Henri Bergson is writing playfully here, of course, and so are we, in part. Yet the analogy with phantoms and spirits is a recurrent trope within his writing, even in "serious" work in the philosophy of psychology or the history of philosophy. When citing Plotinus's *Enneades*, for example, he also likens memories to "souls" that are "lying in wait in the depth of the unconscious," a "phantom memory, materializing itself in sensation which brings it flesh and blood, becomes a being which lives a life of its own, a dream."[15] The mention of dreaming is striking here, for the reference to the *Enneades* comes in Henri Bergson's 1901 lecture on "Dreams" (*Le Rêve*) where the question of movement, of how pure memory-images gain a foothold in the living, moving world, is given an even more suggestive rendering—*as phantoms entering a dance*:

But the memories which are preserved in these obscure depths are for us in the state of invisible phantoms. They aspire, perhaps, to the light: they do not even try to rise to it; they know it is impossible, and that I, a living and acting being, have something else to do than occupy myself with them. But suppose that, at a given moment, I become *disinterested* in the present situation, in the pressing action, in both of the forces which concentrate on one single point all the activities of memory; suppose, in other words, I fall asleep: then these repressed memories, feeling that I have set aside the obstacle, raised the trap-door which held them back below the floor of consciousness, begin to stir. They rise and spread abroad and perform in the night of the unconscious a wild phantasmagoric dance. They rush together to the door which has been left ajar. They all want to get through.

But they cannot; there are too many of them. Of the many called, which will be chosen? It is easy to guess. Just now, when awake, the memories admitted were those which could claim relationship with my present situation, with my actual perceptions. [. . .] So, then, among the phantom memories which aspire to weight themselves with colour, with sound, in short with materiality, those only succeed which can assimilate the colour-dust I perceive, the noises without and within that I hear, etc., and which, besides, are in harmony with the general affective state which my organic impressions compose. When this union between memory and sensation is effected, I dream.[16]

It is the "phantom memories" that perform this wild dance here. I am asleep and only dreaming. Yet dreaming is only one state of my consciousness. Other planes of consciousness, of trance, fugue, hypnotic states, dissociative states (all of which Henri Bergson was well acquainted with in his research) would each offer different means for materialization, diverse forms of movement at M. The movements that we "sketch" (or perhaps "trace") can be multiple—and doubtless ones produced in artistic and mystical performances could be counted in their number. Phantom memories need to find a purchase, a relation in, or kinship with, the present in order to return to life. What the journalist Gaucher described as "a shapeless, chaotic mass . . . slowly emerging from the blackness" in Mina Bergson's Rites—such phantoms need to live as "blood and flesh." So the question naturally arises: what type of movement might reanimate those who, in Henri's words, "rise and spread abroad and perform in the night of the unconscious a wild phantasmagoric dance"?[17] Or, in other words, what else might M stand for?

* * *

To return ourselves to the question of leaving no trace in the context of Mina Bergson's biography, it is noteworthy how Henri Bergson's own preoccupation with "discretion" and the "virtues of the private and the secret" struck many of his contemporary commentators.[18] In a final item of correspondence from 1939, and sounding like an astronaut about to return to his spaceship, he wrote: "I continue to work as best I can, but it is wrong to have said that I was preparing a new book. The truth is that I would like, before leaving our planet, to come to an opinion on certain points, and to do it *for me*."[19] One year later in December 1940, Henri Bergson would, against all advice, line up with his co-religionists to register as a Jew. He died within a month after contracting bronchitis. In his will, he forbade the publication of any un-published writing. No final book appeared after he had left "our planet." Like his sister, all his personal notes and correspondence were destroyed on his instruction.[20]

That we have only just now cited ideas from works that were unpublished in Henri's own lifetime is, therefore, a partial betrayal of his request. Yet no less is true of this very enquiry into the vestiges of Mina's ideas, a woman who wished to remain without a trace. Should we disturb their spirits too much, we might hope for some exoneration in the view that it is the *unmarked* performance which has real creative power, that the indefinite, ephemeral movements of enduring life (Henri) and spiritual ritual (Mina) contain an immanent truth that survives unseen. And these truths will remain at least partially untraced, despite what we are documenting here. Alternatively, be-yond any virtue signaling in *my* retelling of Mina's "her-story" (though hers is a story that should be told, irrespective of motive), and beyond endorsing Henri's possibly *bourgeois* values of "discretion" or "privacy" (though staying faithful to "the inner," to "knowing thyself," was truly paramount for both him and Mina), there remains the necessity of invention when trying to un-derstand the alterity of another. This is no less true of my documentations of the two Bergsons. When I cannot be the other, I must fabulate, remake, or invoke him or her. In *our* fabulation, therefore, our infidelity to both Bergsons could be redeemed through Vladimir Jankélévitch's recommenda-tion that we *remake* Bergson rather than simply reproduce him—that it is "*the Bergsonian direction, the Bergsonian movement*" alone that continues, that survives.[21] Only, in this performance, it is the two Bergsons together, as alter egos, that need to be brought to life—not in "flesh and blood" but as covarying movements of thought. If this book is about memory and a for-gotten Bergson, it is also a book that performs its recollection as an invoca-tion through heterogeneity, discontinuity, and covariance.

3° = 8° *Practicus Covariant*

In an essay by physicist Paul Halpern, wonderfully titled "Spiritual Hyperplane," we find a useful history of both older and more recent engagements by spiritualists with the science of physics. Or, we should say, spiritually inclined physicists. One of these can be found in *The Unseen Universe*, a popular book from 1875 by mathematical physicists Balfour Stewart and Peter Guthrie Tait. It was published anonymously, and for obvious reasons: as Halpern reports, it attempted to link the principle of the conservation of energy with the spiritual question of life after death. In one passage, it also connected a "fourth dimension" of space with an "unseen realm" that could be interpreted as spiritual. Halpern cites Stewart and Tait thus: "just as points are the terminations of lines, lines the boundaries of surfaces, and surfaces the boundaries of portions of space of three dimensions: so we may suppose our (essentially three-dimensional) matter to be the mere skin or boundary of an Unseen whose matter has four dimensions."[1]

Stewart and Tait were not alone in their off-duty speculations as physicists (some of whom, such as Oliver Lodge, emerged in their wake). We heard previously of "neo-alchemists" and telepathists looking to atomic theory and X-rays, respectively, for scientific confirmation of these paranormal phenomena. Here, however, the interest in the spiritual comes directly from the scientists, and the object of fascination at this point for many was *space*. In 1879, German physicist Johann Zöllner published *Transcendental Physics*. He, too, was engrossed in the significance of a space beyond the usual three dimensions. Halpern describes how Zöllner posited "that space's restriction to three dimensions could simply be a persistent mirage. Perhaps, then, the world of the spirit, including all manner of psychic occurrences, had a perfectly natural explanation in a hitherto unexplored dimension."

These underground conjectures by physicists about other spatial dimensions soon drew to a close, however, when one theory in particular appeared: Einstein's general theory of relativity. It was the general theory, Halpern argues, "which enabled physicists to reclaim higher dimensions

Vestiges of a Philosophy. John Ó Maoilearca, Oxford University Press. © Oxford University Press 2023.
DOI: 10.1093/oso/9780197613917.003.0014

from the spiritualists" (no more "spooky physics" to trouble Gerald Edelman).[2] These days, Halpern concludes, "most physicists eschew any spiritual connotations of higher dimensions," though he adds that, perhaps in some cases, the "mystique" of the spiritual "as expressed in books such as *The Dancing Wu Li Masters* (1979) by Gary Zukav—has helped to draw new recruits to the genuine science."[3]

Even earlier than Zukav (who was not a scientist) came the work of Austrian physicist Fritjof Capra, whose 1975 book *The Tao of Physics* explains itself perfectly in its subtitle: *An Exploration of the Parallels Between Modern Physics and Eastern Mysticism*. Seeing parallels between the "new physics," as it was still called in the 1970s (primarily meaning quantum mechanics and relativity theory) and spirituality has become a common enough strategy in a good deal of science and humanities writing since then. It is something that Karen Barad's version of new materialism in *Meeting the Universe Halfway* from 2007 excels at (despite their protests to the contrary that they are *not* conducting any such work in mere "analogy").[4] Where Capra gave us physics and the Tao in order to see the world anew as a highly interconnected ecology, Barad gives us physics and high theory (poststructuralism, feminist theory, posthumanism, and performance studies), in order to think about the problems of epistemology afresh as forms of "entangled" knowledge. And there's no shame in either enterprise. A professor of Feminist Studies, Barad is unusual in the academic humanities for also having a doctorate in theoretical physics. They apply their interdisciplinary approach across various arts and humanities, performance theory being a crucial one. As Christopher Gamble, Joshua Hanan, and Thomas Nail write, Barad's materialism is invested in a "new sense of aliveness" rather than any vitalism, new or old: "in sharp contrast with Bennett, then, Barad's notion of matter's vitality does not derive from alleged essential differences between life and death, but is what performatively engenders those differences."[5]

Like Bennett, though, Barad begins with their new conception of matter, in this case one that emerges from quantum mechanics (especially the version championed by Niels Bohr). In this approach,

> Matter is neither fixed and given nor the mere end result of different processes. Matter is produced and productive, generated and generative. Matter is agentive, not a fixed essence or property of things. Mattering is differentiating, and which differences come to matter, matter in the iterative production of different differences.[6]

We will look more closely at these claims anon, but we should first hear Barad out when they claim that their "diffractive approach" to physics is no mere compare-and-contrast exercise. Their research has no patience, they write,

> for tricks with mirrors, where, for example, the macroscopic is said to mirror the microscopic, or the social world is treated as a reflection of the metaphysics of individualism perfected in atomic theory, and so on. The drawing of analogies, like that between special relativity and the cubist school of painting, for instance . . . can be very interesting. But these common modes of analysis are only of limited value, and insufficient for understanding the deeper philosophical issues at stake. . . . This diffractive methodology enables me to examine in detail important philosophical issues such as the conditions for the possibility of objectivity, the nature of measurement, the nature of nature and meaning making, the conditions for intelligibility, the nature of causality and identity, and the relationship between discursive practices and the material world.[7]

No model of "as above, so below" here, then. Nor will readers, they add, looking to be "dazzled, entertained, and mystified by a quixotic sideshow of isolated facts and cutesy quirks of quantum theory," find any satisfaction in their work.[8] Their approach is serious and explores "deeper philosophical issues," as we heard, without any showmanship.

Iris van der Tuin is one philosopher who has taken Barad's work very seriously and, indeed, seen parallels between it and Henri Bergson's ideas. When Barad states that "reality is not composed of things-in-themselves [thingification] or things-behind-phenomena [representationalism] but 'things'-in-phenomena," or when they write of an "ongoing flow of agency," and a "processual historicity," van der Tuin sees ideas here that are "very much in line with Bergson."[9] Indeed, the dynamism at the heart of Barad's view of the world is thoroughly Bergsonian in spirit if we look to Barad's writing directly:

> Materialization is not the end product or simply a succession of intermediary effects of purely discursive practices. Materiality itself is a factor in materialization. The dynamics of mattering are nonlinear: the specific nature of the material configurations of the apparatuses of bodily production, which are themselves phenomena in the process of materializing, matters to the materialization of the specific phenomena of which they

are a part, which matters to the ongoing materialization of the world in its intra-active becoming, which makes a difference in subsequent patterns of mattering, and so on; that is, matter is enfolded into itself in its ongoing materialization.[10]

Barad's conspicuous use of the verbal form "mattering" (which we will later see David Bohm call a "rheomode," or deeply verbal grammar) and their emphasis on matter as process—materialization—is obviously evocative of Henri Bergson, too. This materialization is best understood as a process of emergence for Barad: "*matter refers to the materiality/materialization of phenomena*, not to an inherent fixed property of abstract independently existing objects of Newtonian physics."[11] Similar comparisons between Barad and Henri Bergson can be made with regard to the dimensions of time as well. On the question of the persistence of the past, their interpretation of the new physics contains many echoes of *Matter and Memory*: "the existence of the quantum discontinuity," for instance, means that "the past is never left behind, never finished once and for all [. . .] rather the past and the future are enfolded participants in matter's iterative becoming."[12]

Though there is much more emphasis on matter or the language of "materialization" here than might be found in Henri Bergson himself, the fact that it is framed within a processual context of "becoming," or "the inexhaustible dynamism of the enfolding of mattering," makes for familiar reading, with further talk of "the world and its possibilities for becoming [that] are re-made with each moment," and the need to be "alive to the possibilities of becoming," which is itself an "ethical call . . . written into the very matter of all being and becoming."[13] And so on. Barad's critique of "thingification" is likewise very Bergsonian: even though they retain the idea of substance, like him, they rerender it as process, as becoming: "*matter is substance* in its *intra-active becoming—not* a *thing but* a *doing.*"[14]

Whereas Bennett puts far greater store on "thing-power" at the larger scale she is mostly writing about, Barad's subatomic level of discourse sees things differently. Things for them are emergent from processes, or as they put it, "relata do not preexist relations; rather, relata-within-phenomena emerge through specific intra-actions."[15] When Henri Bergson writes about animism in *The Two Sources* in terms of things being substantialized by having their activity extracted from them, we clearly see an antecedent position to Barad's: "our philosophy and our language first posit the substance and surround it with attributes, and then make such and such acts arise therefrom like emanations. But we cannot too often repeat that the action may be forthcoming first and be self-sufficient." An action, for Henri Bergson, "can be localized in a thing . . . but it has its own independent existence." When such actions are hypostatized, extracted as immobile ideas, the "subject" of the process thereafter can only "*relapse the more completely into the state of a thing pure and simple.*"[16] Things emerge from actions, from processes deemed intentional and predicated of a substance, a subject.

Barad's neologism "intra-action," cited earlier, signifies "*the mutual constitution of entangled agencies,*" and it is the cornerstone of their approach.[17] It is more than simply a concept of relation or dialectic that has been given a physicist's spin, however. Relata do not exist and *then* interact: their existence emerges reciprocally, intra-actively. Hence, as Barad proclaims, their notion of intra-action "*constitutes a reworking of the traditional notion of causality.*"[18] And there is something performative at work here at a basic, metaphysical level, too. Agency, they write, "*is a matter of intra-acting; it is an enactment, not something that someone or something has.*"[19] This agency, this performativity, is also posthuman for Barad; indeed, they call it a "posthumanist notion of performativity" as it involves "all bodies, not merely '*human*' bodies." What interests them is how these bodies "come to matter through the *world's* iterative intra-activity—its performativity."[20] Finally, we should also note that this phrase "come to matter" is a play on words by Barad: things "matter" for them in as much as they emerge as both material and of value in one and the same process of materialization. That is why we earlier heard them mention an "ethical call" in their project: this is more than a contribution to knowledge; it is also a portrayal of how what matters is simultaneously known, valued, and meaningful.

All these concepts are tied together—meaning, mattering, valuing—so that the word play is not only played by words but is part of a larger performance: "meaning is not a property of individual words or groups of words but an ongoing performance of the world in its differential intelligibility."[21] The ultimate name or "ism" for all of this, then, is proposed by Barad as follows:

> I propose "agential realism" as an epistemological-ontological-ethical framework that provides an understanding of the role of human and nonhuman, material and discursive, and natural and cultural factors in scientific and other social-material practices, thereby moving such considerations beyond the well-worn debates that pit constructivism against realism, agency against structure, and idealism against materialism.[22]

Now, Barad's reference to ethics here is slightly ironic for me because, in many respects, I have not done their philosophy complete justice in my rehearsal of its ideas. It could be said that I have got their argument the wrong way round by focusing on its philosophical ramifications rather than on its inspiration, in physics. When they write that *"phenomena are differential patterns of mattering ('diffraction patterns') produced through complex agential intra-actions of multiple material-discursive practices or apparatuses of bodily production,"* there is a long backstory behind this technical vocabulary.[23] It begins with the "two-slit diffraction or interference experiment" that originated in Thomas Young's scientific work in the early 1800s. A light source is passed through a plate with two parallel slits, thus splitting it in two. An "interference pattern" of dark and bright patches of light is formed on a screen beyond the plate when the light from the slits hits it. This "double-slit experiment," as it is also known, was a demonstration showing that light could behave in ways that displayed the characteristics of both a wave and a particle. In Young's time, it was thought that light consisted of *either* waves *or* particles, and his experiment was to provide evidence favoring the wave theory of light. Yet the experiment was also prescient in that it indicated, well before its time, the quantum mechanical nature of light as *probabilistic*, at least according to a later interpretation developed by Niels Bohr. Light, in this view, was now equally wave *and* particle on the basis of real probability, not only statistical probability. And though many baulked at the idea that a thing or event could really exist as a probability (Einstein, who famously said that God does not "play dice" in response to these ideas, was one such skeptic), Bohr's interpretation prevailed nonetheless: light could live a double life as wave and particle. Here is how Barad brings the story up to date in more contemporary language. These days, it is not just light, in fact, but all matter which behaves so peculiarly:

> under certain circumstances matter (generally thought of as being made of particles) is found to produce a diffraction pattern! That is, we find bands or areas where significant numbers of particles hit the screen alternating with areas where hardly any particles hit the screen. But this is not at all how we would expect particles to behave: we would expect the bulk of the particles to wind up opposite one slit or the other (i.e., no alternating band pattern). And yet diffraction effects have been observed for electrons, neutrons, atoms, and other forms of matter. And even more astonishing, this diffraction pattern is produced even if the particles go through the diffraction

grating one at a time (that is, even if there is, if you will, nothing else around for each particle to interfere with, whatever that might mean).[24]

Oddly enough, Barad's anti-foundationalist metaphysics (relations over relata, emergence over substrate, irreducible processes, etc.) is, all the same, founded on the truths of fundamental physics, even as it posits an epistemology and practice that is intra-active or diffractive. In this, however, they would not be the first to practice such inconsistency, and one could even argue that they *must* at least be *paraconsistent* (doing X *and* not doing X), given the unstable "foundations" of their theoretical touchstone, quantum mechanics, and its ability to practice double-think (X is a wave *and* is not a wave).[25] In such a case, the defense would have to say that paraconsistency is the only consistency available. Nonetheless, this would be as odd as things go: any similarities between the discontinuous logic of paraconsistency and, say, the irrationality of the paranormal, would have to be disavowed. Quantum matter may behave oddly, but it is still not the "spooky physics" of higher dimensional space investigated by the spiritualist physicists of the nineteenth century. Only matter matters here, and what others might have once deemed immaterial has now become immaterial.[26]

Nonetheless, if we cannot go directly to the spiritual from Barad's ideas, we can at least take an alternative route through art. Our own endeavors at destabilizing the normal/paranormal binary through the concept of heterogeneous continuities (and supernormalization) can now turn to art and, in particular, performance art practices in order to flesh out Barad's ideas. In fact, Silvia Battista's *Posthuman Spiritualities in Contemporary Performance* does just this when looking at the art installations of James Turrell, especially his use of the aesthetics of light. His work, she writes, celebrates "light as entangled in both the physical and the metaphysical, without feeling compelled to discern between the two." Rather than reflect on light as a "provocateur for the human spiritual senses," he sees "light as a thing worthy of attention in itself for its intrinsically mysterious, liminal qualities."[27] For Battista, Turrell's installations create "a stage for light to perform its extraordinary qualities," structures that "offer the privileged opportunity to watch and witness light as a thing . . . entangled with space and time."[28] These spaces of Turrell are Baradian in her eyes, becoming "temples where, to use Barad's terminology, we meet 'the universe halfway to move toward what may come to be.'"

With the reference to "space and time" here, perhaps we should not be surprised that Battista's descriptions of Turrell's work then take a turn that, like van der Tuin earlier, connects Barad's work to Henri Bergson's ideas:

> ... despite the fact that light's frequencies, particles and waves, refractions and reflections are absorbed by and entangled with/in our organism, this is a theatre that does not need us human beings for starting its performances. Light and its particles are actors that vibrate and travel, project and move, regardless of whether we are present or not [...] Our participation in these processes invite[s] reflection on the ephemerality, mutability of life; a certain humility, recognition of scale (of a life, a thought, and everything in between); but also offers the possibility of liberation from functional/instrumental time in our culture, and related conceptions of the self.[29]

This "liberation from functional/instrumental time," she argues, involves a change in duration, and thereafter she cites an essay by Pierre Montebello on Henri Bergson, "Matter and Light," to bring out how the "change of light becomes our changing in light" as a "form of duration connected to our own."[30] If we look to Montebello's essay itself, we see how it confirms the relevance of Henri Bergson to this performative aesthetic of light as a non-human actor:

> In *The Creative Mind* [*La pensée et le mouvant*], Bergson has recourse to the example of colors, which are wave lengths. Everywhere his vocabulary translates the opposition between body and color, between geometric figure and figure of light, solid reality and supple interrelatedness. [...] This omnipresence of the theme of light, of radiating, of color and of waves in Bergson's philosophy translates something of an era: the passage from a world of images to a world where one must perceive the imperceptible light that animates things. *Creative Evolution* is inscribed in a larger movement of dematerialization of matter, a movement of going beyond the image and the object, toward their source, toward the intimate and secret movement of things.[31]

The language of light as an actor that "animates things," going beyond "image" and "object" to the "secret movement of things" sounds simultaneously Bergsonian and Baradian. With respect to the former, however, we might ask—which Bergson? The "intimate and secret movement of things" also echoes Mina Bergson's language of the "eternal attraction between ideas and matter," which is for her "the secret of life."[32] And as for the "movement of dematerialization of matter," it takes very little to see here also ideas belonging to both the Bergsons, yet voiced specifically by Mina Bergson as the "spiritualizing" of "material science."

The direct connection between Mina Bergson and not only art but *performance* art (and, therewith, Barad's posthuman performativity) has been discerned by Dennis Denisoff and Charlotte de Mille. She writes of Mina Bergson's art work for the Golden Dawn as "an elaborate form of performance art." It is an art practice, however, "with a very particular intention." As de Mille reports: in a letter to Yeats, Mina Bergson was adamant that the creation of rituals was " 'a long and difficult business . . . Anything of the kind got up without the solid foundation of Truth we will not have anything to do with, and neither will you of course.' "[33] What Truth were the rituals invoking? Obviously, nothing too "solid," given their spiritualist leaning. The mystery rites invoke the past, past spirits, only as movement, in performance.

So we might now ask this kind of question: can a dance, or even a gesture in a dance, be a memory? According to the many kinds of bodily memory we listed earlier, the answer is yes. But can such a memory be transpersonal, acting beyond the individual's biographical space and time to a distribution not only within a collective space *but also across* a supra-personal time? This would not be a past life remembered, but a prior movement in a person that is continued into another life, another "body." To do something, *this thing*, "in memory of me," for example, need not entail reproducing biographical events faithfully and "to the letter": it would be to continue a movement, even as it has been interrupted, and perhaps even corrupted, in its multiple interpretations ("materializations"), partly accurate and partly inaccurate.

This is not "spooky performance," however. Let me give another example. Simone Forti's performances as a "movement artist" rely on the body as a primary source of memory that is both personal and supra-personal, human and nonhuman: "I am interested in what we know of things through our bodies," she states.[34] This knowledge can even be nonhuman knowledge, such as "of" animal movements, for instance, even as they are continued within her own human body. Indeed, *especially* as they are continued within her body. As Filipa Ramos says, this is not an *imitation* or *reproduction* of the movement of a flamingo, say, or a bear, but its heterogeneous continuation—a mimesis of processes. Or as Forti herself claims, "it seems that vertebrate animals transitioned from ocean to dry land; their first and second adaptations were respiratory and ambulatory. It appears that the development of the respiratory organs and members to keep the body off the ground were simultaneous and of maximum integration; the limbs were laterally oriented. Ah backbone! Oh past and future memories!"[35]

Henri Bergson's (and Jung's) biological memory again. Forti's "dances," or "movement art," are also embodied, nonhuman memories—past lives, the past life of the backbone for instance, reincarnated. It is significant here that Jane Bennett cites Manuel de Landa's work on "evolutionary rather than biographical time," too, only for her it is as an example of "mineral efficacy," in particular the development of bones in living bodies, bone as *actant*. De Landa recounts how, around five thousand million years ago, "a new material for constructing living creatures emerged" to replace "the conglomerations of fleshy matter-energy that made up life." A sudden mineralization occurred, with soft tissues, "gels and aerosols, muscle and nerve," being replaced by bone.[36] Such evolutionary time—even longer than that involved in the development of "dorsality," the backbone—can also be recalled in dance, continued in movement. And this mnemonic and embodied persistence of the dorsal past cannot be written off, or normalized, as simply a hugely elongated chain of cause and effect. For Barad, remember, mechanical "cause and effect," the billiard ball causality or interaction of bodies across space and time, is no longer ontologically sound: instead, we have an intra-activity that restores material agency to nonhuman actors, bones and dancers, past and present.[37]

Perhaps, though, we have tipped the balance too far in favor of philosophical speculation in all this talk of causation, memory, and mimesis over experience itself, both artistic and scientific. Admittedly, a lot of positive things have been written by philosophers about dance and, indeed, movement art, especially when thinking of it as an inspiration for philosophy: it can be an "action transposed into a world, into a kind of space-time, which is no longer quite the same as that of everyday life" (Paul Valéry), a "metaphor for thought" (Alain Badiou), or even a model of nonphilosophical thinking that resists philosophical appropriations of dance as "intensification of movement," or "metaphysical excess" in favor of an " 'ordinary' rather than metaphysical aesthetics" (François Laruelle).[38] All the same, maybe we should put a lid on the philosophy and leave until later ideas of dance or performance philosophy. In fact, the work of Lindsay Seers, though admittedly located more in video and performance art than movement or dance, is extremely philosophical *in its own right*. It offers us an "ordinary" aesthetics that is very

Baradian in its themes, employing optical experimentation (she once turned her mouth into a rudimentary camera) and the concept of twinness and entanglement in various guises. Moreover, her installation/performance work *Nowhere Less Now* in particular also engages with themes concerning biological memory, quantum mechanics, transpersonal biography, and (here's the kicker) the life and work of *both* Henri and Mina Bergson. In its first installation it was also located within a church, the Tin Tabernacle in Kilburn, London.

In an interview given at the opening of *Nowhere Less Now* in 2012 (the work has gone through a number of iterations since), Seers tells her interlocutor that "I start with a question—where does the past exist?"[39] In notes accompanying the installation, its themes of opticality, genetic twinning, and memory are introduced as follows:

> The starting point for all of Seers's work is a personal family connection, and for "Nowhere Less Now" it's an old photograph of Seers's great-great-uncle George, himself a sailor, as was Seers's father. The photograph was taken in 1890, when George was 24, on a ship called The Kingfisher. "As soon as I began looking into George's story, I uncovered lots of uncanny facts," Seers explains.... "The first being that George and I share the same birthday, September 27, and that we were born exactly 100 years apart— he in 1866 and myself in 1966." [...] Another photograph Seers drew on for this project was of an early female freemason, possibly George's wife, Georgina. "George was a mason, like many naval men," she says. "I'm very influenced by the ideas of French philosopher and mystic Henri Bergson (1859–1941), whose sister, Moina Mathers, was married to one of the founders of esoteric organisation Golden Dawn, based on freemason practices," Seers explains, "This was also one of the first of such groups to admit female members." Mathers studied at the Slade School of Art, as did Seers. When she tried to find out what records they had of Mathers, all that came up was a card saying that during that time she was living in Kilburn. "Moina was born in 1865, George in 1866 and the Kilburn church was built between 1863 and 1866, so everything meets at this one point in time."[40]

Past and present intertwine through various sets of correspondences (maybe not yet covariants), a crucial one being between two female artists born nearly a century apart. Seers begins with Bergson the philosopher, though, rather

than Bergson the occult-artist: "the starting point is from a notion of the philosopher Henri Bergson's intuition as practice, to make art ontological." To
make art ontological—to give it "being." This is highly apt. Given that Henri
Bergson was portrayed by Paul Valéry and others as having "questioned as
a professor and replied as . . . a poet," it is not all that surprising that Henri
Bergson himself should have described philosophy unapologetically as an
art for the masses, offering altered perceptions "more continual and more
accessible to the majority of men."[41] Philosophy, he continued, enables a democracy of vision irrespective of artistic aptitude: "all things acquire depth—
more than depth, something like a fourth dimension which permits anterior
perceptions to remain bound up with present perceptions."[42] The fourth dimension again, only here not in any immaterial sense, but as an enhanced
aesthesis, a purer perception.[43] In its own fashion, *Nowhere Less Now*
performs these "anterior perceptions" and gives them "being" through eyes,
cameras, costumes, avatars, ships, churches, and cults.[44] As such, it professes
an absolute equality of images ("everything is images, and all images are
equal") no less than that found in *Matter and Memory* which begins and ends
"in the presence of images."

    The installation takes the form of two thirty-three-minute films that are
projected simultaneously within the Kilburn church, along with a multilayered soundtrack relating George's story as a sailor, his family life, journeys to
Zanzibar, and so on. Storytelling, or narrative memory, again:

> One of the aims of my work is to explore an idea of narrative that exists
> way beyond itself. [. . .] Bergson didn't believe in the idea of polarities,
> like fact or fiction, and that's a process I try to work within, between imag-
> ination and experience, the faultiness of memory and the instability of the
> moments that we're in. The way that we experience life is through compli-
> cated connections that leap backwards and forwards, along with constant
> shifts in our sense of self, identity and emotional state. I hope "Nowhere
> Less Now" has a similar connectivity, to be as close as possible to our actual
> experience of "being."[45]

These are familiar themes by now—the power of imagination as real,
the inconsistency of memory, and the ordinary ("actual") experience of
life and being. The use of twin projectors continues this theme of optical
doubling, especially of the photographic image—an artistic variation of
Young's interference experiment. However, Seers's focus on imagery leads,

ironically, to an eventual absence of photographs as an aspiration: "the future of my intuition is a world without photography."[46] The world will not need photographs simply because everything will become a type of photograph or image in Seers's vision. And, of course, this is also *Matter and Memory*'s first "intuition." Its second intuition, too, is shared with Seers, namely that images are located *nowhere*. The work's accompanying text clearly states that images are not localized: "no images are stored in brains, no images in water. Where is the image? *Nowhere*. Yet images are everywhere."[47] An equality of images, equally distributed, in space and across time, past and present. But they are never localized. They exist *across* time "through complicated connections," because the answer to the question "Where does the past exist?" is equally, "Nowhere and everywhere." There are multiples forms of each—pasts and presents. As a consequence, Seers goes looking for her past in different places, things, and optical presents hitherto unattended. She must reconnect with "the" past on many levels. First, via physiognomy, through a genetic twin terminated at the embryonic stage but leaving a trace in the heterochromia (a tiny imperfection within the eye) of her alter ego, George. Yet that is but one level of history, a biological one. She also invokes the past through ghost ships, the Yoruba people, photographs of past relatives, and present reenactments of past events.

Contrary to a dream in the book accompanying the work that discusses the possibility of "complete vision," Seers's film actually proclaims that, for something to be visible, something else must be invisible, unseen.[48] There is always an economy of attention and vision. *Occultus* and *Theoricus* again. And this attention can be either benign or malign. In George's eyes we see the marks left by a malign regard—one twin destroying and absorbing the other. In heterochromia, a trace of the suppressed other survives nevertheless, a virtual twin that has been biologically assimilated, incorporated, yet still showing the mark of its separate existence in the pigment of one iris: the past within the present.

In Claire Hazelton's review of *Nowhere Less Now* for *Aesthetica* magazine, Mina's presence in the work is made conspicuous for the audience.[49] She writes of Seers's own identity becoming "confused" as it begins to "spill into and fuse with that of artist and occultist Moina Mathers (Mina Bergson). Dressed in masonic dress, the artist's explorations lead her to perform a gruesome sacrificial act at two ponds aptly named 'the twins' in Tanzania. The film ends unresolved." Hazelton continues as follows:

From the seed of one name, George Edwards, *Nowhere Less Now* has constructed a strange reality set simultaneously in the past and future. [. . .] But the question of "who is George?" still remains unanswered even after exploring this space. Upon researching once at home, a motto taken up by Mathers/Bergson for The Hermetic Order of The Golden Dawn eerily appears to speak for the unidentified character, reading "Vestigia Nulla Retrorsum,"—"I leave no traces behind."[50]

And it is here, in these "confused" identities, that things take a further quantum turn in the work itself, especially in respect to the "image of Moina Mathers" (as its accompanying text relates). Indeed, at one point "Walter," a character who may or may not be a "quantum cosmologist" appears, relating how "there is actually a Golden Dawn prophesy, or shall we say *rumouri*, that if the society frequently invokes the authentic images of their founders, then one day they will show up." Who Walter actually is remains unclear, for there is also mention of dual identities, the "wave function" collapse in quantum mechanics, and even Young's "famous slit-screen experiment." These mysterious events ultimately lead to the narrator, whose identity remains no less uncertain either, to say that all he or she wants is "to know my extension as a set of events on the other side of the slit from my external identity as Lindsay Seers."[51] An answer of sorts eventually comes in the shape of a photographic image: on the rear of a monochrome picture of a black clad woman

Figure 15   Lindsay Seers in *Nowhere Less Now* (Courtesy of Lindsay Seers)

(see Figure 15), in a costume embroidered with Masonic and Golden Dawn insignia, the following is written: " 'This is me dressed as my great great aunt Georgina. She is my manifestation of Moina. Do what you need to do. Further the image? Repeat yourself? I trust you. Let me know what I can do.' It was signed 'Lindsay Seers.' "[52]

Seers's work is obviously not an attempt to be true to the past (whatever that might mean, given the multiple pasts, human and nonhuman, micro and macro, that she invokes). It is, rather, an overt exercise in fabulation and confabulation, a "faultiness of memory" that is simultaneously accurate and inaccurate. It is this mixture of images that may, nonetheless, capture something real on account of the suspension of any one identity possessing them: what they continue and recollect is not the same, homogeneous thing, but a heterogeneous group of movements. Ironically, the mystic artworks of, and performances led, by Mina Bergson herself were seldom offered the same charitable interpretation. The garments used in her Golden Dawn ceremonies were indeed (as critics now argue) an unfaithful mix of Hermetic and Egyptian influences, the rituals themselves being anachronistic as well as a hodgepodge of Rosicrucianism, Freemasonry, and amateur Egyptology. What Mina and Samuel's reconstruction of the Egyptian mysteries offered was a "kind of not-quite-right approach to ancient Egyptian religion."[53] In fact, according to C. J. Tully, the main problem with Mina and Samuel's attempt at creating their initiatory system was that "there were no *Egyptian Mysteries* to begin with." It was a mistake to believe both that these *public* Egyptian festivals for Osiris were actually "mystery initiations," as well as "the idea that participants in the Graeco-Roman Isis processions were all *mystae*, rather than simply members of the *collegia*."[54] In sum, the Parisian Isis movement was hopelessly compromised with "historically inaccurate syncretic constructions." Like the Golden Dawn initiation ceremonies themselves, far from being "authentic ancient Egyptian rituals," they "were constructed from a combination of classical and pharaonic sources filtered through a Hermetic lens."[55]

Yet did Mina and Samuel care? Of course not. Their works were, as we heard, "artistic in the extreme" (and in more than one sense), and they were clearly content to work with their ahistorical reconstruction of Isis as an "eternal, mysterious, magical figure representative of universal harmony, unity and nature."[56] Faced with the ridicule of professional Egyptologists, their response (in interview) was to commend "beautiful truths . . . dead to the Egyptologist, but so living and so full of vital force to them."[57] Indeed, it may have struck the reader earlier that Mina Bergson's text, "Of Skrying," described "the imagination of the *artist*" as central to this occult practice—not the "practitioner," nor the "adept," but the "artist." Art, then, was surely fundamental to what she believed she was doing (and after all, the goddess of memory, Mnemosyne, was also the Greek goddess of all the arts and mother of the nine Muses). As fellow Golden Dawn member John William Brodie-Innes wrote: "whether the Gods, the Qliphothic forces" (i.e., the evil demons of the Hebrew Qabalah) "or even the Secret Chiefs" (i.e., the supposed invisible superhumans who are believed to direct the activities of authentic magical fraternities) "really exist is comparatively unimportant; the point is that the universe behaves as though they do."[58] Brodie-Innes even goes on to claim that this stance (the "philosophy of the practice of magic") is "identical" with the pragmatism of C. S. Pierce. We would add that it is *as if* the very notion of "as though" (or "as if") renders representation as behavior, as cosmic process. The "as if" of the philosophers, at least from Kant onward (and Henri Bergson, too, uses the phrase "*comme si*" in a perspicuous manner in much of his work) or "seeing as" of imagination, is rerendered as a real, if partial, becoming.

To criticize Mina Bergson for inaccuracy in her rituals, therefore, would be no less churlish than it would be to censure the modern artist Marcus Coates for performing a shamanic ritual in a Liverpool council flat (in his 2004 work *Journey to the Lower World*). Hers was an art that was both faithful and unfaithful, aesthetic and spiritual, intertwining memory with imagination (as it is increasingly acknowledged we all do). It was a creative behavior forming a hetero-continuity with the real rather than a static representation of it. As "supernatural artists," though, Mina and Samuel practiced this in extremis, being witnesses of events at which they could not have been present. If their art was an *avant-garde* aesthetic, it took the term literally, seeing ahead what had come before: a continuity (truth) that is heterogeneous (a beautiful truth).

Moreover, though scholars like Wouter Hanegraaff describe the practice of the Golden Dawn as distinctly modern in as much as it operated within the context of a "disenchanted world," and so also with a *psychologized* approach to magic (though he adds that this would not make it any less real in their eyes), others have even questioned whether modernity can be marked off so straightforwardly as disenchanted. If disenchantment is seen more as a "regulative ideal" than an actualized state, then there is space left for those who practice a magic that is *both* psychological *and* "*naturalis*," of the natural world: there is no need for an either/or.[59]

Returning to Seers's work, we can see that it, too, similarly confabulates false memories together with real historical detail, biological facts, and biographical musings—with photographic imagery and optical apparatuses supporting both tropes within the artwork, real and unreal. The micro-doubling found in Karen Barad's engagement with subatomic physics is rendered, independently and through art, on a human and macro-scale, creating alter egos straddling space and time as two aspects of one "being." And why not? According to Barad, "quantum mechanics is thought to be applicable at all scales."[60] In fact, the central idea of entanglement is not, they say, "simply to be intertwined with another, as in the joining of separate entities, but to lack an independent, self-contained existence [...] Individuals do not preexist their interactions; rather, individuals emerge through and as part of their entangled intra-relating."[61] This is the elimination of "absolute separation," where those "distances that separate bodies and minds from each other" are rendered derivative, emergent.[62] If you had not already noticed, I have just been citing Barad's research *alongside* Pamela Thurschwell's description of psychical research. Doubtless, separation and distance have not been *eliminated* by Barad in the figurative manner seen when paranormal researchers linked telepathy with the new telecommunications of the nineteenth century, but distance is still seen as secondary by Barad in a corresponding fashion: "phenomena are the ontological inseparability of agentially intra-acting components."[63] What we wish to do now, in conclusion, is *temporalize* this intra-action at an even larger scale through the work of the two Bergsons.

Barad points to this temporal possibility, though most often only in passing:

> time and space, like matter and meaning, come into existence, are iteratively reconfigured through each intra-action, thereby making it impossible to differentiate in any absolute sense between creation and renewal, beginning and returning, continuity and discontinuity, here and there, past and future.[64]

The disavowal here of any absolute differentiation between "continuity and discontinuity" is particularly odd, however, given that they lean heavily toward discontinuity in their later work. In "Quantum Entanglements and Hauntological Relations of Inheritance," for example, they experiment with a "disruption of continuity": this will be "a performance of spacetime (re) configurings that are more akin to how electrons experience the world" (we might call this "what is it like to be an electron?"). And yet, it is an experiment that simultaneously avoids "flat-footed analogies between 'macro' and 'micro' worlds" while also providing "a way of thinking with and through dis/continuity." They write of a . . .

> . . . a dis/orienting experience of the dis/jointedness of time and space, entanglements of here and there, now and then, a ghostly sense of dis/continuity, a *quantum dis/continuity*, which is neither fully discontinuous with continuity or even fully continuous with discontinuity, and in any case, surely not one with itself.[65]

This performance of Derridean undecidability is somewhat disingenuous, however, in as much as, like Derrida himself, difference still wins over identity (as does writing over speech, absence over presence, and so on): in the bivalent logic of the continuous-discontinuous, when something is said to *not* be "fully discontinuous with continuity," that is another win for discontinuity. What is needed is not an ambivalence or ontological complementarity between one term and its negation, but their reintegration—a continuity that is *heterogeneous*, not discontinuous, a fullness and positivity rather than a lack and negation.[66]

As Thomas Nail states in *Being and Motion* (a work in process thought that acknowledges a large debt to Henri Bergson), "division only appears as lack or discontinuity from the binary perspective of the divided region." An "intensive" division, as he calls it, is very different: it "adds a new path to the existing one, like a fork or bifurcation, producing a qualitative change in the whole *continuous* flow. The bifurcation diverges from itself while still following the 'same' continuous movement."[67] The same is continuous in as much as it "flows" heterogeneously (producing "qualitative change").

Therefore, we reach the obvious question: *what is unvarying*, or continuous, in a heterogeneous continuity, be it across temporal or spatial scales, if it is *not* at least *some* form of the same (even of the same movement)? And the response involves a kind of *recursion*—but not one that only *logically* turns on itself in an aporetic fashion (the paradox of reflexivity): it is a real, cosmological recursion that reveals a new type, scale, or level of continuity, a mutation (Nail's "bifurcation").[68] What continues is hetero-continuity: logical reflexivity or recursion becomes fractal, a scalar self-similarity—logical regress becoming cosmological progress, through mutation. Which is why we *continue to use new names, new practices, new philosophies.* To continue using the *same* language of "matter" (or indeed of "spirit," or of "movement") for all levels of space and time becomes untenable, or rather, it simply is rendered mutant by its own eventual recursion. Hence, scale invariance, *qua* "movement," can be seen at the same time as a *conceptual variance (or mutation) that opposes the transcendentalism of philosophy.*[69] As we learned with Catherine Malabou in the *Philosophus* covariant, thought must mutate, change will change.

So now we place physics center stage again, only this time with a new protagonist—one who will emphasize a *kind* of quantum continuity over the lacks and privations attendant upon Barad's use of Neils Bohr and post-structuralist thought. We will also see a temporalization of the quantum that is not based upon ontological ambiguity (an impossibility to "differentiate in any absolute sense between . . . past and future"), but a fundamental and positive holism within time. For all its well-argued championing of the dominant Bohrian interpretation of quantum phenomena, tucked away in a few corners of Barad's *Meeting the Universe Halfway* is this alternative vision of the quantum realm: the radically holist model developed by physicist David Bohm. The differences between the two perspectives boil down to this dyad: localization and holism. Where Bohr maintains that (what we nowadays call) "entanglement" demonstrates that differently located entities are nonetheless nonseparable (their quantum properties are intrinsically coengendered), Bohm pushes this half-holism even further. His "radical holism" completely denies *any* such localization and argues instead for "radical nonlocality" within quantum theory (what a Bergsonian might call "complete holism"). It is not that different things intra-act—*different* things do not exist: "for Bohr . . . holism is about (specific) differences (and specific connectivities) that matter—differences within oneness, rather than [as for Bohm] oneness as a seamless, all-encompassing whole."[70] The latter, "oneness as a seamless, all-encompassing whole," is the radically holist view.

This position, initially dubbed the "hidden-variable theory" but later the "ontological theory" (as nothing is actually hidden for it), was initiated by Bohm in the 1950s, and especially with his book *Causality and Chance in Modern Physics* in 1957. It was further developed in subsequent works with physicist Basil Hiley in the 1970s and 1980s.[71] Bohm's stance is situated somewhat "halfway" between Einstein and Bohr on two issues. On the one hand, he partly sides with Einstein against Bohr on the reification of probability: God does not play dice. On the other, whereas both Einstein and Bohr were unwilling "to give up on locality" (though they "passionately disagreed about the question of separability," with Einstein remaining in favor), Bohm is all for radical nonlocalism.[72]

We turn to Bohm, however, not in order to pile even more highfalutin theory onto what is already a strange set of ideas—to out-Barad Barad, so to speak—but to Bergsonize and temporalize the discussion even further: to make it covary.[73] Engaging Bohm also allows us to return to our beginnings and Henri Bergson's encounter with Einstein's special theory of relativity (STR). Now at last we can fully recover his idea of a "complete relativity" that is underscored by real time—*durée*—and which stands in contrast to STR's half-relativity. STR, despite its name, retains a transcendent perspective that spatializes time (rendering all frames of reference relative within an absolute geometry of space). Bohm is valuable, therefore, because he offers an alternative, not only to Bohr's reading of quantum phenomena, but equally to Einstein's reading of cosmic events.

He is also something of a process thinker. Process theory, of course, sees things as secondary to movements, and even as complexes of movements. *Things* do not underlie, support, or transport movement (as when a cat crosses the road): rather, there are types of movement that evolve, mutate, but still continue heterogeneously (catlike road-crossing being one instance). Indeed, in his 1980 book, *Wholeness and the Implicate Order*, Bohm outlines a model of "flowing, verbal" language and thought, or "rheomode," that rests on a process grammar more suited to representing process reality.[74]

Iris van der Tuin also reports on this kinship in her "diffractive" reading of Barad and Henri Bergson, pointing out that Bohm's "contemporary refutations of Einstein's relativity" equally affirm the Bergsonian theory of duration. In fact, van der Tuin is referring to Timothy S. Murphy's work here.[75] In the following, we can hear Murphy himself further explaining what is at stake in these differences of interpretation between Bohr and Bohm, especially toward locality and nonlocality:

> The phenomenon of non-locality implies that faster-than-light connections exist not only between separated subatomic particles, but also between widely separated parts of the larger universe. . . . Many recent interpretations of quantum theory include non-locality, but they do not place it at the conceptual centre of the interpretation as David Bohm's work does, and therefore they can temporarily avoid the confrontation with relativity. On the macroscopic scale of the universe, however, we cannot avoid confronting quantum non-locality with the theory of relativity, which can

be and often is ignored on the subatomic scale. Bohm and Hiley [Bohm's co-researcher from the 1970s and later] insist that their "ontological interpretation helps bring out a fundamental inconsistency between relativity and quantum theory, centred on the question of nonlocality."[76]

For Einstein, his theory of relativity simply states that, in his own words, "*the general laws of nature are to be expressed by equations which hold good for all systems of coordinates, that is, are covariant with respect to any substitutions whatever (generally co-variant)*."[77] According to Murphy, this means that "physical laws remain the same for all frames of reference and so all frames of reference may be transformed into one another."[78] This is how we arrived at the twin's paradox discussed at the outset—a *geometric* ("general") covariance that actually retains an absolute point of view, reducing all other changes to mere relations relative to its immobile stance—a transcendent view from nowhere. For Henri Bergson, a *real* ("*intégrale*") covariance, as in two trains moving in concord with the same vector, is shared (or continuous) simply because it is *not* interchangeable, because it is between two heterogeneities. To adopt the position of the other completely, I must become the other. In quantum nonlocality, there is a violation of the theory of relativity in as much as it "posits apparently instantaneous (or at least extremely rapid) communication, real simultaneous determination, between widely separated objects."[79] In Henri Bergson's terms, this is a *lived* simultaneity that is not a spatialized now, but real covarying processes: the "communication" is based on real experience, on higher and wider experiences that have not fully dissociated (Bergsonian panpsychism). What looks like telepathy or spooky "action-at-a-distance" is simply what has not been fully individuated. Of this, Henri Bergson writes

> Between our consciousness and other consciousnesses the separation is less clear-cut than between our body and other bodies, for it is space which makes these divisions sharp. Unreflecting sympathy and antipathy, which so often have that power of divination, give evidence of a possible interpenetration of human consciousnesses. It would appear then that phenomena of psychological endosmosis exist.[80]

It is not that one mind accesses another mind from without (separation), but rather that the two were never fully differentiated from each other to begin with (partial dissociation over total unity or disunity). *Durée* is shared as one and many, *one between many*: its internal structure, its heterogeneity, simply is the alterity we comprise in our degree of differentiation, our level of *durée*. (Parenthetically, such a dissociative, nonsolid logic also allows for a supernormalization of an apparent "power of divination" between minds.) For Bohm, the nonlocal movement of particles takes place within "a unique frame in which the nonlocal connections operate instantaneously." As Murphy sees it, Bohmian nonlocality "undoes the reduction of time to space performed by relativity theory and establishes an irreducibly *privileged frame of temporal reference* for physical experiments."[81] Real time is restored—not as a view from nowhere extracted from real experience by eliminating its individuality, but as a "temporal reference" to precisely what is unique in any one real perspective. This is where Bohm clearly shows that he is Bergsonian, as we seen in this final quotation from Murphy:

> Bohm and Hiley go so far as to describe the privileged reference frame of non-locality as a "universal order of succession," which is a "hyperplane of constant time . . . obtained by considering[,] at each point in space-time, the line connecting it to the presumed origin of the universe." . . . Such a "universal order of succession" bears a striking resemblance to Bergson's concept of duration. . . . In practice, though, this privileged frame or "time of inherent excellence" would have to coincide with or be transformable to the laboratory frame of reference in order to avoid temporal paradoxes, and indeed in order to be observable at all. Thus the "universal" or "unique" time of non-local interactions would be multiple in principle . . . since it would be determined in each singular case by the experimental arrangements of the particular labs involved in investigating it. [. . .] Bergson called this aspect of duration the "impersonal time in which all things will flow."[82]

A "hyperplane of constant time." A "universal" or "unique" time of non-local interactions that would be "multiple in principle." This is the return of duration, and not only in human form, for it manifests many levels of duration, not one. What Barad calls the "elements of physical reality" that a hidden-variable theory uncovers must be nuanced.[83] The simultaneity between temporal flows need not be abstract and spatial, and the variables need not be hidden, but simply unseen or unknown. So, where nonlocality can be (and has been) derided as "passion-at-a-distance," "fashion at a distance," and, of course, "spooky-at-a-distance," there is room to make this idea ordinary, albeit at a certain scale.[84] The "at-a-distances" or separations that would be involved are indeed relative and only apparent to one perspective, but the perspectives that comprise them are real. They are neither illusory nor merely optical (virtual): what embodies, what incarnates those "gaps," are *physical processes*. They are not hidden but simply unseen because they are spread everywhere in different spaces and across different times; hidden in plain or ordinary sight, across the whole (which is itself becoming). As Seers would put it, they are nowhere because they are everywhere. They are real physical movements, levels of *durée*, foliated or "implicated" (in Bohm's words) within the other levels of *durée* that comprise an incomplete whole. One and many.

For Henri Bergson, the whole is indefinite or open, itself continually evolving as well. Barad comes close to this idea, or rather its implications, when writing that, for intra-actions, "interior and exterior, past, present, and future, are iteratively enfolded and reworked, but never eliminated (and never fixed)."[85] Later, she adds, "the past is never finished once and for all and out of sight may be out of touch but not necessarily out of reach."[86] Barad, using Bohr, entangles things across space for sure (such that things are not fully "across" from each other at all); and here she gestures toward a temporal version of the same: entangled time. The "spiritual hyperplane" that Paul Halpern described nineteenth-century psycho-physicists searching for is not Mina Bergson's astral plane or Henri Bergson's virtual plane. Nor is it Bohm's "hyperplane of constant time." What connects these planes is neither family resemblance nor overweening analogy, but a continuity that is uneven, interrupted, and heterogeneous.

The spiritually inclined physicists that we started out with, Stewart, Tait, and Zöllner, might themselves be spooked to find that spirit was never disembodied in a higher dimension of space, but perfectly incarnated among a covarying set of processes stretched throughout the "life of the cosmos" (to use Lee Smolin's phrase). In *Duration and Simultaneity*, Henri Bergson criticized the idea of a geometric covariance as illusory, where Peter is but a fictional image for Paul, and vice versa. For Henri Bergson, we recall, to represent fully another's lived time, one must experience it in every detail, in person. *But this is impossible without becoming that other person*: "If I want to actually measure Peter's time . . . I must become Peter."[87] This is *real covariance*—not possible through a fanciful picturing of the other, but possible through a real continuation of their movements in oneself. When it comes to time, to a real covariance between a past and a present, we have the continuity that Henri Bergson called "experienced and lived" (an expanded present that retains a past). Such expansion is not wholly due to individual agency in recollection (you), but the agency of time itself, the past, remembering you. Invocation, if it works at any level, would be the voluntary attempt to "call upon" (*invocare*) the involuntary, to make time intervene through ritual, performance, or even, in Henri Bergson's philosophical version, what he also called "intellectual effort."[88] Real covariance as nonlocalized memory (continuing heterogeneous movements across time). And invocation as intra-action. This is how the two Bergsons, Henri and Mina, respectively entangle time "across" past and present. They themselves may be entangled, too, as covarying siblings, albeit operating at different levels of duration in their lives' researches, each one invoking the other.

Patrick McNamara adds a further dimension to this radical holism of time, splicing it here with the operations of memory and the selection of multiple identities:

> According to this theory [selectionism], election of target variants constitutes consciousness. Because people in a given culture possess similar cumulative memory stores, the variants they generate in a given memory cycle will also contain similarities, and when these variants match one another, those persons experiencing the match will experience one another's thoughts. The extreme case would occur when two people transiently select relatively similar or even identical "selves." Such an event is theoretically possible, given the selectionist assumptions we've outlined in the previous pages.[89]

McNamara mentions "response to an affective cue" as one way in which "two people would generate similar associates or select similar selves." In place of identities or "persons" understood as substances, we would see these "thoughts" themselves as movements: their continuous variation "across" (or "down") nonlocal time-spaces, when different levels covary (as "one"), before and after, above and below. Invocation, "possession" even, or just ordinary metempsychosis—but all on different scales.[90] Radical holism meets "matching variants" meets the "power of divination," or Bohm plus McNamara equals the two Bergsons. And in Seers' *Nowhere Less Now*, we see these meetings in a practice, at once human and nonhuman, that remarkably complements Barad's theory of sub-atomic performances.

We can now end this covariant with a question and a suggestion. Though God does not play dice, perhaps She might play cards instead, in particular, the game of Tarot? With origins going back to fifteenth-century Italy where it began as a simple game of chance, its occult repurposing came three hundred years later near the end of the eighteenth century. With that, the cards gave seemingly chance events new meaning for the purposes of divination, or as Catherine Christof puts it, "a symbolic cipher for universal truths, representing . . . the transformational and evolutionary journey of a soul."[91] Chance is tamed, a little, with nonstandard causality (foretelling Bohm's first crucial work, *Causality and Chance in Modern Physics*). Divination through cartomancy offers us a little fabulated order coming out of chaos, signs of a probable fate from a random *selection* of cards. Again, memory, even Yeats's "Great Memory," is not stored anywhere: it is selected. If one asks, "From where?" the answer comes: the past that lives on through new (heterogeneous) lines of continuity. And who selects? Again, the past, though at another of its levels, which are indefinite in number simply because "*the* past" does not exist—there are only the numerous lines of presents-pasts interfering with each other "all the time."

So does the Tarot divine the future through its selection? I would say that it is highly improbable that it should, but not impossible. The Tarot, or any other form of *supernatural* divination, is rightly deemed absurd by most, for in (nearly) all probability it is ridiculous to think that one level of *durée* could control a constructive interference with another at such a higher degree of tension. And yet, within the enduring universe or open whole, no amount of improbability, or implausibility, can exhaust an indefinite period in the long run—and, as David Hume realized, "the long run" is a very long time, indeed. That said, a very long time could pass in the blink of a fabulated God's eye. Perhaps that is why hope—or what Jean-Paul Sartre called humanity's "useless passion"—springs eternal.

9

Spirit in the Materialist World

We have already suggested that, in a feasible model of time travel, we in our world might already be a future being visited by its relative past—the time traveler as ghost memory—*or vice versa*. That "vice versa" would entail travelers from the future already being here, too.[1] And so they may be, though not as clandestine emissaries, however, but, in the fullest naturalization possible, as *ordinary* individuals *wholly unaware* of their "secret": after all, they have to "fit in" *fully* if they are to have *truly arrived here*. Such a complete arrival would preclude maintaining any personal acquaintance or bodily connection with other eras—modern body implants such as hip replacements, pacemakers, or their future equivalents could not time travel into the distant past where they could not exist. Their identity would remain too futural, relatively speaking. In fact, it can be argued that a feasible time travel does not involve temporal displacement at all if such a transport only understands time as spatial, as a link or container: to change "in" duration is not to change "inside" time but a change *of* time—a qualitative becoming, a change "in" identity. As Richard Matheson's protagonist concluded in the time travel novel *Bid Time Return*:

> More and more, I am becoming convinced that the secret of successful time travel is to pay the price of eventual loss of identity. . . . My presence in 1896 is like that of an invading grain of sand inside an oyster. An invader of this time, I will, bit by bit, be covered by a self-protecting—and absorbing—coat, being gradually encapsulated. Eventually, the grain of me will be so layered over by this period that I will be somebody else, forgetting my source, and living only as a man of this period.[2]

To truly be *here* in this space and time, one must truly be *of* this space and time, at least eventually. The arrival from elsewhere, then, may be gradual. Yet the change in identity will not be of essential substance (which, by its own definition, cannot change) but of movements.

Vestiges of a Philosophy. John Ó Maoilearca, Oxford University Press. © Oxford University Press 2023.
DOI: 10.1093/oso/9780197613917.003.0015

Let us return, therefore, to this idea of the ordinary and push it a little further. Possibly the best sign or revelation of *any* time travel being possible is precisely when our mind makes it happen—when one's ordinary memory expands "the" so-called present. Perhaps all of us (unbeknownst to ourselves) are time travelers who are "here" already, having always already arrived, or are perpetually arriving anew. "Mental time travel," thus, would be neither figurative nor second-best: it would be as good as it gets.[3] This is one way to supernormalize time travel: through the idea that we already "travel" in our own mind through our own lifespan, *our* past (and perhaps also that we see others, our alter egos, traveling the other possibilities of life alongside us). Alternatively, out of that glimpse of a different *durée*, we can invent, or rather fabulate, the idea of a hyperbolic time travel that is free-ranging across an impersonal time, *the* past, and which is contained along a spatializing timeline, measured by a clock and propelled by a machine.

Yet this switch from the subjective to the objective, from the view from somewhere to a view from nowhere, is not the only option possible. Rather than eliminating the role of one's mind in mental time travel to leave us with an abstracted or generalized time travel (no ghost, only the machine), mind could be extended otherwise as spirit, as psychic, metaphysical movement. This is not a Platonic metaphysics of abstraction, but the Bergsonian one of an enlarged attention to life. "Introduction to Metaphysics" concludes with a contrast between a *general* abstraction and such an attentive holism: "in this sense, metaphysics has nothing in common with a generalization of experience, and yet it could be defined as the whole of experience (*l'expérience intégrale*)."[4] This would be a different kind of amplified time travel, not through objectivized spatial lines and general mechanisms, but via an extended mental attention, collective, intersubjective memory, and embodied performance—each of them components of "*l'expérience intégrale*." It would still be real and immanent, despite its transcendence of any one individual life. Our own mental time travels in memory could then be compared to this real time travel, as one might compare a part to the whole, a glimpse that is immanent to what it sees. What Henri Bergson refers to as a real past surviving in the elasticated present ("our whole past [that] still exists"), and Mina Bergson practices as the invocation of a distant past through her own body, would then be the real expansions of this glimpse: one, academic and respectable, the other, occult and outlandish, but both realized through movement.

The ordinary can also help us rethink other temporal continuities, such as survival after death. Normally, any supposed persistence of our personal identity would be denied by traditional materialism on account of a *finite* continuity of the body (in particular, that of the mortal brain), but affirmed by traditional spiritualism and its trust in an infinite continuity of mind (or a putatively "immortal" aspect of mind such as memory or intellect).[5] In each case, however, one kind of *substantial* continuity is assumed, be it a negative, terminable one (based on matter), or a positive, interminable one (based on spirit). The specific language of continuity might change (from what "remains," or "survives," to what "persists," "subsists," or even "transcends"), but its tacit homogeneity stays constant. The idea that we are forwarding instead—of hetero-continuities taking myriad forms, *ones that are not dependent on any particular vehicle* (material or immaterial substance) *nor any one (homogeneous) form of continuity*—is given brief attention. Standardly, a substance is denied or affirmed in its continuity, be it mysterious or not: but a multiplicity of different *continuities*—covarying, interfering, ephemeral, and existing at different levels (yet always mundane, wherever they may be)—is left unnoticed or unseen.

In the work before you, we have attempted to think survival through continuity and indivisibility, through ritualized, habitual, movements or behavior: a "supernormal" that, only when projected at an improper level, will fabulate the implausible, the "spooky." This would be a destructive interference that cancels out the continuity in a single, fleeting thought rather than amplifying it through a sustainable, collective bodily response. The act of offering water by the Spring, for example, is fabulated as a spirit, a perfectly individuated metaphysico-real movement. Isis, goddess of healing and nourishment, simply *is* the *giving* of sustenance, *is* that *movement*, too—continued, surviving, or "invoked," across another body, that of Mina Bergson. The *Practicus* covariant—a machine for making a goddess (manifest).[6] This watery logic is one of the new, heterogeneous logics needed to rethink the relationship between "knowings," between "*sophia*" (philosophy) and "*gnosis*" (mysticism).[7] The philosophy of mysticism (Henri's) becomes indiscernible from the mysticism of philosophy (Mina's): not on account of a fuzziness that would only be an exotic variant of classic, hard-bodied logic, but as a real, practiced, water logic (or air logic, or sonic logic).[8] As Marcel Mauss put it in our opening epigraph: "mystical states" are simply "body techniques that we have not yet studied."[9] But then, following his deflation, comes the inflation: "I think that there are necessarily biological means of entering into 'communication with God.'"[10] What God is, however, is super-normal, too.

So there really is nothing unreal to see here, only aspects of the Real left mostly unseen—its becomings, its arrivals, its movements. One might even ask oneself this: if a *human* subject does not pre-exist as substance but only comes to be (say, through "fidelity" to an "Event," as Alain Badiou argues); and, correspondingly, if a *divine* subject (the philosophers' God) can only *come* into existence through radical contingency (Quentin Meillassoux's extension of Badiou's idea)—then, what of the existence of a nonstandard Goddess? What if the Goddess-spirit never pre-existed as substance or sub-ject at all, but *comes* into existence—is *invoked* each time anew—through *heterogeneous continuity*, through *wholly random and contingent* acts of per-formance, a set of hyper-ritualistic practices involving other communicants, their use of voice, script, and dialogue, as well as animals, the environment, sets, costumes, and ceremonial regalia? Some of these acts might not even be voluntary or intentional and include both small and large nonhuman actors (or "*actants*" if you prefer), such as brain events, metabolic events, viral and bacterial agents, climate and atmospheric occurrences, and so on. What if all that, *already*, simply was the invoked goddess insofar as she might par-tially manifest at all: immanent-divine movements covarying across bodily-temporal scales, "above" and "below"? This is as good as it gets. Infinitesimally improbable, perhaps, but not impossible. The fabulations of such improbable "faith," taken as a mystical state, rest on a fluid, hopeful logic in as much as covariance is not about the *same* continuity (Isis returned in all her flesh and blood existence for doubters to probe), but *different*, hetero-continuities. Or rather, *qua* supernormalization, personal and collective "memory," with all its worldly facilitators, would be the invocation of the goddess, because the goddess does not transcend the act. Invocation as immanence: all memories are ghosts; some ghosts are time travelers; and perhaps some time travelers are gods.

* * *

Henri Bergson's strangest ideas in *Matter and Memory* point to the possi-bility of transcending the present, the "now," with a distended perception, an expanded attention that reanimates my past. Mina Bergson's work attempted to transcend her personal identity in performative invocations of the past—"the Isis movement," as she and Samuel so often called it, being literally that in essence: elaborated movements. In one scalar sense then, Henri Bergson plays the part to Mina Bergson's (open) whole, the micro to the macro enveloping it—alter egos at different scales. If such images of nesting or containment make the reader uncomfortable, we might return instead to physics and Karen Barad's language of "quantum entanglement" to describe Mina and Henri: not literal twins, but entangled minds nevertheless. This might thereby make ours a *diffractive* reading of their different trajectories, rather than the simple exercise in "compare and contrast" that it can appear to be: an accumulation of interference patterns of light and dark, amplification and annihilation.[11]

10

Veridical Hallucinations and Circumstantial Evidence

Le physique soit simplement du psychique inverti
—Henri Bergson, *Creative Evolution*

In this research into the conceptual relations of Mina and Henri Bergson, we might seem to be traveling among "veridical hallucinations," which was how Henri Bergson described paranormal perception. Our own fabulations may amount to no more than a set of reciprocating projections, or dream-like coincidences, between the two. Dreams, in Henri Bergson's view at least, are "only" relaxed forms of perception in any case: they are perceptions that have been overwhelmed with wildly associating images from pure memory, the phantasmagoria of the past.[1]

According to François Laruelle, however, *every* philosopher (not only the crazy ones) hallucinates a world that is "withdrawn" from the Real, only then to hold itself as the authoritative account of all reality. This is not simply a Kantian admonition against the misplaced ambitions of traditional met-aphysics: all philosophy, for Laruelle, simply is the gesture in thought that gives itself the authority to pronounce on the essence of reality, to master it from a hallucinated outside—a view from nowhere.[2] It is the withdrawn or *de-parted* part of the Real. The hyperbolic part that stands "over and beyond" the Real, transcending it. Irrespective of whether any particular historical philosophy is materialist, idealist, realist, nihilist, or whatever else, *qua philosophy*, we could say that its real conditions are supernatural for Laruelle, "spooky." This ghostly philosophy is neither spectral nor "hauntological" on account of an aporetic presence-as-absence, that is, as a Derridean ontology of difference. It is simply the de-parted. Mixing Laruelle and Henri Bergson together like this, we arrive at a position that sees standard, conceptual phi-losophy become the thought, *from whatever source*, that abstracts itself from

Vestiges of a Philosophy. John Ó Maoilearca, Oxford University Press. © Oxford University Press 2023.
DOI: 10.1093/oso/9780197613917.003.0016

the Real as a transcendent view from nowhere, a view it believes is sufficiently general to capture the essence of reality without remainder and by dint of its authority alone: rather than integrate itself into the whole, it is the part that attempts to *be* the whole through its own abstraction, the ghostly de-parted.

In Sigmund Freud's *Future of an Illusion* (1927), he talks about Romain Rolland's term "oceanic feeling"—that sensation of an indissoluble bond between oneself and the external world, the quasi-mystical sensation of losing oneself in union with the cosmos. For Rolland, this affect is the source of various symptoms associated with all the religiously minded (not just "mystics"). In Freud's naturalization of this view, unsurprisingly, it becomes the remnant of an infantile consciousness that has not yet differentiated itself from others. For Laruelle, once again, *any* such unity, any "All" is an illusion—including that of the philosophers. A commitment to what he calls a "unitary illusion" is characteristic of a "bad philosophical mysticism" (*le mauvais mysticisme philosophique*), which he contrasts with gnosticism or "ordinary mysticism," which suffers no such delusions.[3] Gnostic knowledge need not imply authority, therefore, whereas the exemplary philosophical gesture does rest on privileged access (to God, Being, or the Real). If seeing ghosts, be it as "memory" in philosophical psychology or as the revenant dead in Hollywood cinema, merely displays different forms of credulity, then all of philosophy is no less credulous as regards its own authoritative vision. Standard philosophy (as the transcendent view from nowhere) *is a ghost* that walks alone, a departed vision of a putative absolute which can have any number of names—matter, spirit, power, energy, force, life, difference. . . . Yet, like the ghosts in Alejandro Amenábar's *The Others* (2001), it does not know what it is or realize that the ones who are supposedly haunted by others are the actual phantoms.

"Unitary illusion" belongs to every view that would reduce a multiplicity to an *arché*, X, rather than leave all things (plural), equal in the Real, which itself, of course, cannot be defined (lest we fall back into philosophizing again). Striving for "union" with the neo-Platonic "One," ecstatic or otherwise, is redundant for Laruelle because we are already in the One, already and ordinarily mystic. The immanent as "always already," again. Significantly, Henri Bergson's *non*reductive temporal naturalism is not guilty of this reduction to or union with the One or any other *arché*, be it material or abstract. As we saw through Malabou's reading of Spinoza, even to say that "everything is moving" involves a self-reference ("*everything* . . .") that thereby ramifies into other types of movement, or the performance of new names. And this is no less true either of Mina Bergson's engaged, progressive mysticism. Just as Henri Bergson in "Introduction to Metaphysics" tries to think unity and multiplicity *together* in the images of *durée*, so Mina Bergson, in *Kabbalah Unveiled*, when thinking of the divine as either "single" *or* a plural set of "Forces," writes of "a plurality whose action is unified, an unity whose action is pluralised."[4]

And what of our own accounts, philosophical and nonphilosophical, in all of this? Perhaps we, too, should heed the warnings against hubris, hallucination, and reductive monomania for our own endeavor. Certainly, we would do well to interrogate our fictions and not let them fabulate too far, capture the Real from a purportedly external view from nowhere. After all, it is ultimately undecidable whether Henri and Mina Bergson really did work in concert in any manner, or whether this is *all* my hallucination—the truth probably lies somewhere in between. All the same, we should not abandon the power of imagination too quickly, especially within the context of a process view that values immanent creativity. As James Burton points out with regard to the early Christian Gnostics, fictioning does not have to imply falsehood or an inexistent, but rather the immanent creativity of spirit:

> when Bishop Irenaeus attacks Valentinian gnostics for creating "imaginary fiction," "new forms of mythological poetry" and for relying on feeling and intuition rather than divine authority, he is criticizing precisely what those same gnostics see as a great resource, the soteriological use of fiction (or in other words, fabulation). [. . .] Whereas the special *gnosis* (knowledge) by which the gnostic Christians defined themselves may give them the outward appearance of cultish mystics, what it really amounts to is the knowledge that anyone may have a relationship with the divine, through creative activity, through fictionalizing, and that all claims to privileged, exclusive access to God are themselves pure, static fictions.[5]

"Claims to privileged, exclusive access to God" are, as Mina Bergson would say, "a subtle egotism."

Nevertheless, it is still not wholly implausible that some of my own thinking is egotistic, too (subtle or otherwise): a wishful performance of circumstances, coincidences—the fictional operating within the Real. I began with a memory from *my* past—as real or as false a memory when compared to *the* past as I could honestly hope it could be (there is no "outside" account, alas). Yet I did not invent it, entirely. The memory, one of very few from that era of my life, returns to me unbidden, channeled along tracks in my brain that are laid "deeper" with each reminiscence. The original experience grated on me, of course, no doubt from Freudian motives, but now it returns for both personal and impersonal reasons.

While I did not discover a reciprocity between the Bergson siblings as a ready-made fact, as I say, it was not entirely invented either. According to Meghan McGuire, "although Moina and her brother did not agree on all philosophical issues, there are frequent echoes of his theories in her words and her actions within The Golden Dawn." McGuire adds that the connections between brother and sister are often quite subtle, such as in Mina Bergson's magic name, *Vestigia Nulla Retrorsum*, which, she claims, is "reminiscent of her brother Henri's philosophy of change, where the past is always present, and the present is only a process of becoming."[6] Or, perhaps the resemblance moves in the other direction or in both directions at once. Henri Bergson frequently argued that, when an increasingly large number of probabilities, no matter how improbable, begin to converge and interfere, there is cause for certainty. So let me draw up a table (see Table 1) of the most obvious concordances between the two protagonists of our story and look for this convergence. Though these are not the "*infinite* number of coincidences" that Henri Bergson spoke of as transforming the improbable into a certainty, they are indicative of some parallelism, and even covariance.[7]

"Realism toward the Past" is listed on both sides of the table. Perhaps it should be "my past" on Henri Bergson's side. The "return to the past," the "reality of the past," a sense of the "nearness" of the past within "the present": such ideas can be understood personally (as memory in Henri Bergson), impersonally (the brain traces of objective science), or, dare we say, transpersonally (suggested in Bergsonian pure memory and pure perception, but fully implemented in Mina Bergson's invocations).

Returning to Ellen Langer's "Counter Clockwise Study," it is easy enough to think of this "memory house" as a Proustian space retrieving "lost time" for us, a "time travel" within one's own experience, one's own memory alone. And we can simply leave it at that—memory is subjective, it's all in the head after all. Supernormalization, by contrast, sees personal memory as a *glimpse* of transpersonal "time travel," *a* past (because there is no one thing behind the expression, "*the* past") restored through an expanded or "defragmented" attention, be it formed voluntarily, involuntarily, or some mixture of the two. Is it merely all "in your head"? Yes. Deflation. But the head is the brain— the expansion can be objective, or at least differently "personal": it involves

Table 1 A List of Concordances

Henri Bergson	Mina Bergson
Monism incorporating duality	Monism incorporating duality
Supernormalizer	Divinizer
The absolute and access to it	The absolute and access to it
Realism toward the Past	Realism toward the Past
Against Reductive Materialism	Against Reductive Materialism
Open to the "paranormal"	Open to Material Science
Hyperaesthesia/Pure Perception	Scrying through Objects
Pluralist and Monist: "scales of being"	Pluralist and Monist: "Three Planes of Being"
Process as Immanence	Victorian/Edwardian Immanentists
Use of Diagrams/Imagery	Use of Diagrams/Imagery/Symbols
Use of Rhythm/Structure	Use of the Vibratory/Vibration
Virtual plane	Astral plane
Thinking in Duration/Changing Philosophical Vocabularies	Multiple Names
Philosophical Spiritualism/Empirical Metaphysics	Occult Spiritualism/Hermetic Kabbalist
Philosophy of Mysticism	Mysticism of Philosophy
Religious Convert (possibly), but still within Abrahamic tradition	Converted to syncretic religious thought, including Abrahamic elements
Few posthumous traces	Few traces of any kind left

selections performed through *your* brain part, *your* engram (*this* one, not *that* one). Reinflation. External objects, props, visuals, sounds, and ("Proustian") spaces correlate with internal organs of "representation" centripetally, so to speak (top-down); but also "spontaneously" (congenitally, bottom-up), mechanically, or chemically induced. Above and below. The (brain) part can also mutate to excess and centrifugally affect the whole in a kind of dementia. What J. W. Dunne, for one, thought of as real time travel within *nth* higher dimensions of the brain becomes a real restoration of the past through physical mutation of brain cells, often life-threatening to the organism as a whole, of course. Thought through the prism of scale, of macro- and micro- (and a little anthropomorphism), one can say that these parts are attempting to *overtake the whole* (which is also Henri Bergson's definition of pain in *Matter and Memory*).[8] Destructive interference from the radicalized part, the mutant, the cancer.

Following a Deleuzian reading of Henri Bergson, Leonard Lawlor describes duration in terms of "alteration," reading *dureé* through an ethics of the other, the "alter": "the logic of duration is not one of same and other, but a logic of alteration; duration is the same becoming-other."[9] Linked to this is the image of an *other* haunting one's perception, which has been a significant variable throughout the work we have looked at here. The past—not as a dead time but *as a piece* of "present" within a multiplicity of presents—exists *on the periphery* of one's attention, one's vision, and is only temporarily "lost."[10] Depending on how far one wants to push this thesis, we can be afforded either a real, but partial glimpse of such time within our own psychic life, or something much more than that from the past lives of others, our alter egos: *durée* as alter-ation.

Furthermore, if we take this transformation beyond the anthropocentric scale of subjective phenomenology (the whole subject) toward the anthropomorphized brain part (supernormal naturalism), then the part becomes another "alter," indeed, another alter ego, one of many micro-alter egos. An equality of scales, an ordinarizing through equalizing. With that flat equality in place, one can naturalize the exotica of memory—the dovetailing of my past and the past—at micro-levels (the brain, in all its health and ill health) *but also* at macro-levels—the movements, postures, and rituals of various assemblages that, in a kind of nonreductive super-behaviorism of collective subjects, invoke and re-embody former "lives." The transmigration (or travel) of souls, metempsychosis, is altered: metem-*psychosis* becomes metem-*psychoses*—the diseased brain at one micro-level, the deceased past (as movement), at another, macro-level. Mereology once more.

Henri Bergson argued that false problems ("errors") were due to confusing or misperceiving two or more things for one thing: a false problematic is not solved but *dissolved* by multiplying the number of variables at play within it.[11] Hence, we have types or levels of time, not just one. And, likewise, the constant endeavor in his thought to discern types or levels of space, of order, of memory, or of relativity, morality, religion, and even multiplicity itself. False problematics misapply the *level of their enquiry* ("level" from *libra*, "scales"); or rather, they do not even *see* that there are levels at all, that there are *types* or multiplicities in play. They see only the one *same* kind, and its negation, with either one dominating or even eliminating the other (materialism, realism, idealism, spiritualism) or a never-ending dialectic between the two. *Zelator covariance.*

Following this insight, we might say that the mystical/spiritual—when it is not seen as an extension (or continuity) of the ordinary but instead as a "cut," a hyperbolic and transcendent "beyond"—is a hallucination of sameness, of homogeneity. It is a misapplication or confusion due to a monocular vision. Hence, the "cut" in seeing memory as *only* ordinary (and *not* as a kind of time travel), and seeing time travel as *only* extraordinary (*not* as a kind of memory). Seeing only cuts or hard discontinuities rests on a logic of solids, a logic of "separation" (Barad) that engenders the disenchantment of the near and ordinary and the enchantment (or mystification) of what *comes to be seen as* unearthly, extramundane, or ontologically virtual: incredible hinterworlds rejected by the hard-headed and accepted by the credulous.[12] *Theoricus covariance.* These are all symptoms of the cut (a different kind of "partition of the sensible," to speak like Jacques Rancière); it is a totalizing, homogenizing, authoritarian vision—the "destructive interference" of a part trying to be (the) whole. *Hyperbolic* projection might then be seen as the destructive *projection* (*hyperballein*, "to throw above or beyond") of one level onto all.[13] This is the thought that needs to be transcended by immanence and "superstition" (or what we have called supernormalization). Or the *Philosophus covariant.* Spirit vision, rendered supernormal instead, sees things through a fluid logic in terms of continuous *yet different* beings—but they are different *in time, not space*: "*questions relating to subject and object, to their distinction and their union, should be put in terms of time rather than of space.*"[14] *Occultus*—an unseen "distinction and union" or heterogeneous continuity. Where the hyperbolic was, there the supernormal shall be.

We have been doing a lot of analogizing here, to be sure—what Karen Barad called "tricks with mirrors." The hermetic grades of the Golden Dawn's Tree of Life, *Theoricus, Philosophus, Practicus,* and so on, were invoked as covarying with aspects of Bennett's, Malabou's, and even Barad's own thought practices. Admittedly, at the right level of abstraction one can see almost anything as anything else: analogizing can go as far as the word "like" can carry you (x is like y); and at the level of just *Being* as such, that's pretty far (after all, even fictional things *exist* as fictions). Descend the plane of abstraction and add some detail—the appearance of materiality, an outline shape, some color, movement, and texture, or (less concretely) intensity, vibrancy, scope—and gradually things start to fall into their "proper" places or categories. Which things still correlate? Which patterns emerge and at what scale? Is capitalism "like" schizophrenia, for instance? Or is it more like cancer? Are political events driven by paradoxes in set theory, or are they simply *like* such mathematical theories? In one of his later books, François Laruelle compares quantum mechanics to Christological principles, just as Barad compares it with identity politics. The entire history of structuralism and poststructuralism is underpinned either by analogy with Saussurian linguistics or a determination by it (depending on how one sees language and textuality). What would contemporary philosophy of mind do without the metaphors of computers, neural nets, and artificial intelligence? In previous work, I have argued for a kinship between paraconsistent logic, Laruelle's democracy of thought, and hyperkinetic film editing. (It's a job.)

Such seemingly fictional gatherings and bindings, "allying and attuning," as Mina Bergson called them, are neither wholly invented nor discovered. What counts as simple analogy (most abstract), as a correlation (more detail), or as a covariance (more concrete, moving details) will involve a good deal of imagination as well as close observation (depending on the levels in question). There are lines of heterogeneous continuity, the perspicuity or implausibility of which can take a lifetime to "demonstrate," not only so as to persuade others to their "satisfaction," but perhaps first in order to convince oneself.

If one thinks about these acts of allying immanently rather than representationally, then they are never inventions *of* the Real nor discoveries *about* it. Instead, they are nascent acts of creation or "*re*-invention" within and by the Real, a part of the Real, even if at the smallest "scale" imaginable, of the neophyte, the neonate, imagination itself. The Real is enduringly incomplete and unwhole: it is open and indefinite, and in it some processes are only beginning, even while they continue other, older ones through what Thomas Nail called "bifurcation." To award any such fabulation the badge of "reality" on account of its "correspondence," "coherence," "consistency," "rigor," or just physical "solidity" (whatever that means anymore) is missing the point. Likewise, to count it the same as anything else just because *you* (think you) believe this is to enter into a "half relativism." Such unilateralism denies the immanent reality of others' views, a billion other beliefs that do not represent but act (or rather, their partial representations *are* acts). They act *like* matter, *like* the laws of physics, or biology, or mathematics—they are hyper-collective (allied) beliefs that can overwhelm with their "strength of opinion," so to speak. The power of "as if." Unlike Hollywood cinema's phantoms (or neutrinos), there is no way to walk through a wall unharmed, no matter what you believe: "solidity" as matter's groupthink. Again, you are just a (moving) part, a microcosm, and your passing thought or comparison is just a part of a part, too: so it is partly real, yet not like everything else (everything else is not like everything else either). In other words, all things are real but not in any one way that *makes all things the same*. Not all things flow with the same liquidity or speed, for instance (sometimes it pays to be bleedingly obvious). That said, solid beliefs (and the beliefs of solids) are not entirely immovable and impenetrable either, at least not in principle and at the appropriate level or scale. Yet they are supremely *enduring*: once again, difference and sameness are matters of time rather than space.

One might conclude, therefore, that "heterogeneous continuity" (or covariance) is not so much a solution to any problem but simply a new name for a perennial problem—of how past and present interact, and with that inside and outside, spirit and matter. And this may well be true, though such continual renaming of a problematic, especially if the new name "sticks," is also the best we can hope for—it is as good as it gets. If the new name, and concomitant new conceptualizations of everything else around the name, do indeed stick, it should be because they form a varying, partial whole with a set of other current problematics: ones concerning, say, the place of traditional practices within the contemporary, the nature-culture divide, religion and science, decolonizing knowledge, or posthuman and animal thought. It is a name that is also a *becoming*-unproblematic, a dissolution rather than solution. And, like any arrival, that becoming is gradual.

* * *

It is in *Creative Evolution* that Henri Bergson offers an *orientational* reading of life and matter, a duality of direction—"le physique soit simplement du psychique inverti." The physical is simply the psychical, inverted.[15] Indeed, Georges Canguilhem once redubbed *Creative Evolution* as equally a theory of the "*élan matérielle*" were one simply to invert (but not in any way dismiss) its arguments.[16] Obvious wordplay aside, these inversions do capture something of the Mina-Henri bifurcation, one of methods and materials (mysticism/philosophy, spiritualism/science) dovetailing from different "poles" of the one "substance" (which is not a substance but a movement). This would offer a shared vision of life and world united through temporality, the one operating performatively to invoke and embody parts of the past directly in the person of the priestess; the other, operating conceptually to explain my past as immanent within a set of "larger," stratified presents, accessed through an expansion of attention. The difference is one of orientation (as when a rocket rotates to head back to its point of departure), one going from *the* past to *my* past, the other from *my* past to *the* past.

The question that remains, therefore, is who of the two, Mina or Henri, was really in the rocket while the other remained on earth.

Epilogue

The Whole of the Moon

According to Bergson (Henri), "the truth is that we shall never reach the past unless we frankly place ourselves within it."[1] One aim of this work has been to ask how literally we should take this statement. A little over twenty years ago, I published an introduction to Henri Bergson's philosophy that had, as one of its declared aims, to retrieve his ideas from what I described then as the "philosophical ghettos of 'vitalism,' 'spiritualism' and 'psychologism.'"[2] Perhaps, in attempting to model a nonstandard philosophy using spiritualism as its source material, all I have achieved here is a certain gentrification of those ghettos, replacing their original residents with new, respectable types: Didn't you know that Plato was a mystic, too, as were these physicists? And what these modern materialists say over there is very similar to this nonsense over here (heck, even a Wykeham Professor of Logic at Oxford University, the late Michael Dummet, wrote about the Tarot).

Understandably, I hope that such interpretations of this experiment will be rare (though I do not delude myself into thinking that they will be non-existent). The purpose of supernormalization is to show hetero-continuities between the ordinary and the extraordinary, to show that something supposedly unearthly is found in plain sight by looking at the earth (and even its most disreputable denizens) with far more attention than it is usually given. In the pairing of Henri and Mina, we see two allied attempts to naturalize spirit and spiritualize matter at work, two inverse, yet covarying ways of rethinking naturalism and spiritualism beyond deflation or inflation (they are, in their different ways, both supernormal). The work of one of them was well-acknowledged at the time and subsequently (Henri's); the other, Mina's, has been lost to contemporary view for a good while, even as its performative, mystical, and artistic approach to spirit and matter has become all the more timely.

Mina Bergson came from a respectable family and had a very famous, and very respectable, brother. She did not lead a respectable life, however. Yet her

Vestiges of a Philosophy. John Ó Maoilearca, Oxford University Press. © Oxford University Press 2023.
DOI: 10.1093/oso/9780197613917.003.0017

ideas and practices matched those of her closest relative both in breadth and depth. Possibly even more so—there is still so much more to research and for future scholars to unearth about both the Bergsons and their strange ideas about spirit, matter, and, of course, time—especially the past and memory. One might even say that Henri gave us the "special theory of the past and memory" while Mina left us the "general theory." Perhaps Henri knew this, too. There is an odd passage near the middle of his 1911 essay on William James's pragmatism that, in retrospect, can be read in the light of much more than its ostensible subject:

> According to James, we bathe in an atmosphere traversed by great spiritual currents. If many of us resist, others allow themselves to be carried along. And there are certain souls which open wide to the beneficent breeze. Those are the mystical souls. [. . .] The truth is that James leaned out upon the mystic soul as, on a spring day, we lean out to feel the caress of the breeze on our cheek, or as, at the seaside, we watch the coming and going of sail-boats to know how the wind blows. Souls filled with religious enthusiasm are truly uplifted and carried away: why could they not enable us to experience directly, as in a scientific experiment, this uplifting and exalting force?[3]

The vestiges of Mina's mystic philosophy comprise occult training techniques, Hermetic worldviews, and a spiritual performance art that, set side by side with the more usual tropes of her brother's philosophy (intuition, empirical evidence, deduction, argument), unveil nothing less in comparison. All the same, both the philosopher and the mystic only ever glimpsed something "wider" from each of their vantage points, hers incarnated through forms of dance and ritualized movements, his governed by philosophical codes and experiments. If she did see more than he, though, she undoubtedly suffered more as a result.

* * *

There is a song by The Waterboys that now seems appropriate to mention by way of a final remark. "The Whole of the Moon" may, or may not, have been playing at that house party in March 1990 when I tried to explain the Bergsonian philosophy of time and memory—or at least Henri's version of it—to my interlocutor. Yet when Mike Scott sings "I was grounded / While you filled the skies / I was dumbfounded by truth / You cut through lies," it seems like he must have been in the room, too. The lyrics continue to resonate with the story of Mina and Henri, especially when the protagonist describes how "I spoke about wings / You just flew / I wondered, I guessed, and I tried / You just knew," before ending with the perfectly astral conceit: "I saw the crescent / You saw the whole of the moon." The philosopher-mystic and the mystic-philosopher, the part and the whole.

Notes

Prologue: A Reciprocity of Acceleration

1. See Canales 2015.
2. Jimena Canales tells us that "Langevin's original publication did not talk about twins or use the common names later given to them by Bergson of Peter and Paul; rather, he simply described a single 'voyager' taking off from Earth in an imaginary rocket and only imagined what would happen when he returned" (Canales 2015, p. 57).
3. Bergson 1965, p. xvi.
4. The purported irrelevance of this criticism to the general theory of relativity of 1915, on account of it adding the decelerations and accelerations of the rocket *rotating* mid-journey, *and that are not reciprocated on earth*, was side-stepped by Bergson disaggregating, and so further relativizing, these forces as themselves internally comprised of symmetrically related frames of reference. In other words, he downsized the problem and found that it was still present at a smaller scale: see Bergson 1969.
5. Canales 2015, pp. 58–59.
6. See Bergson 1965, p. 30.
7. Bergson 1969, p. 174. He made the same point over thirty years earlier in *Time and Free Will* when discussing the representation of another's experience of freedom (also using the protagonists Peter and Paul): "Peter and Paul are one and the same person, whom you call Peter when he acts and Paul when you recapitulate his history. The more complete you made the sum of the conditions which, when known, would have enabled you to predict Peter's future action, the closer became your grasp of his existence and the nearer you came to living his life over again down to its smallest details: you thus reached the very moment when, the action taking place, there was no longer anything to be foreseen, but only something to be done" (Bergson 1910, pp. 188–89).
8. Bergson 1965, pp. 150, 152, 177 (in French: "toujours virtuels et simplement pensés, jamais actuels et réalisés" and "mais l'essence de la théorie de la Relativité est de mettre sur le même rang la vision réelle et les visions virtuelles"; and "pour effet de dissimuler la différence entre le réel et le virtuel."
9. See Bergson 1992, pp. 102–3 on a related thought experiment concerning alterity: to be in Shakespeare's place (and so able to write *Hamlet*) would entail "thinking all that Shakespeare will think, feeling all he will feel, knowing all he will know, perceiving therefore all he will perceive, and consequently occupying the same point in space and time, having the same body and the same soul: it is Shakespeare himself."

10. Paul Atkinson follows F. C. T. Moore in the view that we need to nuance our usual understanding of "duration" in this regard: "F. C. T. Moore argues that the translation of *durée* as duration omits one of the other senses of the word as '*the fact or property of going through time*' or continuance and, consequently, he argues that the English expression 'durance' is more suitable. Here the emphasis shifts from the description of a temporal expanse to the movement inherent in time and what it means to endure, for the continuity of time is actually felt as a continuance that is irreducible to an external and measurable representation" (Atkinson 2020, p. 20).

Strange Memory: An Introduction in Five Parts

1. My translation from Mauss 1968, p. 386: "Je crois que précisément il y a, même au fond de tous nos états mystiques, des techniques du corps qui n'ont pas été étudiées. . . . Je pense qu'il y a nécessairement des moyens biologiques d'entrer en 'communication avec le Dieu.'"
2. This is how Henri Bergson himself puts it: "The truth is that memory does not consist in a regression from the present to the past, but, on the contrary, in a progression from the past to the present. It is in the past that we place ourselves at a stroke. We start from a 'virtual state' which we lead onwards, step-by-step, through a series of different planes of consciousness, up to the goal where it is materialized in an actual perception" (Bergson 1990, p. 239).
3. It is also claimed that such episodic ("autonoetic") memory is specific to humans (acquired about the age of four years): see Tulving 2005, pp. 4, 21. My thanks go to Markus Rajala for this reference.
4. Langer 1989, p. 155, "The control group was told once again that they were to concentrate on the past. [. . .] In contrast, the orientation remarks for the experimental group stressed that the best way to learn about the past may not be through simple reminiscence. Rather, we should try to return as completely as possible in our minds to that earlier time."
5. "The experimental group as a whole improved while the control group's performance worsened somewhat over time" (Langer 1989, p. 163).
6. I do not pretend that this account of Proust's position is the only tenable one, and I am sure that much nuance could be added by Proustian scholars.
7. Bergson 1992, pp. 151–2.
8. Bergson 1975, pp. 69–70.
9. See Bergson 1911a, pp. 5, 6; in French, see Bergson 1959, pp. 498–9: "l'amoncellement *du* passé sur *le* passé se poursuit sans trêve," and then "c'est avec *notre* passé tout entier, y compris notre courbure d'âme originelle, que nous désirons, voulons, agissons," followed by "de cette survivance *du* passé résulte l'impossibilité, pour une conscience, de traverser deux fois le même état." See also his *Cours* on memory (Bergson 2018, pp. 32–33): "si nous pouvions la retrouver, nous serions transportés dans le passé; nous revivrions notre passé" etc.

10. Bergson 1911a, p. 5. All emphases mine. Both Bertrand Russell and Jacques Maritain specifically upbraided Henri Bergson for this conflation of memory with the past; see Russell 1914, pp. 21–24; Maritain 1968, pp. 219–23, 231–36.

11. Grosz 2005, p. 3; Khandker 2020, p. 85; Perri 2017, p. 510 (citing François 2008, p. 30); Mourélos 1964, p. 136.

12. de Warren 2015, p. 247. See also p. 248: "The pure or virtual past is not *in* me; on the contrary, I live *in* the pure past."

13. Bergson 1990, p. 230.

14. Hyppolite 2002, p. 112.

15. See Bachelard 1963. Conversely, one might say, with Leibniz, *natura non facit saltus* ("nature does not make jumps"), of course: but this Leibnizian axiom of the spatial plenum, where there are no breaks or cuts, can also be temporalized through Bergsonism as the plenitude of creativity, the fullness of novelty, or the continuity of change. Spatial cuts, be they affirmed (Bachelard) or denied (Leibniz), are no longer opposed to continuity, *once they are temporalized* as heterogeneous continuity.

16. Perri 2017, p. 516.

17. McNamara 1999, p. 117.

18. Bergson 1990, p. 197; Bergson 1910, p. 101.

19. Naturally, then, if there is no universal time but only instead partial durations, any feasible time travel would only concern local moments rather than encapsulate a universal slice of time—a certain "bubble" of activity within, say, "1912," a part of 1912, rather than "all" that happened within that calendar year—whatever "all" might be imagined to mean here.

20. Bergson 1992 ("The Perception of Change"), pp. 143–4. The irony of this image of moving trains is palpable given the importance of trains in Albert Einstein's thought experiments explaining his special theory of relativity, which Henri Bergson argues confuses real time with space.

21. See Bergson 2018, p. 308.

22. In addition, after one foray into psychical research (a case of telepathy) early in his career, Bergson immediately stopped all such enquiries for almost thirty years, probably on the sound advice that this would hamper his academic career. We return to this event later.

23. As will become clear, names and naming conventions are extremely important for the practices of the Golden Dawn, and Mina herself had many names, both outside the Golden Dawn and within it. This leads to some challenges for writing about her life and work alongside that of her brother and husband. If I were to use her taken surname, "Mathers," in any discussion of an idea or practice, I would have to differentiate between which Mathers (Samuel or "Moina"—her adopted forename in marriage) was in question. Even more so, however, when discussing ideas belonging to "Bergson," it would be unclear if it is Henri or Mina who is in question. So I have decided to use forename and surname for both her and her brother, "Mina Bergson" and "Henri Bergson" whenever the context might not make it clear. Not only can this act to reinforce their sibling relationship, it should also help to equalise their status within this study as thinker-practitioners of equal value. Moreover, if I use the adjective

"Bergsonian" thereafter, any ensuing ambiguity over ownership will be intentional; it might also help strengthen the idea of shared covariant movements which do not belong to any particular subject or substance.

24. Denisoff 2019b.

25. Armstrong 1975, pp. 37–38.

26. Denisoff 2019b; Lees 1900.

27. Mina Bergson reported that Isis had appeared to her in a dream and asked her to perform the Rites publicly. Given what we will see later in Henri Bergson's theory of dreams as hypercorrelated perceptions (phantasmagoria), one might even say that Mina Bergson's dream of Isis was also a performance, albeit in sleep and so with partial movement paralysis

28. As performed here, these Rites invoked the spirit of Isis into a statue, though it is the movements of Mina's body (as "priestess") that invoke the spirit. But it could also have been invoked directly into her own body: see Butler 2011, p. 58, who notes that for the Golden Dawn, "divine forces can be made to appear in people as well." Nonetheless, as Butler adds (p. 92): "One thing we do know about the cult of Isis is that its rituals required a house or temple because of the tradition in Egyptian cults in which the divinity was believed to reside within statues. This is interesting when speculating that the ritual may have involved the animation of these statues by the divinity, or even, in a theurgic spirit, the animation of those taking part in the ritual. This speculation was one held by MacGregor Mathers and his wife in their reenactment of the rites of Isis in Paris." See also Butler 2011, pp. 146–8, on other subtle differences between invocation and evocation, especially in the Golden Dawn and its use of *unmediated* magic (where no intermediary spirits are needed for the magician to invoke or evoke a spirit or power from a spirit).

29. I say "partially" because it was a two stage process: in one version of the myth, Osiris, a king of Egypt, was murdered and dismembered by his brother Sep; so Isis must first find the parts of his body and reintegrate or defragment them. This brings him partly back to life in what we might call a supernatural fashion. But then, in what we would later dub a "supernormal" continuation, Osiris is fully resurrected only through *biological reproduction*: for Isis is both Osiris's sister *and* wife, and their son, Horus, is the ordinary means by which Osiris's continuation and survival can be completed.

30. See Greer 1995, pp. 237, 238, 250. Technically, as C. J. Tully informs us, their Isis movement was not "connected to the Golden Dawn and reflected the Matherses' long-standing interest in ancient Egyptian religion" (Tully 2020, p. 148).

31. See Colquhoun 1975, p. 76. An odd passage in Henri Bergson's *The Two Sources* (Bergson 1977, p. 260) on vegetarianism (his sole reference in all published works) probably goes back to a "lecture" from his brother-in-law at one of Henri's dinner visits (reported by W. B. Yeats) to the Mathers', where meat would not have been served: "I enjoy a well-prepared dish of meat; to a vegetarian, who used to like it as much as I do, the mere sight of meat is sickening. It may be alleged that we are both right, and that there is no more arguing about taste than about color. Perhaps: but I cannot help noting that my vegetarian is thoroughly convinced he will never revert

to his old inclinations, whereas I am not nearly so sure that I shall always stick to mine. He has been through both experiments; I have only tried one. His repulsion grows stronger as he fixes his attention on it, whereas my satisfaction is largely a matter of inattention and tends to pale in a strong light. I do believe it would fade away altogether, if decisive experiments came to prove, as it is not impossible they will, that I am directly and slowly poisoning myself by eating meat." It may well turn out that he was correct. Bon appétit.

32. See Pattison and Kirkpatrick 2018 for a very respectable collection of essays on the mystical sources of existentialism. For the Gnostic, or rather "Hermetic," Hegel, see Magee 2001. See also Ramey 2012, p. 234n on such readings: "certain post-Kantian thinkers such as Hegel, Schelling, Novalis, and Josef Hoëné-Wronski were all strongly influenced by esoteric traditions. As [Christian] Kerslake has now definitively shown, this post-Kantian esoteric line had a profound influence upon Deleuze." Such enterprises can also be pursued for less edifying reasons, such as Peter Hallward's *Out of This World* (2006), the primary purpose of which was to damn Deleuze by association with spiritualist ideas, and thereby (even more importantly) bury his philosophy in advance of the emergence of Alain Badiou's thought, which could thereby assert its dominance within the Anglophone reception of contemporary French philosophy all the more easily.

33. Ramey 2012, p. 10.

34. Gamble, Hanan, and Nail 2019, p. 111.

35. Gamble, Hanan, and Nail 2019, p. 116.

36. See the essays collected in *The Routledge Handbook of Mechanisms and Mechanical Philosophy* (Glennan and Illari 2017). In particular, see the essay by Mark Povich and Carl F. Craver, "Mechanistic Levels, Reduction, and Emergence" (Povich and Craver 2017): p. 188: "In aggregates, the property of the whole is literally a sum of the properties of its parts. The concentration of a fluid is an aggregation of particles; allelic frequency is a sum of individual alleles. Aggregate properties change linearly with the addition and removal of parts, they don't change when their parts are rearranged, and they can be taken apart and reassembled without any special difficulty. This is because in true aggregates, spatial, temporal, and causal organization are irrelevant. . . . Mechanisms, in contrast, are literally more than the sums of their parts: they change non-linearly with the addition and removal of parts, their behavior is disrupted if parts are switched out, and this is because their spatial, temporal, and causal organization make a difference to how the whole behaves."

37. Coleman 2006, pp. 40–44; cited in Pinch 2014–15, p. 15.

38. Zammito 2017, pp. 309–10.

39. It was Ravaisson who showed how habit must be seen as spiritual rather than mechanical.

40. See Edelman 1992, pp. 212–18. Oddly enough, Edelman cites W. B. Yeats's "A Vision" to show how even intelligent people can be attracted to the "spooky and mystical" (p. 213). Yeats's "A Vision" was dedicated to Mina Bergson.

41. See Delitz 2021, pp. 109–14 for an engagement with a new materialism that takes a positive line on Bergson's influence.

42. Adela Pinch, "The Appeal of Panpsychism in Victorian Britain," p. 1.

43. Sommer McGrath 2020, p. 10.

44. Sommer McGrath 2020, p. 10.

45. Sommer McGrath 2020, pp. 15–16, 13.

46. Sommer McGrath 2020, p. 135.

47. Dunham 2020, pp. 1005, 988; Sinclair and Antoine-Mahut 2020, pp. 862, 863. Sinclair and Antoine-Mahut also describe "two halves" (p. 857) of French spiritualism, one dominated by Victor Cousin, with its "eclectic" mix of German idealism and Scottish common-sense philosophy, and a more "positivist" spiritualism following Ravaisson and the idea that biology has more in common with psychology than physics (p. 860).

48. Gayon 2005, p. 47.

49. Woods 2017, pp. 200–24.

50. Woods 2017, pp. 201–2.

51. Jankélévitch 2015, p. 257.

52. Jankélévitch 2015, p. 257.

53. Bergson 1992, p. 87. See also Bergson 2018, p. 198: "*suivre un calcul, c'est le refaire pour son propre compte.*"

54. Bennett 2010, p. 154n26.

55. See Morrison 2007, p. 17.

56. Different occult societies had different hermetic grading systems, and the Golden Dawn had ten grades using ten positions or divine emanations ("*sephira*") on the Tree of Life (Malkuth, Kether, etc.). However, it is noticeable that the numbers of the grade always add up to eleven rather than ten ($3° = 8°$ *Practicus*; $4° = 7°$ *Philosophus*, etc). This is because the Golden Dawn also counted an extra step, "Daath" in the middle as a special position synthesizing all of the *sephira*. Both this and the final three positions of the "third order" ($10° = 1°$ *Ipsissimus*, $9° = 2°$ *Magus*, and $8° = 3°$ *Magister Templi*) were only achievable "in principle" as many argued that they were the unique provenance of "astral beings," or "*Superieurs Inconnus*"—the "secret chiefs" guiding the Order and instructing its leaders. Non- astral beings could progress no further than $7° = 4°$ *Adeptus Exemptus* (which Mina Bergson did attain). The equals sign, as mentioned, is not an equation but functions graphically. It can be likened to the dividing line of the letter *Aleph* א—indicating a connection upward and a connection downward, as well as a division. As such, it shows how each side is linked to the ascent the student is working on and a descent to where she began. A spiritual diagrammatology of sorts. My thanks to Dr. Mark Price for these insights.

57. Malabou, Barad, and Bennett probably represent the most important and original figures among the first generation of new materialist thinkers, with second-generation work being done by Felicity Colman, Iris van der Tuin, and others. Some of the newer work is collected in the journal *Matter: Journal of New Materialist Research*.

58. See Laruelle 2013.

59. Hanegraaff 2008, p. 296.

1° = 10° *Zelator Covariant*

1. Grogin 1988, p. 59n10. Grogin also notes that "spiritism" has an added "reincarnationist component" over the English "spiritualism."
2. Gayon 2005, p. 46.
3. Noakes 2014, p. 2.
4. Noakes 2014, pp. 1–2.
5. Noakes 2008, p. 11.
6. Morrison 2007, p. 63.
7. See Jones 2016, pp. 176–7.
8. See Jones 2016, pp. 135–6.
9. Jones 2016, p. 134.
10. Thurschwell 2001, p. 3.
11. Thurschwell 2001, p. 23.
12. Katz 1978, p. 22.
13. Katz 1978, pp. 38, 46.
14. Katz 1992, pp. 34n9, 15.
15. Jones 2016, p. 60.
16. Jones 2016, pp. 60, 59.
17. Forman 1990, p. 25.
18. Forman 1990, pp. 37–38.
19. Forman 1998, p. 29.
20. See Mullarkey 2004b.
21. Forman 1998, p. 32; Bergson 1992, p. 161.
22. Jones 2016, p. 173.
23. Luhrmann 1991, pp. 274–5.
24. This use of the term "supernormal" also contrasts starkly with the other contemporary usage in biology and psychology that builds on Nikolaas Tinbergen's pioneering work in ethology: there, a supernormal stimulus is an exaggeration of a normal condition, one sometimes eliciting maladaptive behavior—so the "super" is indeed a real excess (see Barrett 2010). In our usage here, the emphasis is on ordinarizing the "super" through a reinterpretation of the normal, bringing it back to earth, so to speak, by enlarging our view of how the normal functions.
25. As Mina Bergson puts it in the Golden Dawn's language, "Malkuth is in Kether . . . Kether is in Malkuth" (Bergson/Mathers 2016c), p. viii.

One: Ordinary Mysticism, the Hyperbolic, and the Supernormal

1. See Ó Maoilearca 2019a.
2. Bergson 1990, p. 145.
3. This is indeed the plot of Richard Matheson's novel *Bid Time Return*, which he adapted into a screenplay for the film *Somewhere in Time* (Szwarc 1980). Yet, whereas the film

simply allows its protagonist ("Richard Collier") the supernatural ability to *will* himself to return to a distant past (partly also through self-hypnosis—mental time travel *in extremis* as it were), in the book we are told that the hero has a brain tumor, leaving it open that his entire experience was in fact only "in his head," literally. Skeptical work, such as seen in Shermer 2011, grasps this nettle by talking simply of "the believing brain" or "believing neuron" when it comes to explaining belief in supernatural or preternatural phenomena: belief in such patent falsehoods *is itself a brain phenomenon*. Yet the existence of these clear cerebral correlations can be reoriented in order to inflate the cerebral rather than deflate the phenomenal.

4. See Mullarkey 2004a; Ó Maoilearca 2015, chapter four.

5. Kelly et al. 2007, p. 72. See also p. 78: "To illustrate this view of our ordinary self as a 'segment' of a larger Self, Myers used an analogy with the electromagnetic spectrum. Specifically, he suggested that the Individuality or larger Self can be thought of as analogous to a ray of light which, when filtered through a prism, appears as a continuum, or spectrum, of colors. Our ordinary waking consciousness corresponds only to that small segment of the electromagnetic spectrum that is visible to the naked eye (and varies from species to species); but just as the electromagnetic spectrum extends in either direction far beyond the small portion normally visible to us, so human consciousness extends in either direction beyond the small portion of which we are ordinarily aware. In the 'infrared' region of consciousness are older, more primitive processes—processes that are unconscious, automatic, and primarily physiological. [. . .] Sleep, for example, and its associated psychophysiological processes are an important manifestation of an older, more primitive state. . . . In contrast, in the 'ultraviolet' region of the spectrum are all those mental capacities that remain latent because they have not yet emerged at a supraliminal level through adaptive evolutionary processes. In the 'ultraviolet' region, therefore, are those new modes of functioning that appear rarely, fitfully, and briefly. They are the "super-conscious operations. . . . ""

6. A passage of dialogue from the biopic of the animal scientist Temple Grandin, who is not neurotypical, runs as follows:

Temple: "[People] keep on giving each other looks and I don't know what they mean."
Eustacia (Temple's mother): "People tell each other things with their eyes."
Temple: "I will never learn how to do that"
(*Temple Grandin*, dir. Mick Jackson, 2010).

What appears mysterious, or even magical, clearly lies in the neural connections of the beholder.

7. Delivering a phenomenon from the category of the supernatural, understood as a projected hyperbolic discontinuity, into the supernormal, understood as many *different* or heterogeneous continuities, is also bound up with a conversion from only seeing a phenomenon associatively (going from the parts to the whole) to seeing it *dissociatively* (running from wholes to parts). At heart, then, these are two different orientations in mereology when it is understood as a process.

8. Bergson/Mathers 2016c, p. viii, my italics.

9. Though I am using Laruelle's method of nonphilosophy as an inspiration here, others, like Egil Asprem (2014), have asked if we can think of esotericism in terms of a "research programme" (following Imre Lakatos), and whether such comparisons should only be based on genealogy or might also incorporate analogies between structures or functions.

10. Lincoln 1994, p. 5. See also pp. 116–17: "I do not view authority as an *entity*, still less one that came into existence in one historic era and disappeared in another. Rather, I take it to be an *effect* (and the perceived capacity to produce an effect) that is operative within strongly asymmetric relations of speaker and audience. Further, this effect can be exercised whenever certain rather general features are brought into conjuncture: the right speaker, the right speech and delivery, the right staging and props, the right time and place, and an audience, the historically and culturally conditioned expectations of which establish the parameters of what is judged 'right' in all these instances. I thus take authority to be much more supple, dynamic, and situationally adaptable. . . ."

Two: Meet the Bergsons

1. Soulez and Worms, p. 37.

2. See Gayon 2005, p. 43: "There can be no doubt that Henri Bergson . . . was the most influential of all twentieth-century French philosophers. Until about 1960 there was general agreement about this. [. . .] In the past 30 years, however, this situation has changed dramatically. Most philosophers under the age of 50 know little or nothing of Bergson."

3. She was said to be "as much of a Celtophile as her husband"—see Greer 2013, p. 7.

4. Female membership of the Paris Temple would eventually comprise almost half of its body. See Bogdan 2008, pp. 253–4: "From 1888 to the schism in 1900 almost 400 members had joined the GD through one of the five Temples. Isis-Urania in London had 229 members, of which 133 were men and 96 women; Osiris Temple in Weston-super-Mare had a total of only 12 members, of which all were men; Horus Temple in Bradford had 55 members, consisting of 40 men and 15 women; Amen-Ra Temple in Edinburgh had 54 members of whom 29 were men and 25 women; and finally, Ahathoor Temple in Paris had 26 members, consisting of 11 men and 15 women. The total number of members was thus 376, of which 225 were men and 151 women."

5. See Butler 2011, pp. 11–15, for an account of these events and their damage to the Golden Dawn.

6. Greer 1995, p. 358. Coincidently, this was the same year that her mother Katherine died, aged ninety-four.

7. See Colquhoun 1975, p. 53. Yet Mary Greer notes that, on her return to England at least, she was an affectionate aunt, and suggests that "any family disagreements from when she first married Mathers were long past and that she was a welcome part of the family" (Greer 1995, p. 357).

8. Greer 1995, p. 42: "Although Mina saw little of the brother she idealized while growing up, she was later to live near him in Paris for twenty-five years. It seems obvious that with their mutual interest in aspects of the spirit and in psychology (Henri became the president of the British Society for Psychical Research), they no doubt met often for discussion and probably argued over their differing perspectives."

9. Tereshchenko 1986, pp. 82–83.

10. Pasi 2009, p. 64.

11. For an articulation of something like this view, see Franklin 2018, p. 42: "Perhaps the real point is to keep the ultimate source mysterious by ever pointing backward and insisting that it only can be known to the fully initiated adept. This, after all, is the strategy used to effect by the adepts of Theosophy, the Golden Dawn, and, for that matter, the Church of Scientology, a more recent occult-scientific religion that rivals the hybridity of its late nineteenth-century antecedents."

12. The Golden Dawn invited individual adults as members, not minors nor indeed whole families; its members came and went with relative ease; and the founding members did not profit from the group's activities—indeed, something closer to penury was more often the norm. Whether or not contemporary new religious movements (aka "cults") actually conform to the antithesis of each of these characteristics (and the prejudices of many toward them) is another matter altogether.

13. Pasi 2009, p. 65.

14. Greer 1995, pp. 13–14.

15. Greer 1995, p. 15. The theme of invisibility and power returns later.

16. See Hedenborg White 2021; Owen 1989.

17. Bergson/Mathers 2016c, p. viii. Of course, "materialization" is rich in meaning for occultists, and its significance for both Bergson's shall gradually manifest in what follows.

18. This is how R. C. Grogin reports on Henri Bergson's attitude: "What Bergson was trying to do in large part in the generation following 1889 (and this only becomes clear with the appearance of *Creative Evolution* in 1907) was *validate* esoteric ideas through empirical and rational means. This was why he rejected the more extreme forms of the occult in favour of the empirical methods of psychical research. According to his brother-in-law, MacGregor Mathers, Bergson was not the least bit interested in magic" (Grogin 1988, p. 43). Grogin's last point oversteps the mark, however, especially since Henri Bergson's *The Two Sources* spends so much effort elaborating a sociobiological account of the origins of magical thinking.

19. Le Doeuff 2002, pp. 107–8.

20. Herring 2019, p. 10.

21. Herring 2019, p. 3.

22. Herring 2019, pp. 5–6.

23. Cariou 1976, p. 226.

24. See Jantzen 1998.

25. See Deleuze 1988. To a lesser extent Deleuze's two *Cinema* books in the mid-1980s helped to maintain this impression, especially in Film Studies.

26. Significant works by these authors include Mossé-Bastide 1959; Mossé-Bastide 1955; Barthelemy-Madaule 1966; Kremer-Marietti 1953; Delhomme 1954; and Cariou 1990. This is not to reduce the important role of male commentators in this period, such as Leon Husson, Jean-Claude Pariente, Henri Gouhier, Georges Mourélos, or Alex Philonenko—the Henri Bergson bibliography is so huge (with over three thousand items up to 1986 and probably in excess of a thousand more since then) that a numerical majority of works by male philosophers in almost inevitable given the systemic biases against women in academia both before and after World War II: but this makes the relatively large representation of women among the *best* secondary literature all the more striking.

10° = 1° Ipsissimus Covariant (Neophyte)

1. See McNamara 1999, p. 11. See also Michaelian 2016, p. 5: "In psychology, Tulving has influentially dubbed this form of memory *episodic* (Tulving 1972, 1983). . . . Episodic memory refers, roughly, to the form of memory responsible for allowing us to revisit specific episodes or events from the personal past. It is typically contrasted with semantic memory, which allows us to recall facts without necessarily giving us access to the episodes in which they were learned." Procedural memory is "the kind of memory at work when one learns a new behavior or skill" (p. 26).
2. Bergson 1990, p. 145.
3. McNamara 1999, p. 122.
4. Hacking 1998, p. 201.
5. Perri 2017, p. 516.
6. Perri 2017, p. 516.
7. Bergson 2018, p. 309.
8. See Bergson 1975, pp. 70–71, on how the brain keeps our attention pointing forward and on life.
9. Sartre 2012, p. 51.
10. Plato 1997, p. 212.
11. Ricoeur 2006, p. 426. Cited in ter Schure 2020, p. 128.
12. ter Schure 2020, p. 128.
13. As first revealed through animal experiment: see Bickle 2017, pp. 34–47.
14. Barbour 2000, p. 105.
15. ter Schure 2020, p. 128.
16. ter Schure 2020, p. 128. For Bergson's own discussion of Aristotle on memory, see his lectures on the history of theories of memory given at the Collège de France in 1904 (Bergson 2018, pp. 255ff).
17. Russell 1921, pp. 159–60.
18. For a contemporary version of Russell's presentism, we need only turn to Julien Barbour's cosmology (Barbour 2000): see Marchesini 2018 for a Bergsonian critique of Barbour's "Platonian" notion of "special Nows" or "time capsules."

19. Bergson 1990, p. 135.
20. Hacking 1998, p. 251. Indeed, the type of "two cultures" approach that Hacking wishes to temper is prevalent on both sides. Ian McEwan is on fine form here illustrating the case for the arts: "Think how humanised and approachable scientists would be if they could join in the really important conversations about time, and without thinking they had the final word—the mystic's experience of timelessness, the chaotic unfolding of time in dreams, the Christian moment of fulfillment and redemption, the annihilated time of deep sleep, the elaborate time schemes of novelists, poets, daydreamers, the infinite, unchanging time of childhood" (McEwan 1987, p. 120).
21. Mourélos 1964, p. 133.
22. McNamara 1999, pp. 84–85. Italics mine. He goes on: "Unfortunately, none of these implications have received any substantial scientific investigation. One possible exception might be the case of psi abilities like telepathy, but such abilities are controversial." The other exception is his own work.
23. McNamara 1999, p. 56. McNamara's co-option of Bergson's selectionist approach is also motivated by an underlying Darwinism of selective adaptation (in the fashion of Gerald Edelman's "Neural Darwinism"), and it explains part of the subtitle of his book "Mental Darwinism." Pace Bergson's critique of Darwinian gradualism, McNamara nonetheless emphasizes the compatibility between the two forms of selectionism. McNamara is not alone in finding Bergson's direct (nonstorage) account of memory credible, psychologist Stephen Robbins having also made the case for the selectionist account (for instance, in Robbins 2006) as well as Bergson's holism (while relating it to the work of David Bohm—see Robbins 2017).
24. McNamara 1999, pp. 56, 41.
25. McNamara 1999, p. 12.
26. McNamara 1999, p. 24.
27. Bergson 1990, p. 241; see also p. 162.
28. Kern 1983, p. 41.
29. See Bergson's Collège de France lecture on memory for December 11, 1903 (Bergson 2018, p. 33): "Le vrai processus de la localisation n'est donc pas quelque chose de mécanique, comme ce que j'ai décrit. Cela, ce n'est pas le processus d'intercalation, de juxtaposition, c'est un processus qui ressemble beaucoup plus à un processus biologique, à la segmentation d'un ovule : l'ovule se segmente, se divise indéfiniment de manière à parcourir toutes les phases de la vie embryonnaire. C'est cela l'intuition : la période s'est divisée, s'est segmentée en souvenirs qui s'éparpillent et qui constituent alors un développement, sur un plan, de tous les événements qui remplissaient cette période." See also Bergson 2018, pp. 309–10, on using this biological model.
30. Bergson 1990, p. 135 ("Imaginer n'est pas se souvenir").
31. See Kelly et al., 2007, pp. 270–1 for more on Bergson's theory of memory retrieval, which, they say, "comes remarkably close to the picture . . . emerging from the latest neuropsychological and functional neuroimaging studies. On Bergson's view the overall pattern of brain activity associated with some particular act of conscious remembering constitutes a sort of "frame," into which the memory knowledge somehow 'inserts' itself."

32. See Bergson 2018, p. 124.
33. See Bergson 2018, pp. 134, 191.
34. Robins 2017, pp. 76, 78.
35. Robins 2017, p. 84.
36. Kuhn 2002, p. 4.
37. Robins 2017, pp. 80–81.
38. De Brigard 2017, p. 138.
39. Michaelian 2016, p. 5.
40. McNamara 1999, p. 25.
41. McNamara 1999, p. 27.
42. See Michaelian 2016. Werning 2020 argues for a midway position with "Trace Minimalism," which "rejects the need for memory traces to carry representational content" (p. 329) while avoiding strongly constructivist approaches, like Michaelian's, that run the risk of nihilism (no reliable content in memory): "The minimal trace is the causal link between experience and remembering. The minimal trace does not carry any representational content, but just cognitively non-categorical, and sequential hippocampal information. The resulting prediction, i.e., the constructed scenario, can be regarded as a simulation of the past. The memory trace is reliable if properly functioning in so far, as the result of the prediction has a high probability of being close to the truth (in spite of the misinformation effect etc.), given that also the previous experience was reliable" (p. 328). However, whereas the reliance on (causal) traces is minimized, the presumption that the brain stores content is retained, only it is stored in a distributed fashion.
43. Luhrmann 1991, p. 876.
44. Resurgam 1987, p. 47.
45. Luhrmann 1991, pp. 857–8.
46. See Hanegraaff 1997, pp. 109–10: In "the *Hermetic Order of the Golden Dawn*, visualization is essential to such central practices as the 'Middle Pillar Ritual' (where the practitioner aligns himself to the kabbalistic Tree of Life, and visualizes how the 'universal energy' descends as iridescent light through all the sefirot that correspond to his own body) or astral travel (where the practitioners must visualize a hexagram that then becomes a 'doorway' through which they enter another world of the reified imagination, where they encounter angels and other entities)." Some of these exercises could be likened to an attempt at constructing a self-imposed *Ganzfield*, putting them on a par with Robert Forman's ur-PCE (pure consciousness event).
47. Butler 2011, pp. 155, 157. See also Plaisance 2014 for criticism of Butler's claim that the Golden Dawn revolutionized Victorian magic rituals in these and other respects.
48. Sinnett 1881, p. 129.
49. Sinnett 1919, pp. 57, 38.
50. Steiner 1914, pp. 320–1. See also pp. 405–6, 453–4.
51. Asprem 2008, p. 159.
52. See Asprem 2017 and Asprem and Davidsen 2017, p. 8.
53. McNamara 1999, pp. xi, 75.
54. McNamara 1999, p. 62.

55. Bergson 1990, pp. 17–18.
56. McNamara 1999, p. 30.
57. See Locke 1979, II.xxvii.ii; Butler 1736.
58. McNamara 1999, p. 31.
59. Bergson 1972, p. 858. McNamara 1999, p. 33, mentions in passing Henri Bergson's interest in multiple personality disorder. See also Hacking 1998, p. 132, for more on Morton Prince and the Sally Beauchamp case. In his Collège de France course on memory for February 12, 1904, Bergson also addresses the earlier case of "dédoublements de la personalité" found in Eugène Azam's studies of the patient named "Félida" (Bergson 2018, pp. 154–5) and so showing his abiding interest in the topic. See also Hacking 1998, pp. 159–70, for further comments on the Félida case.
60. Lawlor 2020.
61. And, indeed, when the two levels *interfere*—we experience déjà vu, oneself as another at a different level—or my perception experienced as (another's) memory.
62. As Paul Atkinson points out (2020, p. 126), on the one hand, free, artistic creation for Bergson "involves the 'whole personality,'" and yet, on the other hand, such a whole contains a multiplicity, an alterity: citing (p. 28) *Le Rire*, he quotes Bergson thus: "If the characters created by a poet give us the impression of life, it is only because they are the poet himself,—a multiplication or division of the poet,—the poet plumbing the depths of his own nature in so powerful an effort of inner observation that he lays hold of the potential in the real, and takes up what nature has left as a mere outline or sketch in his soul in order to make of it a finished work of art." See Bergson 1911b, p. 151.

Three: Hyper-Ritual

1. Apart from appearing in David Fenton's novel *The Ghost Club* (2014), an earlier novel by F. Gwynplaine MacIntyre, *The Woman Between the Worlds* (2000), and artist Lindsay Seers's installation *Nowhere Less Now* (2012), her only other modern appearance that I have found is a very odd one in an online fan page ("wiki") for the video game, *Assassin's Creed*: https://assassinscreed.fandom.com/wiki/Moina_Mathers. We examine Seers's engagement in the *Practicus* covariant.
2. There is also a fourth, technical Flying Roll by Mina Bergson, "No.31, Correspondence between Enochian and Ethiopian Alphabets," which is of less interest. More significant is a joint interview from 1900, "Isis Workshop in Paris," between Frederic Lees and Samuel and Mina, a.k.a., Hierophant Rameses and the High Priestess Anari, which holds some interesting information. There is also some surviving personal correspondence; though, from what I have seen of it thus far, these hold less interest for general readers.
3. Bogdan 2008, p. 251.
4. See Luhrmann 1991, p. 268: the "'Middle Pillar' is a term used by Golden Dawn students (and their descendants) to describe the balanced use of the kabbalah, along the central core of the Tree of Life—Malkuth, Yesod, Tiphareth, Kether. The term is often shorthand for a balanced, integrated approach to life and its problems."

5. The link between modern performance theory and ritual, religious or secular, is uncontroversial, going back to Richard Schechner's "broad spectrum" approach in the 1970s whereby "any action that is framed, presented, highlighted, or displayed is a performance" (see Schechner 2002, pp. 1–2). The hyper-rituals of the Golden Dawn could then be seen as hyper-performative, a further extension of the spectrum into different space-times (allegedly).

6. See Schechner 2002; Turner 1986.

7. As might time travel be understood: the suspension of disbelief or acting as if it were 1912.

8. Yeats 1978, p. ix.

9. In Kabbalah the most intricate of the divine names comprises seventy-two letters, but the letters in varying combinations can become seventy-two names as well.

10. See Greer 1995, p. 357.

11. Grogin 1988, p. 40. Coincidently, Henri Bergson's lecture rooms were also covered in offerings of flowers from his adoring audiences, at least at the height of his fame; see Antliff 1993, p. 99.

12. Oddly enough, despite a certain gender bias toward male mysticism in *The Two Sources*, Bergson's actual examples are more often than not female—St. Teresa, St. Catherine of Sienna, Joan of Arc, etc. Published four years after his sister's death, one might also wonder about the effect her death had on its composition.

13. Bergson/Mathers 1987, p. 155. One clear example of this activity lies in the fact that both Henri and Mina were very active during the First World War, Henri participating early on in a number of diplomatic missions to the United States in order to convince Woodrow Wilson to join the Allies in the war, while Mina and Samuel transformed their home in Paris into an army recruitment center, which, according to W. B. Yeats, succeeded in recruiting six hundred Americans and Britons living in France (see Greer 1995, p. 349).

14. Bergson/Mathers 1987, p. 158.

15. Bergson/Mathers 2016c, pp. vii–viii.

16. Bergson 1990, p. 17—my emphases. It is notable that Macgregor Mathers, in his 1900 interview with Lees, claimed that "the universe . . . [is] a great eidolon [image or ideal]." Mina Bergson will later use this term when discussing imagination.

17. Bergson 1911a, pp. 197, 210.

18. From Greer's citation of Lees, Greer 1995, pp. 208–9.

19. Kolakowski 1985, pp. 37–38; Pilkington 1976, p. 7. Mourélos writes (1964, p. 103): "we absolutely agree with M. Jankélévitch declaration that, of all of Bergson's works, *Matter and Memory* is the most brilliant."

Four: "O My Bergson, You Are a Magician"

1. Green 2015, p. 19.

2. See Bergson 1975, p. 34.

3. See Hude 1989–1990: the "hypothesis" of Hude's eccentric study is that there is a "spiritualist Bergson from the start" (vol. I, p. 19) and even that "the problem of god" is Bergson's continual problem (vol. II, p. 185).

4. Jankélévitch 2015, p. 228.

5. Jankélévitch 2015, p. 227.

6. Bergson 1990, pp. 184, 185.

7. Bergson 1992, p. 190; see Moore 1996.

8. Grogin 1988, p. 61n31. He continues, "Bergson once acknowledged that he had taken instruction in Hebrew, but was quite clear in maintaining that he had ignored the Kabbala. Nevertheless, critics have insisted that the connection exists."

9. Murdoch 1999, p. 225.

10. Hutton 1999, p. 82. For the Golden Dawn as a syncretic" or "hybrid" religion, see Franklin 2018, p. 185.

11. See Hanegraaff 2020, p. 78: "A large-scale empirical study directed by Heinz Streib and Ralph W. Hood has demonstrated that the term "spirituality" is broadly understood today as referring to the practice of what they call "privatized, experience-oriented religion. . . . Hence it refers to types of religion that (1) are focused on the individual rather than the collective, (2) are concerned with the cultivation of personal experience(s) more than with legal or doctrinal matters, and (3) emphasize praxis over belief."

12. Franklin 2018, p. 154. It is Michael Bevir who coined the term "Victorian and Edwardian immanentism" (Bevir 2011, p. 22).

13. See Bergson 1972, p. 1528.

14. Owen 2004, pp. 135, 136, my emphases.

15. Owen 2004, p. 136.

16. Bergson 1977, p. 194n.

17. For more on Underhill's time in the Golden Dawn, see Armstrong 1975, pp. 36ff. Her 1907 "A Defence of Magic," was reprinted in its majority in her key work, *Mysticism* in 1911, though by that time some of her initial belief in mystical magic had waned.

18. James 2015, p. 181.

19. Bergson 1977, p. 148.

20. Bergson 1977, p. 140.

21. In 1939, Sartre would generalize this idea in *Sketch for a Theory of the Emotions* to make the function of all emotion a magical transformation of the world. See Sartre 2001.

22. Bergson 1977, p. 141.

23. Bergson 1977, pp. 141, 146.

24. See Mullarkey 2007.

25. See Bergson 1975, p. 11 "consciousness is coextensive with life." That matter also endures is a major thesis of *Matter and Memory* and *Creative Evolution*.

26. We will return to the question of probability and chance when discussing the Tarot at the conclusion of the *Practicus* covariant later.

27. Caygill (2013, pp. 256–7) links hyperaesthesia and panoramic vision thus: the one operates in space, the other in time: "His most telling example is the panoramic view

of the past that is evoked in a moment of mortal danger. This is not the spatialization of time, but the phenomenon of hyperaesthesia assuming its temporal dimension in memory. [. . .] A new attention to life thus emerges, one not restricted to voluntary action and oriented ahead, but which assumes the complex nexus of past, present and future that constitutes the monad." See also Bergson 2018, pp. 132–3.

28. In 1901 (twelve years before his address to the Society for Psychical Research), Henri Bergson records his participation in the "Groupe d'études des phénomènes psychiques," whose task was to look at "psychic phenomena"; see Bergson 1972, pp. 511–12. His 1903 report talks of radiation and psychic phenomena (Bergson 1972, pp. 606–9). Grogin (1988, pp. 51–52) discusses the case of "Eusapia Palladino" who was "tested in forty-three seances which were conducted between 1905 and 1908. She was examined at various times by a distinguished company of physicists, psychologists and physiologists who included Professors Richet, Ballet, Courtier and Madame Curie of the Sorbonne, and D'Arsonval, Perrin and Bergson of the Collège de France. On several occasions Bergson and Madame Curie were the controllers— they held Eusapia's hands to insure against cheating." Henri Bergson was skeptical of her performance as genuine. He records these sessions in Bergson 1972, pp. 673–4. Grogin also notes (1988, p. 65n85) that Henri Bergson was a member of the "Thirteen Club," which met on the thirteenth of each month to discuss psychic matters. Its other members included Charles Richet, Eugène Osty (director of the Institut métapsychique internationale), Emile Boirac, and Flammarion. See also de Mille 2022, p. 2. In fact, Henri Bergson's interest in psychic phenomena goes back as far as 1886, as we will see later, but he held it at a distance from his public research work until 1913.

29. Caygill 2013, p. 250.

30. Bergson 1992, p. 32.

31. See Evrard 2021 for an overview of Bergson's undulating public enthusiasm (or "une certaine ambiguïté," p. 249) toward psychical research throughout his career, especially in the light of his more positive private investigations in the area, which some have even described as an "open secret" in certain French academic circles.

32. See van Gemert and Eland 2021.

33. Bergson 1975, p. 82. Henri Bergson, quoting an interlocutor who told him the story of this vision, only says that the officer died "in an engagement"; but from the details of his own discussion of the case thereafter, it is clear that it was an engagement on a battlefield.

34. Bergson 1975, p. 85, my emphasis. Not that telepathy is discounted as a myth by Henri Bergson, but, as always, its putative reality will need to be naturalized: see Bergson 1975, pp. 79–80. See also Barnard 2012a, pp. 239ff: Barnard ruminates on the possibility that a "radio reception" or "filter theory" of consciousness fits Henri Bergson's approach best, and would allow him to think of telepathy as real (p. 239): for "Bergson, it is quite likely that telepathic communication between minds still does take place 'under the radar' almost continuously, not just for especially gifted psychics, but for everyone (in much the same way that radio or television waves are ubiquitous)."

35. Bergson 1975, p. 86.

36. Bergson 1992, p. 134.

37. Caygill 2013, p. 258. Toward the end of this study we will offer a remake of this final line from *The Two Sources* in the image of Mina Bergson's mystical thought.

38. In Flying Roll No.XI, "Of Clairvoyance," MacGregor Mathers distinguishes between clairvoyance and astral projection as follows: "In this Travelling of the Spirit . . . you perceive a different result to that of the clairvoyant, mirror-like vision-scenes and things instead of being like a picture, have the third dimension, solidity, they stand out first like bas relief, then you see as from a Balloon, as it is said, by a bird's eye view. You feel free to go to the place, to descend upon it, to step out upon the scene, and to be an actor there. If voluntary, it comes across as an out-of-body experience, but the first difference is one of detail—being less like a picture and more like actually being there" (MacGregor 1987, pp. 79–80).

39. Owen 2004, pp. 138–9.

40. Bergson/Mathers 2016c, p. xii, my italics

41. There is a cross pollination of ideas here with those of theosophist Annie Besant and "thought-forms" that we have not the space-time to pursue further. But as Denis Dennisof explains, "herself a synaesthetist, Besant explains that the images in their book "are not imaginary forms, prepared as some dreamer thinks that they ought to appear," but "representations of forms actually observed as thrown off by ordinary men and women" (Denisoff 2019a, pp. 146–64).

42. See Bergson 1990, pp. 172, 241–2.

43. Bergson 1992, p. 103.

44. Bergson 1975; Lees 1900.

45. See Bergson 1992, p. 175. Incidentally, one could thereby also argue that Henri Bergson's response to the twin's paradox in the special theory of relativity—refuting the interchangeability of the sibling's personal experience—is motivated by a radically individuated affect, a "haecceity," "thatness," or Tattwa vision.

Five: On Watery Logic, or Magical Thinking

1. Lees 1900.

2. From Greer's citation of Lees, see Greer 1995, pp. 208–9.

3. Bergson 1911a, p. 142.

4. Bergson 1992, p. 119.

5. Bergson 1992, p. 109.

6. Bergson 1992, p. 119.

7. Bergson 1992, p. 121.

8. And this survival is no less true of Henri Bergson himself, as Jankélévitch said (Jankélévitch 2015, p. 257)—"it is Bergsonian to look in the direction he shows," not to reproduce his ideas as he wrote them.

9. Riquier 2009, pp. 43–44, 35–37. All translations mine.

10. Riquier 2009, pp. 43–44. Italics mine. For more on the centrality of images in general for Henri Bergson's method and philosophy, see Podoroga 2014, pp. 129ff.

11. Bergson 1992, p. 168.

12. Riquier 2009, pp. 43–44. Italics mine. See Szerszynski 2021, p. 16 for an interesting take on Bergsonian individuation in terms of "colloidal social theory" (colloids are substances such as foams, powders, or gels that exhibit macroscale physical properties that go beyond the binary of solid or liquid): "a colloidal social theory can help us to be more sensitive to the animacy and sociality of matter and materials. Thinking in and across the whole family of colloidal species and their subspecies provides a framework for understanding and relating a wide range of material powers and behaviours. In the substance of the colloid, what Bergson called the *élan vital* derives its creativity by dividing itself not into individual entities and lineages, or into life's explosive force and the resistance of matter, but into solid and fluid, continuous and dispersed, and across causal domains at different spatial scales."

13. Bergson 1977, pp. 152, 176.

14. Bergson 1977, pp. 152–3, translation altered. Italics mine.

15. Bergson 1977, p. 153.

16. Bergson/Mathers 2016b.

17. Wallace 2001, p. 181.

18. My italics. Yetzirah is the third of four worlds in the Kabbalistic Tree of Life. Assiah is the fourth, an active realm incorporating the world of sensation and the unseen energies of matter.

19. See Neimanis 2017 for a contemporary use of "bodies of water" as the mediating image for a feminist and posthumanist phenomenology.

20. See Barnard 2012b, p. 295: "Seen from a Bergsonian perspective, we are (subconsciously) connected with the entire universe and the apparent clear-cut separation between objects is not ontologically real but instead is created by the filtering mechanisms of the brain as well as by unconscious, deeply engrained patterns of memory and belief. Given this alternate set of metaphysical assumptions, then, it makes sense to posit that different spiritual disciplines (e.g., chanting, fasting, meditation, dancing, ritualized ingestion of sacred plants, and so on) simply serve to open up the inner floodgates in a ritually controlled and culturally sanctioned fashion, allowing practitioners to more easily and effectively absorb and integrate the powerful information that is pouring into them from different currents of the ocean of the ever-changing images that make up the universe as we know it."

21. Bergson 1992, p. 34. See Mullarkey 1999a, chapter eight.

22. Bergson 1977, pp. 61–62.

23. I am obviously referring here to the ideas of Richard Dawkins and Richard Semon (meme/mneme theory) and Deleuze and Guattari (affect theory), respectively.

24. For the remake as a reinvention of form or movement rather than content, see Ó Maoilearca 2015.

25. Though as we will see, movement is general (as quantity) and individual (as quality) at different levels ("above" or "below").

26. Santayana 1913, p. 87.

27. Santayana 1913, p. 88.

28. Santayana 1913, p. 88. See George Steiner's "Foreword" to Murdoch 1999, p. x.

29. Santayana 1913, p. 105.

30. Bergson 1990, p. 9.

31. That said, many other "neutral monisms" are rarely sufficiently neutral—be they composed from "experience," energy, powers, information, events, or even "life," "difference," or the Real—as they are frequently determined (either from the start or eventually) with properties from one or other side of a dyad, thereby revealing a hidden bias after all.

32. Interestingly, G. William Barnard, while admitting that "pure perception" is only a hypothetical construct for Henri Bergson, still claims, nonetheless, that it is a very useful analytical tool "because it enables us to recognize that there is a "that-ness," a stubbornly objective "external" matter-like aspect to our everyday perceptions, a core of our perceptual experience that, while it may be partial, is nevertheless also not relative, not simply our own subjective creation" (Barnard 2012a, p. 137).

2° = 9° Theoricus Covariant

1. Zammito 2017, pp. 309–10.

2. Bennett 2010, p. vii.

3. Bennett 2010, p. 56.

4. Bennett 2010, p. 48.

5. Bennett 2010, pp. 12–13, x.

6. Bennett 2010, pp. 12–13, x.

7. Bennett 2010, p. viii.

8. Bennett 2010, p. xiv.

9. Bennett 2010, p. 106. I say that hers is an equality "of sorts" because it retains some chauvinism: "To put it bluntly, my conatus will not let me 'horizontalize' the world completely. I also identify with members of my species, insofar as they are bodies most similar to mine. I so identify even as I seek to extend awareness of our inter-involvements and interdependencies. The political goal of a vital materialism is not the perfect equality of actants, but a polity with more channels of communication between members" (p. 104). The slippery slope from identifying "with members of my species" first (i.e., speciesism) to other chauvinist identifications (why not with my gender, sex, race, etc.?) is obvious, and blaming "my conatus" for such political expediencies will not wash, unless one is happy to depoliticize (and even naturalize) other, less convenient divisions, too.

10. Bennett 2010, p. xiii.

11. Bennett 2010, pp. 5, 107, xvi.

12. Bennett 2010, p. 28.

13. Van Elferen 2020, p. 204. See Latour 2005, pp. 45–46.

14. Bennett 2010, p. 107.

15. Bennett 2010, pp. vii–viii.
16. Bennett 2010, pp. 64, 76.
17. Bennett 2010, pp. 63, 76, 77.
18. Bergson 1990, p. 208.
19. Bergson 1992, pp. 92–93, italics mine. In the original, the parenthetical remark goes: "*Et vous ne le pouvez que par un effort artificiel d'abstraction, car le monde matériel, encore une fois, implique peut-être la présence nécessaire de la conscience et de la vie.*"
20. Riquier 2009, p. 190.
21. Bergson 1992, p. 303n6 (hardback edition).
22. Bennett 2010, p. x.
23. If Deleuze's reading of Henri Bergson helped to popularize his work again in certain corners of Theory, which it surely did, then it was at the price of some gross distortion in places and, ultimately, a conflation with Deleuze's similar, but still (in crucial places) different ideas. Getting the balance right of which ideas in this reading are Bergson's and which are Deleuze's has continued to be such a thorn in the side of Bergson Studies that one might even begin to think that it might have been healthier for the ongoing reception of Henri Bergson if Deleuze's reading could be bracketed and set aside for a while, at least until we can remember what is *not* Deleuzian about Henri Bergson.
24. Bennett 2010, p. xiii.
25. Bennett 2010, p. xvii.
26. Bennett 2010, p. 81. All the same, Bennett's hard-headedness does not stop Gamble, Hanan, and Nail 2019 from commenting (p. 112) that "while vital materialism explicitly rejects any form of essentialism, we think it nevertheless manages to sneak back in through a metaphysics of life projected onto inorganic matter."
27. Bennett 2010, pp. 87, 88, 83.
28. Sinclair 2019, p. 217.
29. Cariou 1976, p. 99, my translation. One can imagine a book on "The New Pantheism" quite easily.
30. See Čapek 1971, p. 193; Čapek 1987, p. 132; Mourélos 1964, p. 90.
31. Hude 1989–1990, vol. II, p. 36.
32. Hirai 2020, pp. 2–3.
33. Bennett 2010, p. 99. See also Bennett 2010, p. xvi. "We need to cultivate a bit of anthropomorphism—the idea that human agency has some echoes in nonhuman nature—to counter the narcissism of humans in charge of the world." It is these "structural parallels" or "isomorphisms" that, put through the processual mill, I am calling "heterogeneous continuities" or "covariants."
34. Bennett 2010, p. 117.
35. Bennett 2010, p. 118. We return to superstition later when discussing Malabou.
36. Bergson 1972, p. 1031.
37. Bergson 1911a, pp. 48–49.
38. Bergson 1977, pp. 112–14, 116.
39. Green 1995, p. 170.

40. Bennett 2010, p. 122.
41. Bennett 2010, pp. 80, 57, 112.
42. See Ó Maoilearca 2015, p. 244. Other philosophical uses of mystery range from avowed intractable issues ("hard problems") within analytic philosophy of mind (for instance, "new mysterians" like Colin McGinn argue that the mind-body problem is unsolvable); or more humanistic uses of mystery as an existential corrective against philosophical hubris: see, respectively, McGinn 2000 and Cooper 2017.
43. Bergson 1911a, p. 137.

Six: Of the Survival of Images

1. Flusser 2000, p. 9.
2. Flusser 2000, p. 66.
3. Resurgam 1987, p. 47.
4. Bergson/Mathers 2016a.
5. Godwin 2017, p. 467.
6. Bergson/Mathers 2016a. Anyone in any way familiar with Henri Bergson's "Introduction to Metaphysics" of 1903 (Bergson 1992, pp. 159–200) will recognize a similar dialectic of intuition and intellect here.
7. Bergson/Mathers 2016a.
8. Bergson/Mathers 2016a.
9. See Brang et al. 2010. Both an artist and occultist (like Mina Bergson), Pamela Colman Smith was also the most famous actual synesthete member of the Golden Dawn, using this faculty in her artistic and spiritual practices (see Denisoff 2019a). Paul Atkinson discusses Kandinsky from a Bergsonian point of view at Atkinson 2020, pp. 215–16, and especially, p. 52: a "debt to Bergson" may have also "inspired some of the ideas in Wassily Kandinsky's *Concerning the Spiritual in Art*, in particular when he talks about the importance of the 'vital impetus,' in which the artist as part of a spiritual avant-garde is guided by 'feeling' as they strive toward the 'immaterial.'"
10. Bergson/Mathers 2016a.
11. Bergson/Mathers 2016a.
12. Bergson/Mathers 2016a.
13. See Bergson 1992, p. 42; see also Bergson 2018, pp. 225–6 on the essential obscurity of "movement" and how any clarity and distinction brought to its analysis must involve its spatialization.
14. "Entretiens avec Lydie Adophe," p. ix; cited in Riquier, p. 35.
15. See Mullarkey 1999a, pp. 241–2. See Bergson 1992, p. 43: "Let us not be duped by appearances: there are cases in which it is imagery in language which knowingly expresses the literal meaning, and abstract language which unconsciously expresses itself figuratively. The moment we reach the spiritual world, the image, if it merely seeks to suggest, may give us the direct vision, while the abstract term, which is spatial in origin and which claims to express, most frequently leaves us in metaphor." In

Bergson 1972, p. 980, Henri Bergson says that metaphors should be taken seriously, that is, nonmetaphorically.

16. Bergson 1990, pp. 133–4. Remember that "attitude" means something closer to "posture" for Henri Bergson.

17. In later works, like "The Perception of Change," this "survival" is rerendered as an *indivisibility*—the indivisible continuity within different levels of duration (and their related levels of "condensation" of, or "attention" to, temporal change or passage). This is why our earlier analysis of Henri Bergson's interpretation of a case of telepathy in "Phantasms of the Living and Psychical Research" equated pure *perception* with astral projection, whereas here we compare the plane of pure *memory* with the astral plane. In truth, these two equations can themselves be merged because memory and perception become indivisible in Henri Bergson's later work—just as the past and the present become nominal: they are things we call "past" and "present" depending on our degree of attention to life. That said, there is already an earlier version of this striated version of duration in the fourth chapter of *Matter and Memory*, which puts much more emphasis on what unites the different planes (condensation or tension) and not what divides them (as in the first and third chapters on perception and memory, respectively, as separated temporal modalities). Vladimir Jankélévitch goes so far as to say that the fourth chapter of *Matter and Memory* contradicts the rest of the book. I would not go that far: it simply takes the first steps toward cosmologizing the more first-person perspective of the earlier chapters (that later work would elaborate, as psyche leaves the human ego to enter the nonhuman world as movement).

18. Bergson 1990, p. 132.

19. Mullarkey 2006, chapter five.

20. "Flashing Tablets" should also be mentioned here. These were talismans, magical objects, often decorated in complementary colors and with divine names, or symbols, that had special powers that would aid in invocations or evocations.

21. See McGuire 2017, p. 24, who argues that "due to Yeats's relationship with Mina Bergson and the Order of the GD, he was exposed to Bergsonian ideas long before he read and studied the philosopher's work for himself." Moreover, "in addition to the diagrams of cones and gyres scattered throughout Yeats's copy of *Matter and Memory*, his annotations suggest that the poet found an interesting correlation between Bergson's complex understanding of memory and his own representation of the *Four Principles*" (p. 59). The four principles are "*Spirit, Celestial Body, Husk*, and *Passionate Body*." See also Yeats 1978, p. xi: "The symbolic forms of psychic geometry projected in *VA* [*A Vision*, 1925 edition] were not in fact based primarily on Plato or Swedenborg or others of the classical writers Yeats liked to cite but rather on the experiments and thinking of his many friends and fellow students, first in the Hermetic Order of the Golden Dawn and more significantly in the Society for Psychical Research." This is especially true of the vortices, gyres, or cones (p. 31n129).

22. Similar documents from Golden Dawn members can be found at the Museum of Witchcraft and Magic, at Boscastle, Cornwall. Other archival materials are reputed to exist in San Francisco, New York, and Geneva, though I have yet to gain access to them. There are also at least three private collections concerning the Golden Dawn

which are held by individuals wishing to remain anonymous and are difficult for scholars to access. See Gilbert 1987, pp. 163–68.

23. Pamela Colman Smith, artist, synesthete, and Golden Dawn member, was also responsible for the artwork in the classic Waite-Smith Tarot deck; see Denisoff 2019a, pp. 146–64.

24. It is notable that Mina Bergson retains her maiden name in this illustration from 1898. She translated some of Fiona Macleod's (William Sharp's) poetry, including "The Melancholy of Ulad." Sharp was also a member of the Golden Dawn. The aquarelle work here, a painting with thin, transparent (rather than opaque) watercolors, appears to be an advertisement for a staging of a fragment of the poem. Mina planned several such stagings, including ones of Yeats's works (having translated Yeats's early play *The Land of Heart's Desire*, she apparently planned a production of it in Paris in 1898). See Yeats 1977, pp. 42–43.

25. Yeats 1977, p. 43.

26. De Mille 2022, p. 16. Citing Greer (1995, p. 225), De Mille notes how Mina Bergson wrote to Yeats stating that she "had to abandon any idea of an independent career in that direction, to be kept busy not only with the techniques of magic itself but with the techniques of art in magic's service."

27. Bennett 2010, p. 35.

28. In addition, the group that Samuel and Mina founded after the Golden Dawn, the "Rosicrucian Order of the Alpha et Omega," placed great emphasis in its name on what Mina calls the "living images" of all religions, the Rose, Cross, Lily, and Lotus. The image of the Rose is crucial for Mina Bergson—"its mysterious centre, its nucleus, the central Sun, is a symbol of the infinite and harmonious separations of nature"—and it appears throughout the visual occulture of Alpha et Omega. See Bergson/Mathers 2016c, pp. ix–x.

29. The vibratory is essential to invocation, as Nicolas Tereshchenko points out (Tereshchenko 1986, pp. 85–86): "The most important rituals of invocation are also the quite essential training towards the supreme moment of eventual Union with the One Creator. For this to become possible, and before daring to attempt it, everything must change in the aspirant. More precisely and specifically, the vibratory rate of all his bodies must become considerably higher than man's usual rate, approaching the high frequency of vibrations of the Absolute Being. Through the prescribed rituals, exercises and prayers . . . little by little the vibratory rate of the practicing magician rises through the frequent and intimate contact with the invoked 'god-forms' of Egyptian and other Divinities."

30. See Bergson/Mathers, "Flying Roll No.31." See also the W. B. Yeats online archive at https://my.matterport.com/show-mds?mls=1&m=CfD9eU6iPhf (accessed July 24, 2021): "Adepts of the Golden Dawn practised the 'Enochian Magic' developed by the Elizabethan magician Dr. John Dee and his medium Edward Kelly, revealed to them by angels and using an angelic language supposedly first given to the patriarch Enoch by the angel Ave. Words from this language of the angels were used in Golden Dawn ceremonies, referred to as Enochian calls. The structure of the Enochian system was based upon a cipher of numerological and set permutations of elements arranged on

a grid of letters called the Enochian Tablets. From these elemental tablets were derived the names of various elemental powers, angels, beings, and spiritual dominions known as Aethyrs."

31. MacGregor Mathers, "Flying Roll No.12, Telesmatic Images and Adonai."

32. Bergson 1975, pp. 56–59.

33. Bergson 1992, pp. 86–87. It is undoubtedly disappointing that its title *La pensée et le mouvant* was translated in English as *The Creative Mind*.

Seven: On the Meta-Spiritual

1. See the section, *Vestigia Nulla Retrorsum*: "Leave no Trace" for an explanation of this.

2. Bergson 1992, p. 145.

3. Valiaho 2010, pp. 17, 60.

4. Moore 1993, p. 166. Paul Atkinson points out (Atkinson 2020, p. 17) that Bergson "formulated the theory of *durée*, his response to the philosophy of the Eleatics, while taking a walk during his tenure at Clermont-Ferrand" and that "according to Chevalier, in 1926 Bergson complained that he was beginning to have problems with his movement and claimed that this also affected his thought. Bergson was someone who liked to move around while thinking and while teaching, and he did not like the way that the École normale and the Collège de France limited his movement" (p. 13).

5. Gamble, Hanan, and Nail 2019, p. 125.

6. Bergson 1911a, p. 232.

7. As Khandker (2020, p. 161n6) points out with regard to Charles Hartshorne's "psychicalism": "Hartshorne defends this position as a 'true physicalism.' It is not simply that he is a 'spiritualist' or idealist, but that what we understand physicality and spatial position to be require reformulation: 'If physical means spatial then mentalism or psychicalism is physicalism, for space is how sentient beings have neighbors (Peirce) with whom they react, and their basic operations (Whitehead) are prehensions, feelings of (others) feelings.'"

8. Bergson 1977, pp. 79–80: "If telepathy be a real fact, it is a fact capable of being repeated indefinitely. I go further: if telepathy be real, it is possible that it is operating at *every* moment and everywhere, but with too little intensity to be noticed, or else in such a way that a cerebral mechanism stops the effect, for our benefit, at the very moment at which it is about to clear the threshold of consciousness. . . . *if telepathy be real, it is natural*" ["si la télépathie est réelle, elle est naturelle"].

9. See Grogin 1988, pp. 42–43, 61n36.

10. See Ó Maoilearca 2019a.

11. Hacking 1998, p. 143. Earlier we heard William James not only call Henri Bergson a "magician" but his book *Creative Evolution* "a marvel." That the Bergsonian approach to evolution, being neither mechanist nor finalist, has never found a natural home within standard evolutionary theory or its standard antitheses, makes calling it a "marvel" all the more prescient, given Hackings description here.

12. Morrison 2007, p. 4.
13. Wahida Khandker cites François Jacob usefully in this regard (Khandker 2020, p. 67): "In *The Logic of Life*, François Jacob reflects on the impact of the invention of new technologies on scientific analysis, noting that even the invention of the microscope was simply an application of abstract theories of light, and the world of "swarming forms" that it opened up was slow to alter existing conventions of interpretation of the relation between the lives of macro-organisms and microbes. The presence of this hitherto unseen microcosm was even (for Buffon) "a flagrant insult to the whole living world.""
14. See Mullarkey 1999a, chapter eight.
15. Burton 2015, p. 108.
16. Burton 2015, p. 108.
17. Other cinematic traditions of the supernatural may well avoid such pitfalls given that their story-telling conventions are less dualistic to begin with: the Japanese, "J-Horror" cycle, for example, exemplifies specters that are, as Jay McRoy puts it, "not quite ghosts in the strictest sense of the *onryou* or *kaidan* tradition, but not quite conventional biological monsters either" (McRoy 2005, p. 180).
18. Pereen 2017, p. 168.
19. Morin 1956, pp. 43, 69, cited in Blassnigg 2006, pp. 113, 116.
20. Bergson 1990, p. 72.
21. Bergson 1911a, p. 324. See also Atkinson 2020, p. 134: "The processes of a plant growing from a seed, an insect coming into being or a colour changing are quite different, and they must not lose their distinctiveness when integrated into a 'colourless' image of Becoming in general—Becoming should always be conceived as a multiplicity of becomings."
22. For more on this dyadic refutation of monism, see Ó Maoilearca 2014.

4° = 7° *Philosophus Covariant*

1. Bergson 1992, p. 124.
2. Bergson/Mathers 1987, pp. 151–2.
3. Bergson/Mathers 2016a.
4. Van Egmond 1997, p. 332.
5. See Lincoln 1986, pp. 21–22.
6. See Godwin 2017.
7. It is a little ironic that one of the main problems at the interface of neuroscience and cognitive psychology is called "the binding problem," one aspect of which concerns how background knowledge, abstract concepts and categories, and affective components all combine into a single experience in the brain.
8. Ramey 2012, p. 3. An "encosmic" divinity is immanent, one might even say earthly.
9. Latour 2017, p. 96. Latour is commenting here on the work of Olafur Eliasson: "Olafur Eliasson is right to insist on the fact that the mechanisms of disorientation he employs are as much temporal as spatial."

10. Barad 2007, p. 245.
11. "The molar and the molecular are not distinguished by size, scale, or dimension, but by the nature of the system of reference envisioned" (Deleuze and Guattari 1987, p. 217). That said, Deleuze and Guattari do continue to use language suggestive of scale: majority, major, massive, big, mass, collective, whole, global, macro-, super-, over-, and molar itself, on the one hand; partial objects, part organs, larval selves, minority, minor, local, part, component, small, miniaturization, sub-, micro-, and molecular itself, on the other. And the value is almost always on the side of the small, what Sam Coleman called "smallism."
12. In Bergson 2010, the critique of intensive magnitudes in the first chapter (psychophysics) rests on subverting the relation of container and contained that underpins it.
13. Wittenberg 2019, p. 352.
14. See Brouwer 1975.
15. See Lambert 2005.
16. It is not that X would be an illusion that is displaced by the truth of Y, but that, at different scales, a redescription or renaming of an event becomes evident.
17. Such temporalization is more than simply time sampling, which would still be quantitative. A *temporalized* scale must be distinguished from a *temporal* scale—which is only the quantification of a process: the former is the qualification of a quantity, a spatial entity integrated into real time.
18. Gunter 1982, p. 644. For a more up-to-date account of such biological memory, with reference to Henri Bergson, see Longo 2019.
19. Bergson 1911a, pp. 181–3. Deleuze and Guattari's much more famous wasp and orchid example in A Thousand Plateaus is a modern variation on this theme.
20. McNamara 1999, p. 118.
21. Gunter 1982, p. 646.
22. de Mille 2022, p. 7.
23. Cited in de Mille 2022, p. 9.
24. Cited in de Mille 2022, p. 9.
25. Ramey 2012, p. 183.
26. Ramey 2012, p. 31.
27. Eslick 1987, p. 362.
28. Bergson 1990, pp. 207–8.
29. Bergson 1990, p. 207. It would be interesting to unpack the phrase embedded in this quotation, "it is possible to imagine . . . " using Mina Bergson's Golden Dawn ideas for building an image of the higher degrees of tension.
30. Bergson/Mathers 2016c, p. xi. In Deleuzian or even Spinozist language, there is a univocity or substantial equality among the "expressions" of the infinite.
31. Malabou 2016, pp. 104–5.
32. Benveniste 1973, p. 527; Cited at Malabou 2016, p. 106.
33. Malabou 2016, p. 107.
34. See Malabou 2008 for her original position.
35. Malabou 2019, p. xvii.
36. Malabou 2019, pp. 82–83.

37. Malabou 2019, p. 91.

38. Smolin 2013, p. xv. See Marchesini 2018 for both a positive comparison of Smolin's durational thinking with Bergson, and also a critique of where he falls short of thinking consistently about time, that is, in a fully Bergsonian, and immanent manner.

39. Bergson 1992, pp. 34, 168, 189. For more on this, see Khandker 2020, pp. 6–7. Khandker (2020, p. 106) extends this processual methodology to Bergson's use of diagrams, too, seeing them, not as "fixed representations of well-defined things, but as indications of processes that are continuously changing, whilst settling momentarily into fixed forms for the purpose of practical activity. They reveal pure memory to be a useful myth, so to speak, insofar as its suggested ontological status (as Deleuze, for example, emphasizes it) serves a particular function: to open up reflection on the reconfiguration of matter in temporal terms and thus the reconfiguration of mind in terms of processes."

40. Atkinson 2020, p. 189.

41. See Bergson 1992, p. 35: "The habitual labor of thought is easy and can be prolonged at will. Intuition is arduous and cannot last. Whether it be intellection or intuition, thought, of course, always utilizes language; and intuition, like all thought, finally becomes lodged in concepts such as duration, qualitative or heterogeneous multiplicity, unconsciousness—even differentiation, if one considers the notion such as it was to begin with."

42. See Mullarkey 1999a, pp. 181–5.

43. The phenomenon of interference is the "process whereby two or more waves of the same frequency or wavelength combine to form a wave whose amplitude is the sum of the interfering waves" (Parker 1982, pp. 472–3). Interference can be *destructive* or *constructive*. The latter is when the trough and crest of both waves coincide. The former is when the trough of one wave coincides with the crest of another; that is, they are completely "out of phase." In this case, if these two waves are of equal amplitude, they can cancel each other so that the resulting amplitude is zero. And as a wave must, to be a wave, have an amplitude of some dimension, then the result of this encounter is no wave at all, or annihilation. As we will see in our engagement with Karen Barad's work, interference can be seen graphically when one splits up light with two parallel slits (as in "Young's Two-Slit" experiment). An interference pattern can be seen by letting the light from the two slits fall on a white screen. A pattern is produced of dark and bright patches of light. Dark patches or "fringes" indicate waves that have interfered *destructively*. The bright fringes indicate waves that have interfered *constructively*.

Eight: *Vestigia Nulla Retrorsum*: "Leave No Trace"

1. Gaucher 1900, pp. 446–9, cited in Greer 1995, pp. 248–9.

2. Denisoff 2014, pp. 10–11.

3. Phelan 1993, p. 6; cited in Denisoff 2014, p. 9.

4. Denisoff 2014, p. 9. We saw Greer 1995 (p. 15) also connect power with invisibility.

5. Horace, *Epistles*, I, i, 75.

6. Greer 1995, p. 358.

7. Schneider 2011, p. 102.

8. See Bergson's lecture on memory from January 29, 1904 (Bergson 2018, pp. 116–17, 119) on the importance of distinguishing between "impersonal memories" and memories that belong to my own *personal* experience. This seemingly fatuous distinction (don't all memories belong to some person by definition?) covers an important point about "actualization": nearer the plane of pure memory and unrecollected, memories belong to *my* past, which is really present, in embryo so to speak. Once recollected or actualized, memories come closer to an *impersonal*, or public, sharable perception—a memory-image that is not so much mine, that is, belonging to my past reality, my past-time (or "event" as Bergson puts it at one point—p. 125), as one that, though dated and signed as mine, is nonetheless now a common currency, an impersonal memory (of mine). He also describes it as a process of "interference" (p. 129) between different personal memories as they actualize, erasing or "neutralizing" (p. 134) some of their individual personality as they move from subjectivity to objectivity (p. 129). It is the difference between what has not yet manifested and what has manifested.

9. We have already referred to the *Cours* on memory (Bergson 2018) a number of times in these notes. The lecture scripts are not Henri Bergson's originals (he forbade any posthumous publication of his private notes and correspondence) but have been reconstructed from professionally typed notes taken during his courses at the behest of the poet and essayist Charles Péguy, a devotee of Bergson.

10. See Bergson 2018, p. 123. More generally, the editor of the 1903–4 *Cours*, Arnaud François, refers to how the lectures build on Bergson's positions in *Matter and Memory*, noting in particular a third form of recognition being added to the automatic (or inattentive) and attentive forms discussed in the 1896 book—"recognition through movements of imitation" (echoing Bergson's frequent statement that to understand something is to remake or reinvent it for ourselves). This theory of three kinds of recognition then becomes a "general concept of mental life" through "planes of consciousness" (just as in *Matter and Memory*). See François 2018, p. 12.

11. Bergson 2018, pp. 127, 138.

12. These schemata—first introduced in Bergson's 1902 article "Intellectual Effort"—are dynamic, imageless ideas that organize our memories as they descend from RR," ferrying them from virtual life back to actual life (see Bergson 1975, pp. 186–230). Each schema is a guiding model for constructing mental images as they are actualized in perception, neither particular nor universal, but capable of mediating between memory-images and perception. Though Bergson says that such dynamic schema are "not easy to define" (Bergson 1975, p. 196), he nonetheless explains how a set of images must be "reconstructed" through these schema in order to "meet" a perception (Bergson 1975, p. 208). Sounding at times like a Kantian idea, at other times a Husserlian one, the schema is a "meaning" that "guides us in the reconstruction of forms and sounds," and thereby informs recognition. Though the schema is an aid to the subdivision and coordination of images as they come closer to a perception, it is

itself *not an image*. Bergson gives the example of the peculiar ability of chess masters to remember the state of play of several chessboards at once: "the players all agreed that a mental vision of the pieces themselves would be more disturbing to them than useful" (Bergson 1975, pp. 207, 197–8). Rather, it is the chess piece's function or meaning that is paramount.

13. Bergson 2018, pp. 127, 138.
14. Bergson 2018, p. 128.
15. The full quotation goes as follows (Bergson 1975, p. 118): ". . . souls dwell in the world of the Ideas. Incapable of acting, and moreover not even thinking of acting, they lie at rest above time outside space. But, among bodies, there are some which by their form respond more than others to the aspirations of certain souls. And, among souls, there are some which find their own likeness, so to say, in certain bodies. The body, unfinished, as it has been left by nature, rises towards the soul which can give it complete life. And the soul, looking down on the body and perceiving it as the reflexion of itself in a mirror, is fascinated, leans forward and falls. This fall is the beginning of life. I may liken these detached souls to the memories lying in wait in the depth of the unconscious, and the bodies to our sensations during sleep. Sensation is warm, coloured, vibrant and almost living, but vague; memory is clear and distinct, but without substance and lifeless. Sensation longs for a form into which to solidify its fluidity; memory longs for matter to fill it, to ballast it, in short, to realize it. They are drawn towards each other; and the phantom memory, materializing itself in sensation which brings it flesh and blood, becomes a being which lives a life of its own, a dream."
16. Bergson 1975, pp. 116–17.
17. In the French (Bergson 1959, p. 886), the line goes, "*dans la nuit de l'inconscient, une immense danse macabre.*" The translator of the lecture, H. Wildon Carr, notes, however, that not only was this translation authorized by Henri Bergson, it was also a collaborative effort. Bergson was bilingual, so the deliberate choice to translate the French "*une immense danse macabre*" as something quite different ("a wild phantasmagoric dance") is revealing.
18. Lacroix 1943, p. 197n1.
19. Bergson 1972, pp. 1588–89.
20. See Soulez and Worms 1997, p. 36.
21. Jankélévitch 2015, p. 257.

3° = 8° *Practicus Covariant*

1. Halpern 2018.
2. Halpern 2018.
3. Halpern 2018.
4. Barad's chosen pronoun is "they."
5. Gamble, Hanan, and Nail 2019, p. 123.

6. Barad 2007, p. 137.
7. Barad 2007, pp. 93–94.
8. Barad 2007, p. 249.
9. Van der Tuin 2011, p. 24. She is not alone: Ali Lara (Lara 2017, p. 14) writes that "the idea of diffraction is about matter's behavior, or better about matter's dynamic and vibrational nature. Barad, like Bergson, is clear in this quality of matter."
10. Barad 2007, p. 180.
11. Barad 2003, p. 822.
12. Barad 2007, p. 234.
13. Barad 2007, pp. 234, 398.
14. Barad 2007, pp. 140, 151. As Henri Bergson does, too, in fact: "let me insist I am thereby in no way setting aside *substance*"; Bergson 1992 (HB edition), p. 305n23—but he insists on this while also asserting that "reality is mobility" (Bergson 1992, p. 188), or in other words, substance is reinterpreted as a kind of mobility, a complexity of change or movements.
15. Barad 2007, pp. 140, 151.
16. Bergson 1977, pp. 152–3.
17. Barad 2007, p. 33.
18. Barad 2007, p. 140.
19. Barad 2007, p. 178.
20. Barad 2003, p. 808; Barad 2007, p. 152.
21. Barad 2007, p. 821.
22. Barad 2007, p. 25.
23. Barad 2007, p. 140.
24. Barad 2007, p. 82.
25. François Laruelle would be another anti-foundationalist who turns to the quantum realm for a model of knowing that is pluralist: see Ó Maoilearca 2015, chapter two, on "Paraconsistent Fictions and Discontinuous Logic."
26. I own up to cribbing this counter-wordplay on the "immaterial" from *Pirates of the Caribbean: At World's End* (Verbinski 2007).
27. Interestingly, Laruelle turns to Turrell as well for a "new aesthetic (and theoretical) object: light as such, the being-light of light." See Laruelle 1991, cited in Galloway 2013, p. 231.
28. Battista 2018, pp. 83, 89, 91.
29. Battista 2018, p. 87.
30. Battista 2018, p. 90.
31. Montebello 2007, pp. 97–98.
32. From Greer's citation of Lees at Greer 1995, pp. 208–9.
33. De Mille 2022, p. 13.
34. From *Simone Forti: Thinking with the Body* (Breitwieser 2014, pp. 1, 9); cited in Ramos 2021.
35. From the edition of *Planet*, Edizioni Pari & Dispari, Cavriago, Reggio Emilia, 1976, cited in Ramos 2021.
36. Bennett 2010, pp. 11–12.

37. For more on backbone memories (or "continuities"), see Wills 2008 and Moynihan 2019.
38. Valery 1976, p. 65; Badiou 2005; Laruelle 2013, pp. 148–9. Alongside Valery et al., Einav Katan (Katan 2016), provides an updated example of what Laruelle means by such philosophical appropriation, a "salvation" of dance that sublimates it into "this superior choreography that is philosophy." Katan writes: "expression generates a surplus and its ideas go beyond the intentionality of a dancer and/or a choreographer. Along with its actual rhythm of development, an expression conveys an illusion; it becomes a gesture with a semblance that transgresses its actuality" (p. 194). See also Cvejić (2015), who uses Bergson to interesting effect.
39. Lindsay Seers's *Nowhere Less Now* was an Artangel commission that ran from September 8 to October 21, 2012, at The Tin Tabernacle in London. The interview with *Aesthetica Magazine* can be found at http://www.aestheticamagazine.com/blog/lindsay-seers-nowhere-less-now-london/—accessed July 24, 2021.
40. https://www.lindsayseers.info/content/lindsay-seers-nowhere-less-now—accessed July 24, 2021. For the record, I was born in 1965. That Henri Bergson is described here as a "philosopher and mystic" is rather premature in my view, making the present work seemingly redundant.
41. Cited in Pilkington 1976, p. 104; Bergson 1992, p. 157. Atkinson 2020 notes (p. 16) that "rather than creating a new system of thought, Bergson developed new ways of thinking through philosophical problems as a way of revitalizing philosophy. Valéry argues that one of Bergson's greatest contributions to philosophy was the development of an alternative language to the sciences and systematic philosophy, which brought together poetry with the rigour of the exact sciences in order to reveal the orientation of a philosopher's thought."
42. Bergson 1992, p. 157. See also Atkinson 2020, p. 24: "Bergson confirms his view that the arts are founded on intuition like philosophy and that 'philosophy is a genre and the different arts are its species' (*la philosophie est un genre dont les différents arts sont les espèces*)."
43. Significantly in this regard, Atkinson (2020, p. 39) also reports that "while sitting for his portrait with the painter Jacques Émile Blanche, Bergson asked Blanche about Cubism because the Cubists were at the time seeking some type of theoretical foundation for their ideas on the fourth dimension, but the interest was only passing."
44. Hagen 2012, p. 8; Bergson 1990, p. 17.
45. https://www.lindsayseers.info/content/lindsay-seers-nowhere-less-now.
46. Hagen 2012, p. 181.
47. Hagen 2012, p. 23.
48. Hagen 2012, p. 8.
49. Hazelton 2012.
50. Hazelton 2012.
51. Hagen 2012, pp. 116, 122, 9.
52. Hagen 2012, p. 161, 165.
53. Tully 2009, p. 68.

54. Tully 2009, pp. 69, 71. According to Tully (p. 69): while there certainly were Greco-Roman mysteries of the Hellenized Isis, the false idea that there were ancient Egyptian "mysteries" originated with Greeks such as Herodotus, who misunderstood the Egyptian cult of Osiris at Abydos, interpreting it as "mysteric" because it was carried out by a specially consecrated priesthood, unlike the part-time priests of Greece. While access to the inner recesses of the Egyptian temple was limited to the priesthood, festivals were open to the public, not restricted to groups of initiates.

55. Tully 2020, pp. 145, 151.

56. Tully 2020, p. 160.

57. Tully 2009, p. 72.

58. Cited in King and Skinner 1976, p. 15.

59. Hanegraaff 2003, p. 368; see also Josephson Storm 2017.

60. Barad 2007, p. 350. See also p. 279: "Clearly there are major obstacles to observing quantum behavior for large-scale systems. But however difficult it is to realize in practice, in principle we ought to be able to observe quantum behavior in macroscopic systems."

61. Barad 2007, p. ix.

62. Barad 2007, p. 89; Thurschwell 2001, p. 3.

63. Barad 2007, p. 33.

64. Barad 2007, p. ix.

65. Barad 2010, pp. 240, 244.

66. This "reintegration" could also be seen as the "disintegration" or dissolution of what is for Bergson a "false" dichotomy (or binary).

67. Nail 2019, p. 69.

68. These are the bifurcations we referred to earlier when addressing the ramifications of logical types (Russell) and cosmological levels (Bergson) that emerge from the paradoxes of reflexivity. Oddly enough, though, Nail makes little mention of the work of Ilya Prigogine and Isabelle Stengers on thermodynamic bifurcation, despite its huge influence and the fact that Prigogine and Stengers also acknowledge their debts to Henri Bergson. See Prigogine and Stengers 1984.

69. This is what François Laruelle calls the "structural invariance" of one thought standing outside and dominating all other scales, all other thoughts—a thought he dubs "philosophy."

70. Barad 2007, p. 459n61.

71. Murphy notes that hidden-variable theory actually goes back to Louis de Broglie (1892–1987), who was a student of Langevin, and himself acknowledged the influence of Henri Bergson on his own ideas: "Louis de Broglie, who developed the first 'hidden variable' interpretation of quantum mechanics in the 1920s and later inspired Bohm in his fuller version of it, notes the many similarities between quantum theory and Bergson's work as a whole in his *Physics and Microphysics*" (Murphy 1999, p. 79n18).

72. Barad 2007, p. 319. As Barad also says (2007, p. 174): "Bohr did not find Einstein's concerns troubling because Bohr did not share the same metaphysical beliefs." Hence, no dice for Einstein.

73. Though Bergson rarely uses the verbal form, to "temporalize" as we have here, he can talk about adding a "temporal colour" to the description of a phenomenon: see Bergson 2018, p. 116.

74. Bohm 1980, pp. 34–60.

75. Van der Tuin 2011, pp. 28–29n6. Murphy (and Van der Tuin) are not alone, however, with Paul Atkinson (2020, pp. 224–5) also writing about Bergson and Bohm both believing in "undivided wholeness." Milič Čapek (Čapek 1971, p. 309), too, records Bergson's likeness to Bohm's concept of a qualitative infinity within the cosmos: "'the qualitative infinity' . . . of nature shows clearly his [Bohm's] affinity with process philosophy of the type [Bergson's] discussed in this book."

76. Murphy 1999, p. 74.

77. Cited at Murphy 1999, p. 74.

78. Murphy 1999, p. 74.

79. Murphy 1999, p. 74.

80. Bergson 1992, p. 32.

81. Murphy 1999, p. 75.

82. Murphy 1999, pp. 75–76. We would take issue with the use of this last line taken from *Duration and Simultaneity* (Bergson 1965, p. 47), given Henri Bergson's dialogical approach: he seems to be assenting to a theory of *impersonal* time here, and so giving away some ground to the STR; but this is only so that he can later retake that ground by showing where such impersonal time still falls short of real time (*durée*). Nonetheless, there are indeed more extended rhythms of duration that contract our own in Henri Bergson's theory (especially outside *Duration and Simultaneity*), and these would appear impersonal relative to us (at least before we fabulate a personality out of them).

83. Barad 2007, p. 273.

84. Barad 2007, pp. 318, 319.

85. Barad 2007, p. 182.

86. Barad 2007, p. 394.

87. Bergson 1969, p. 174.

88. See Bergson 1975, pp. 186–230.

89. McNamara 1999, p. 136.

90. Another relatively ordinary example of metempsychosis, or what he calls the "translife of the soul," comes in Laurent Debreuil's concept of an "intellective space" (Debreuil 2015, pp. 111ff): "I may still speak of my soul as an effect of this mind toward another I than the one I think I am using. *My soul is a singular persistence of my thinking into yours, yours, and yours.* [. . .] Our souls are 'immortal,' for they do not *live*. They have a *translife*, they are differentially performed by organisms. They disappear, when painted stones are erased, languages go extinct, memories vanish. But, as long as their *tracé* is to be found, they will appear, and sink. [. . .] This strange place, I call it *the intellective space*, that is, a putative space where thought and knowledge are performed and shared, and not only computed according to universal laws that would 'speak' to us directly and by themselves" (pp. 119, 120, 3).

91. Christof 2017, p. 160.

Nine: Spirit in the Materialist World

1. See Ó Maoilearca 2019b.
2. Matheson 1998, pp. 216, 302.
3. Moreover, we must strip away the confused mixtures of time and space operating in the usual models of time travel. Take the time machine itself, for example. Such transcendent machines are somehow able to coexist in the past (or future) as well as their present such that they never completely enter into the new time at all. The fictional time travel machine is a transcendent, atemporal transport and so, like some *objet petit a*, never immanent within either its original time or any other. Its circulations (voyages) embody both the possibility and impossibility of time travel, at least as we standardly think of it, because they can never either fully arrive at their destination or return to their point of departure.
4. Bergson 1992, p. 200.
5. The "transhumanist" notion of a transcendent *intellect* or *intelligence* that survives any particular hardware platform (bioware/meatware/siliconware, etc.) which would "host" it as digital software might appear to be a materialist route to actual *immortality*. Yet its obvious Cartesian origins (mind reduced to an essence of self-awareness that is cut off from any particular body) clearly show it to be a crypto-spiritualism predicated on one form of continuity—cogitative self-sameness (I think, I am; I think, I am . . .)—with only a solipsistic God, or its software equivalent, to maintain its existence. See Clarke 2009.
6. This, we suggest, would be Mina Bergson's remake of the concluding line from Henri Bergson's *Two Sources of Morality and Religion* that we heard Howard Caygill quote earlier (Bergson 1977, p. 275): "the essential function of the universe, which is a machine for making gods."
7. In *A Biography of Ordinary Man*, François Laruelle writes of a "mystical-ordinary acting" that would allow "for the description of the World in its remoteness and its strangeness, of its heterogeneity—the heterogeneity of philosophical logics—as fundamentally undecidable" (Laruelle 2017, p. 84). It is this strangeness of the World (or Real, as Laruelle would later put it) that requires heterogeneous logics to depict it.
8. Yeats, we recall, used the phrase "mystical philosophy," which now has added weight.
9. See also Sommer McGrath (p. 17) on how, in new French spiritualism, even "faith came to be seen as a bodily practice"—one later example being Bergson's reading of magical fabulation as a "logic of the body" (Bergson 1977, p. 140).
10. My thanks to Alastair Cameron for alerting me to this passage from Mauss.
11. In a future work I hope to demonstrate the ethics of our perceptual categories and beliefs (the "structure of regard") in terms of interference phenomena, *and vice versa*—that the destruction and construction of waves are normative acts, acts of belief. The beliefs acquired or learned as *character* traits, for example (be they normal or "pathological"), would be read as interfering lines that have been significantly amplified. For further interesting remarks on Walter Elsasser's work on "amplification" as a mode of "functioning of the living" (and in the context of Whitehead's thought on microcosmic and macrocosmic relations), see Khandker 2020, pp. 44–46.

Ten: Veridical Hallucinations and Circumstantial Evidence

1. As McNamara relates (1999, p. 129), Henri Bergson "suggested that the dream in-volved a lifting of the normal inhibitory stance of the brain, a relaxation of the usual 'interested' and outward-oriented stance of the individual." For J. W. Dunne, such dreams could be tokens of real time travel—but that's another story: see Ó Maoilearca 2019b.

2. See Laruelle 2013.

3. Laruelle 2017, p. 160. Laruelle writes of an "ordinary mysticism," wherein he claims that "the mystical is pre-philosophical, or, as we will say, 'ordinary'" (Laruelle 2017, p. 59).

4. Bergson/Mathers 2016c, p. x. Indeed, the charge that mystical systems of thought de-sire unity with one absolute principle may well be undeserved in many cases, at least in terms of their underlying metaphysics. See Jones 2016, pp. 193–4: "most mystical systems do not involve an all-encompassing nonduality in which all of the apparent diversity in the world is in the final analysis unreal. [. . .] There may be a sense of union or a sense of individuality melting away, but there is no *ontic change in na-ture* from what was already our true situation all along—only the false conceptual boundaries that we ourselves had created soften or disappear. Through experiencing the commonality of being, one gains a knowledge by participation, but there still is no new ontic union of substances." Jones continues, using Brahmanism as his example (p. 197): "For Advaita, only Brahman is real, and thus there is nothing else to unite with it. There is no 'absorption' of an independent self into 'the Absolute.' Nor is the universe the pantheistic body of Brahman. The Upanishads have an emanationist position, but Advaita and Samkhya interpret the situation differently. The popular image of a drop of water merging in the ocean does not fit the metaphysics of these traditions."

5. Burton 2015, pp. 109–10.

6. McGuire 2017, pp. 23, 24.

7. See Bergson 1975, pp. 84–85. It should be noted that Bergson is more likely to speak of *tendencies*, rather than probabilities, when it comes to anything else, material or spiritual, other than epistemology. But the notion of real probability that emerges in physics with Bohr's work can be plausibly translated into the language of tendency when seen through the lens of heterogeneous continuity.

8. See Bergson 1990, p. 56, 233–4. See also Bergson's course on memory at the Collège de France for February 5, 1904, where he reiterates this mereological theory of phys-ical pain but also adds the same part/whole analysis for emotional suffering, taking grief for a deceased parent as his example (Bergson 2018, pp. 145–7). Recall also that in Richard Matheson's novel *Bid Time Return* we are told that the hero has a brain tumor, leaving it open that his entire experience of time travel was literally "in his head." But such a deflation can be pivoted to inflate the cerebral rather than deflate the phenomenal.

9. See Lawlor 2002, p. 82. See also Deleuze 2004: pp. 25–26: "But for Bergson, alterity is still not enough to make it so that being rejoins things and really is the being of things.

He replaces the Platonic concept of alterity with an Aristotelian concept of alteration, in order to make of it substance itself. Being is alteration, alteration is substance. And that is what Bergson calls *duration*, because all the characteristics by which he defines it, after *Time and Free Will*, come back to this: duration is that which differs or that which changes nature, quality, heterogeneity, what differs from itself. The being of the sugar cube will be defined by a duration, by a certain manner of persisting, by a certain relaxation or tension of duration."

10. Indeed, *The Two Sources* adds a clear ethical dimension to Bergsonian attention as "attention to life." What stands in contrast to an *inattention* toward others is the "open soul," the soul whose centripetal movement of love is inexhaustible (not even a love of "all humanity," nor a love extended "to animals, to plants, to all nature" could exhaust it—Bergson 1977, p. 27). This would be a positive, ethical attention to all, one that could well be set alongside a Kantian tradition of attention as respect or reverence (*Achtung*) or even a quasi-mystical attention such as Simone Weil's "voiding" or Iris Murdoch's "clear vision." Neither Kant nor Plato (a crucial source for both Weil and Murdoch), however, can be numbered as conceptual allies of Henri Bergson. His attention to life is neither rationalist (a reverence for law) nor transcendentalist (an escape from the senses): attention to life is inherently experiential, being based on the findings of psychology, biology, and mysticism, albeit as understood through a process philosophy.

11. See Mullarkey 1995.

12. After all, the virtual is not a different ontological realm but perfectly optical and psychological, only of a different type.

13. That modern philosophy was partly colored by the *hyperbolic* stage of Cartesian doubt, which eventually trapped it within a prison of representation (Kant), is also an excess that was valorized in "postmodern" (sic) thought (see Derrida et al.), which offers us a number of related instances of what Laruelle calls the "philosophical decision" (or cut) whereby philosophical thought withdraws from the Real. This withdrawal is also described as an "hallucination"—a projected image, or rather an invented image that is doubtlessly real yet improperly seeing itself as exhaustive of the real (the part standing for the whole). See Ó Maoilearca 2015 for more on this withdrawal.

14. Bergson 1990, p. 71.

15. Bergson 1911a, p. 221.

16. See Canguilhem 1943. Even for Canguilhem, though, what counted was the first term, the *élan*, movement, or direction: life or spirit *is* matter in an opposed direction.

Epilogue: The Whole of the Moon

1. Bergson 1990, p. 135.

2. Mullarkey 1999b, p. 3.

3. Bergson 1992, pp. 212–13.

Bibliography

Antliff, Mark. *Bergson: Cultural Politics and the Parisian Avant-garde*. Princeton University Press, 1993.

Armstrong, Christopher. *Evelyn Underhill*. Mowbray, 1975.

Asprem, Egil. "Beyond the West: Towards a New Comparativism in the Study of Esotericism." *Correspondences* 2 (2014): 3–33.

Asprem, Egil. "Explaining the Esoteric Imagination: Towards a Theory of Kataphatic Practice." *Aries* 17 (2017): 17–50.

Asprem, Egil. "Magic Naturalized? Negotiating Science and Occult Experience in Aleister Crowley's Scientific Illuminism." *Aries: Journal for the Study of Western Esotericism* 8 (2008): 139–65.

Asprem, Egil, and Markus Altena Davidsen. "Editors' Introduction: What Cognitive Science Offers the Study of Esotericism." *Aries: Journal for the Study of Western Esotericism* 17 (2017): 1–15.

Atkinson, Paul. *Henri Bergson and Visual Culture: A Philosophy for a New Aesthetic*. Bloomsbury, 2020.

Bachelard, Gaston. *Dialectique de la Durée*. Presses Universitaires de France, 1963.

Badiou, Alain. "Dance as a Metaphor for Thought." In Alain Badiou, *Handbook of Inaesthetics*, translated by Alberto Toscano. Stanford University Press, 2005, pp. 57–71.

Barad, Karen. *Meeting the Universe Halfway: Quantum Physics and the Entanglement of Matter and Meaning*. Duke University Press, 2007.

Barad, Karen. "Posthuman Performativity: Toward an Understanding of How Matter Comes to Matter." *Signs: Journal of Women in Culture and Society* 28, no. 3 (2003): 801–31.

Barad, Karen. "Quantum Entanglements and Hauntological Relations of Inheritance: Dis/continuities, SpaceTime Enfoldings, and Justice-to-Come." *Derrida Today* 3 (2010): 240–68.

Barbour, Julian. "Time, Instants, Duration and Philosophy." In Robin Durie, ed., *Time and the Instant: Essays in the Physics and Philosophy of Time*. Clinamen Press, 2000, pp. 96–111.

Barnard, G. William. *Living Consciousness: The Metaphysical Vision of Henri Bergson*. State University of New York Press, 2012a.

Barnard, G. William. "Tuning into Other Worlds: Henri Bergson and the Radio Reception Theory of Consciousness." In Lefebvre and White, 2012b, pp. 281–98.

Barrett, Deirdre. *Supernormal Stimuli: How Primal Urges Overran Their Evolutionary Purpose*. W. W. Norton & Company, 2010.

Barthelemy-Madaule, Madeleine. *Bergson, adversaire de Kant: Etude Critique de la Conception Bergsonienne du Kantisme*. Presses Universitaires de France, 1966.

Battista, Silvia. *Posthuman Spiritualities in Contemporary Performance*. Palgrave Macmillan, 2018.

Bennett, Jane. *Vibrant Matter: A Political Ecology of Things*. Duke University Press, 2010.

Benveniste, Emile. *Indo-European Language and Society.* Translated by Elizabeth Palmer. London, 1973.

Bergson, Henri. *Creative Evolution.* Translated by Arthur Mitchell. Macmillan, 1911a.

Bergson, Henri. *The Creative Mind: An Introduction to Metaphysics.* Translated by Mabelle L. Andison. Citadel Press, 1992.

Bergson, Henri. *Duration and Simultaneity: with Reference to Einstein's Theory.* Translated by Leon Jacobsen. Bobbs-Merrill, 1965.

Bergson, Henri. "Entretiens avec Lydie Adophe." In Lydie Adophe, *La Dialectique des images chez Bergson.* Presses Univérsitaires de France, 1951.

Bergson, Henri. "Fictitious Times and Real Times." Translated by P.A.Y. Gunter, in P.A.Y. Gunter, ed., *Bergson and the Evolution of Physics.* University of Tennessee Press, 1969, pp. 168–86.

Bergson, Henri. *Histoire des heories de la mémoire: Cours au Collège de France 1903–1904.* Presses Univérsitaires de France, 2018.

Bergson, Henri. *Laughter: An Essay on the Meaning of the Comic.* Translated by Cloudesley Brereton and Fred Rothwell. Green Integer, 1911b.

Bergson, Henri. *Matter and Memory* (1911). Translated by Nancy Margaret Paul and W. Scott. Palmer Zone Books, 1990.

Bergson, Henri. *Mélanges.* Edited by André Robinet. Presses Universitaires de France, 1972.

Bergson, Henri. *Mind-Energy: Lectures and Essays.* Translated by H. Wildon Carr. Greenwood Press, 1975.

Bergson, Henri. *Oeuvres.* Edited by André Robinet. Presses Universitaires de France, 1959.

Bergson, Henri. *Time and Free Will: An Essay on the Immediate Data of Consciousness.* George Allen and Unwin, 1910.

Bergson, Henri. *The Two Sources of Morality and Religion.* Translated by R. Ashley Audra and Cloudesley Brereton, with the assistance of W. Horsfall Carter. Notre Dame Press, 1977.

Bergson, Mina/Moina Mathers. "Flying Roll No.21, Know Thyself." In Mathers, King, and Gilbert, 1987, pp. 151–9.

Bergson, Mina/Moina Mathers. "Flying Roll No.23, Tattwa Visions." In Regardie, 2016b.

Bergson, Mina/Moina Mathers. "Flying Roll No.31, Correspondence between Enochian and Ethiopian Alphabets." http://www.tarrdaniel.com/documents/Thelemagick/gd/publication/english/Flying_Rolls.html#flying-roll-XXXI. Accessed June 28, 2020.

Bergson, Mina/Moina Mathers. "Preface" to second edition of Samuel Mathers, *Kabbalah Unveiled* (1926). Routledge, 2016c, pp. vii–xiii.

Bergson, Mina/Moina Mathers. "Of Skrying and Travelling in the Spirit-Vision." In Regardie, 2016a.

Bernecker, Sven, and Kourken Michaelian, eds. *The Routledge Handbook of Philosophy of Memory.* Taylor & Francis, 2017.

Bevir, Michael. *The Making of British Socialism.* Princeton University Press, 2011.

Bickle, John. "Memory and Levels of Scientific Explanation." In Bernecker and Michaelian, 2017, pp. 34–47.

Blassnigg, Martha. "Clairvoyance, Cinema, and Consciousness." In Robert Pepperell and Michael Punt, eds., *Screen Consciousness: Cinema, Mind and World.* Rodopi, 2006, pp. 105–22.

Bogdan, Henrik. "Women and the Hermetic Order of the Golden Dawn: Nineteenth Century Occultistic Initiation From A Gender Perspective." In Alexandra Heidle and Jan A. M. Snoek, eds., *Women's Agency and Rituals in Mixed and Female Masonic Orders*. Brill, 2008, pp. 245–63.

Bohm, David. *Wholeness and the Implicate Order*. Routledge, 1980.

Brang, D., E. M. Hubbard, S. Coulson, M. Huang, and V. S. Ramachandran. "Magnetoencephalography Reveals Early Activation of V4 in Grapheme-Color Synesthesia." *NeuroImage* 53, no.1 (October 2010): 268–74.

Breitwieser, Sabine, ed. *Simone Forti: Thinking with the Body*. Hirmer Verlag, 2014.

Brouwer, L. E. J. "Consciousness, Philosophy, and Mathematics" (1948). In A. Heyting, ed., *Collected Works: Volume One: Philosophy and Foundations of Mathematics*. North-Holland, 1975, pp. 480–94.

Burton, James. *The Philosophy of Science Fiction: Henri Bergson and the Fabulations of Philip K. Dick*. Bloomsbury, 2015.

Butler, Alison. *Victorian Occultism and the Making of Modern Magic: Invoking Tradition*. Palgrave, 2011.

Butler, Joseph. *Analogy of Religion, Natural and Revealed* (1736).

Canales, Jimena. *The Physicist and the Philosopher: Einstein, Bergson, and the Debate That Changed Our Understanding of Time*. Princeton University Press, 2015.

Canguilhem, Georges. "Commentaire au troisième chapitre de *L'Evolution créatrice*." *Bulletin de la faculté des lettres de Strasbourg* XXI, no. 5–6 (1943): 126–43 and XXI, no. 8 (1943): 199–214.

Čapek, Milič. *Bergson and Modern Physics: A Reinterpretation and Re-evaluation*. D. Reidel, 1971.

Čapek, Milič. "Bergson's Theory of the Mind-Brain Relation." In *Papanicolaou and Gunter*, 1987, pp. 129–48.

Capra, Fritjof. *The Tao of Physics: An Exploration of the Parallels Between Modern Physics and Eastern Mysticism*. Shambhala Publications, 1975.

Cariou, Marie. *Bergson and le fait mystique*. Aubier Montaigne, 1976.

Cariou, Marie. *Lectures Bergsoniennes*. Presses Univérsitaires de France, 1990.

Caygill, Howard. "Hyperaesthesia and the Virtual." In Ó Maoilearca and de Mille, 2013, pp. 247–59.

Christof, Catharine. "Feminist Action in and through Tarot and Modern Occult Society." *La Rosa di Paracelso* 1 (2017): 153–69.

Clarke, Julie. *The Paradox of the Posthuman: Science Fiction/Techno-Horror Films and Visual Media*. VDM Verlag, 2009.

Coleman, Sam. "Being Realistic." In Galen Strawson et al., eds., *Consciousness and Its Place in Nature: Does Physicalism Entail Panpsychism?* Imprint-Academic, 2006, pp. 40–52.

Colquhoun, Ithell. *Sword of Wisdom: MacGregor Mathers and the Golden Dawn*. Neville Spearman, 1975.

Cooper, David E. *Senses of Mystery: Engaging with Nature and the Meaning of Life*. Routledge, 2017.

Cvejić, Bojana. *Choreographing Problems: Expressive Concepts in European Contemporary Dance and Performance*. Palgrave Macmillan, 2015.

De Brigard, Felipe. "Memory and Imagination." In Bernecker and Michaelian, 2017, pp. 127–40.

De Mille, Charlotte. *Bergson in Britain: Philosophy and Modernist Painting c. 1890–1914*. Edinburgh University Press, 2022.

Debreuil, Laurent. *The Intellective Space: Thinking beyond Cognition*. University of Minnesota Press, 2015.

Deleuze, Gilles. "Bergson, 1859–1941." In Gilles Deleuze, *Desert Islands: And Other Texts, 1953–1974*. Semiotexte, 2004, pp. 22–31.

Deleuze, Gilles. *Bergsonism*. Translated by Hugh Tomlinson and Barbara Habberjam. Zone Books, 1988.

Deleuze, Gilles, and Felix Guattari. *A Thousand Plateaus*. Translated by Brian Massumi. Athlone Press, 1987.

Delhomme, Jeanne. *Vie et conscience de la Vie: Essais sur Bergson*. Presses Univérsitaires de France, 1954.

Delitz, Heike. "Life as the Subject of Society: Critical Vitalism as Critical Social Theory." In Hartmut Rosa, Christoph Henning, and Arthur Bueno, eds., *Critical Theory and New Materialisms*. Routledge, 2021, pp. 107–22.

Denisoff, Dennis. "Pamela Colman Smith, Symbolism and Spiritual Synaesthesia." In Andrew Radford and Christine Ferguson, eds., *The Occult Imagination in Britain, 1875–1947*. Routledge, 2019a, pp. 146–64.

Denisoff, Dennis. "Performing the Spirit: Theatre, the Occult, and the Ceremony of Isis." *Cahiers victoriens et édouardiens* 80 (2014): 2–12.

Denisoff, Dennis. "Queer Occulture and Feminist Ritual Performance." Presented at Queen Mary University, London. May 23, 2019b.

Dubilet, Alex. "'Neither God, nor World': On the One Foreclosed to Transcendence." *Palgrave Communications* 1 (2015): 1–8.

Dunham, Jeremy. "Overcoming the Divide between Freedom and Nature: Clarisse Coignet on the Metaphysics of Independent Morality." *British Journal for the History of Philosophy* 28 (2020): 987–1008.

Edelman, Gerald. *Bright Light, Brilliant Fire: On the Matter of the Mind*. Basic Books, 1992.

Eslick, Leonard. "Bergson, Whitehead, and Psychical Research." In Papanicolaou and Gunter, 1987, pp. 353–68.

Evrard, Renaud. "Bergson et la télépathie: à propos d'une correspondance inédite." *Bergsoniana* 1, no. 1 (2021): 237–55.

Fenton, David. *The Ghost Club*. Smashwords, 2014.

Flusser, Vilém. *Towards a Philosophy of Photography*. Translated by Martin Chalmers. Reaktion Books, 2000.

Forman, Robert K. C. "Introduction: Mystical Consciousness, the Innate Capacity, and the Perennial Psychology." In Robert K. C. Forman, ed., *The Innate Capacity: Mysticism, Psychology, and Philosophy*. Oxford University Press, 1998, pp. 3–41.

Forman, Robert K. C. "Introduction: Mysticism, Constructivism, and Forgetting." In Robert K. C. Forman, ed., *The Problem of Pure Consciousness: Mysticism and Philosophy*. Oxford University Press, 1990, pp. 3–49.

Forti, Simone. *Planet*, Edizioni Pari & Dispari, Cavriago, Reggio Emilia, 1976.

François, Arnaud. *Bergson*. Ellipses, 2008.

François, Arnaud. "Présentation: De la mémoire à la liberté." In Bergson, 2018, pp. 9–17.

Franklin, J. Jeffrey. *Spirit Matters: Occult Beliefs, Alternative Religions, and the Crisis of Faith in Victorian Britain*. Cornell University Press, 2018.

Galloway, Alexander R. "Laruelle and Art." *continent* 2, no. 4 (2013): 230–36.

Gamble, Christopher N., Joshua S. Hanan, and Thomas Nail. "What Is New Materialism?" *Angelaki* 24 (2019): 111–34.

Gaucher, André. "Isis à Montmartre." *L'Echo du Merveilleux* (1900): 446–49.

Gayon, Jean. "Bergson's Spiritualist Metaphysics and the Sciences." In Gary Gutting, ed., *Continental Philosophy of Science*. Wiley-Blackwell, 2005, pp. 43–58.

Gilbert, R. A. "Magical Manuscripts: An Introduction to the Archives of the Hermetic Order of the Golden Dawn." *Yeats Annual* no. 5 (1987): 163–77.

Glennan, Stuart, and Phyllis Illari, eds. *The Routledge Handbook of Mechanisms and Mechanical Philosophy*. Routledge, 2018.

Godwin, Joscelyn. "Esoteric Theories of Color." In Peter J. Forshaw, ed., *Lux in Tenebris: The Visual and the Symbolic in Western Esotericism*. Brill, 2017, pp. 447–76.

Green, Helen L. *Middlebrow Mystics: Henri Bergson and British Culture, 1899–1939*. Doctoral thesis. Northumbria University, 2015.

Green, Richard. *The Thwarting of Laplace's Demon: Arguments against the Mechanistic World-View*. St. Martin's Press, 1995.

Greer, John Michael. *The Celtic Golden Dawn: An Original & Complete Curriculum of Druidical Study*. Llewellyn Publications, 2013.

Greer, Mary. *Women of the Golden Dawn: Rebels and Priestesses*. Park Street Press, 1995.

Grogin, R. C. *The Bergsonian Controversy in France, 1900–1914*. The University of Calgary Press, 1988.

Grosz, Elizabeth. *Time Travels: Feminism, Nature, Power*. Duke University Press, 2005.

Gunter, P. A. Y., ed. *Bergson and the Evolution of Physics*. University of Tennessee Press, 1969.

Gunter, P. A. Y. "Bergson and Jung." *Journal of the History of Ideas* 43 (1982): 635–52.

Hacking, Ian. *Rewriting the Soul: Multiple Personality and the Sciences of Memory*. Princeton University Press, 1998.

Hagen, Ole. *Nowhere Less Now*. Artangel, 2012.

Hallward, Peter. *Out of This World: Deleuze and the Philosophy of Creation*. Verso, 2006.

Halpern, Paul. "Spiritual Hyperplane." *Aeon* (January 18, 2018), https://aeon.co/essays/the-occult-roots-of-higher-dimensional-research-in-physics. Accessed June 15, 2020.

Hanegraaff, Wouter J. *Esotericism and the Academy: Rejected Knowledge in Western Culture*. Cambridge University Press, 2008.

Hanegraaff, Wouter J. "How Magic Survived the Disenchantment of the World." *Religion* 33 (2003): 357–80.

Hanegraaff, Wouter J. "Imagining the Future Study of Religion and Spirituality." *Religion* 50 (2020): 72–82.

Hanegraaff, Wouter J. *Western Esotericism: A Guide for the Perplexed*. Bloomsbury, 2013.

Hazelton, Claire. "Lindsay Seers: Nowhere Less Now." 2012. https://aestheticamagazine.com/lindsay-seers/. Accessed June 20, 2017.

Hedenborg White. Manon. "Proximal Authority: The Changing Role of Leah Hirsig in Aleister Crowley's Thelema, 1919–1930." *Aries: Journal for the Study of Western Esotericism 21* (2021): 69–93.

Herring, Emily. "Henri Bergson, Celebrity." *Aeon*. https://aeon.co/essays/henri-bergson-the-philosopher-damned-for-his-female-fans. May 6, 2019. Accessed June 28, 2020.

Hirai, Yasushi. "Bergson on Panpsychism." https://www.academia.edu/42887513/Bergson_on_Panpsychism_2020. Accessed June 28, 2020.

Horace. *Satires and Epistles*. Translated by John Davie. Oxford University Press, 2011.

Hude, Henri. *Bergson I et II*. Editions Universitaires, 1989–1990.

Hutton, Ronald. *The Triumph of the Moon, A History of Modern Pagan Witchcraft*. Oxford University Press, 1999.

Hyppolite, Jean. "Various Aspects of Memory in Bergson." Translated by Athena V. Colman in Lawlor 2002, pp. 112–27.

James, William. *The Letters of William James*, Vol. II. Createspace, 2015.

Jankélévitch, Vladimir. *Bergson*. Translated by Nils F. Schott. Duke University Press, 2015.

Jankélévitch, Vladimir. "Bergson and Judaism." In Lefebvre and White, 2012, pp. 217–45.

Jantzen, Grace M. *Becoming Divine: Towards a Feminist Philosophy of Religion*. Manchester University Press, 1998.

Jones, Richard H. *Philosophy of Mysticism: Raids on the Ineffable*. State University of New York Press, 2016.

Josephson Storm, Jason A. *The Myth of Disenchantment: Magic, Modernity, and the Birth of the Human Sciences*. University of Chicago Press, 2017.

Katan, Einav. *Embodied Philosophy in Dance: Gaga and Ohad Naharin's Movement Research*. Palgrave Macmillan, 2016.

Katz, Steven T. "Language, Epistemology, and Mysticism." In Steven T. Katz, ed., *Mysticism and Philosophical Analysis*. Oxford University Press, 1978, pp. 22–74.

Katz, Steven T. "Mystical Speech and Mystical Meaning." In Steven T. Katz, ed., *Mysticism and Language*. Oxford University Press, 1992, pp. 3–41.

Kelly, Edward F., et al. *Irreducible Mind: Towards a Psychology for the 21st Century*. Rowman and Littlefield, 2007.

Kern, Stephen. *The Culture of Time and Space: 1880–1918*. Harvard University Press, 1983.

Khandker, Wahida. *Process Metaphysics and Mutative Life: Sketches of Lived Time*. Palgrave Macmillan, 2020.

King, Francis X., and Stephen Skinner. *Techniques of High Magic*. Destiny Books, 1976.

Kolakowski, Leszek. *Bergson*. Oxford University Press, 1985.

Kremer-Marietti, Angèle. *Les formes du mouvement chez Bergson*. Les Cahiers du nouvel humanisme, 1953.

Kuhn, Annette. *Family Secrets: Acts of Memory and Imagination*. Verso, 2002.

Lacroix, Jean. "L'Intuition, Méthode de Purification." In Albert Beguin and Pierre Thevanez, eds., *Henri Bergson: Essais et Témoignages*. Editions de la Baconniere, 1943, pp. 196–204.

Lambert, Gregg. "What the Earth Thinks." In Ian Buchanan and Gregg Lambert, eds., *Deleuze and Space*. Edinburgh University Press, 2005, pp. 220–39.

Langer, Ellen, J. *Mindfulness*. Perseus Books, 1989.

Lara, Ali. "Wine's Time: Duration, Attunement, and Diffraction." *Subjectivity* 10 (2017): 104–22.

Laruelle, François. *A Biography of Ordinary Man: On Authorities and Minorities*. Translated by Jessie Hock and Alex Dubilet. Polity Press, 2017.

Laruelle, François. "First Choreography or the Essence-of-Dance." *Qui Parle* 21, no. 2 (Spring/Summer 2013): 143–55.

Laruelle, François. "A Light Odyssey: La découverte de la lumière comme problème théorique et esthétique." Le Confort Moderne, 1991.

Laruelle, François. *Mystique non-philosophique à l'usage des contemporains*. Harmattan, 2007.

Laruelle, François. *Principles of Non-Philosophy*. Translated by Nicola Rubczak and Anthony Paul Smith. Bloomsbury Academic, 2013.

Latour, Bruno. "Anti-Zoom." In Michael Tavel Clarke and David Wittenberg, eds., *Scale in Literature and Culture*. Palgrave, 2017, pp. 93–101.

Latour, Bruno. *Reassembling the Social: An Introduction to Actor-Network-Theory*. Oxford University Press, 2005.

Lawlor, Leonard. *The Challenge of Bergsonism*. Continuum Press, 2002.

Lawlor, Leonard. "Henri Bergson." https://plato.stanford.edu/entries/bergson/. Accessed on June 14, 2020.

Le Doeuff, Michele. *The Philosophical Imaginary.* Translated by C. Gordon. Continuum, 2002.

Lees, Frederic. "Isis Worship in Paris: Conversations with the Hierophant Rameses and the High Priestess Anari." *The Humanitarian* 16, no. 2 (1900).

Lefebvre, Alexandre, and Melanie White, eds. *Bergson, Politics, and Religion.* Duke University Press, 2012.

Lincoln, Bruce. *Authority: Construction and Corrosion.* University of Chicago Press, 1994.

Lincoln, Bruce. *Myth, Cosmos, and Society: Indo-European Themes of Creation and Destruction.* Harvard University Press, 1986.

Locke, John. *Essay Concerning Human Understanding.* Nidditch edition. Oxford University Press, 1979.

Longo, Giuseppe. "Confusing Biological Rhythms and Physical Clocks: Today's Ecological Relevance of Bergson-Einstein Debate on Time." Paper presented at conference "Einstein and Bergson 100 Years Later" in Aquila, Italy (April 4–6, 2019). https://www.researchgate.net/publication/338139213_Confusing_biological_rhythms_and_physical_clocks_Today%27s_ecological_relevance_of_Bergson-Einstein_debate_on_time. Accessed August 20, 2020.

Luhrmann, Tanya M. *Persuasions of the Witch's Craft.* Harvard University Press, 1991. Epub edition.

MacGregor Mathers. "Flying Roll No.XII, Telesmatic Images and Adonai." http://www.tarrdaniel.com/documents/Thelemagick/gd/publication/english/Flying_Rolls.html#flying-roll-XII. Accessed June 29, 2020.

MacIntyre, F. Gwynplaine. *The Woman Between the Worlds.* Dell Books, 1994.

Magee, Glenn Alexander. *Hegel and the Hermetic Tradition.* Cornell University Press, 2001.

Malabou, Catherine. "Before and Above: Spinoza and Symbolic Necessity." *Critical Inquiry* 43 (Autumn 2016): 84–109.

Malabou, Catherine. *Morphing Intelligence.* Translated by Carolyn Shred. Columbia University Press, 2019.

Malabou, Catherine. *What Should We Do with Our Brain?* Translated by Sebastian Rand. Fordham University Press, 2008.

Marchesini, Paula. "The End of Time or Time Reborn? Henri Bergson and the Metaphysics of Time in Contemporary Cosmology." *Philosophy and Cosmology* 21 (2018): 140–52.

Maritain, Jacques. *Bergsonian Philosophy and Thomism.* Translated by Mabelle L. Andison and J. Gordon Andison. Greenwood Press, 1968.

Mathers, S. L. MacGregor. "Flying Roll No.XI, Of Clairvoyance." *In* MacGregor, King, and, Gilbert, 1987, pp. 75–83.

Mathers, S. L. MacGregor, Francis X. King, and R. A. Gilbert, eds. *Astral Projection, Ritual Magic, and Alchemy: Golden Dawn Material.* Destiny Books, 1987.

Matheson, Richard. *Bid Time Return* (1975). Republished as *Somewhere in Time.* TOR Books, 1998.

Mauss, Marcel. *Sociologie et Anthropologie.* 4th ed. Presses Universitaires de France, 1968.

McEwan, Ian. *The Child in Time.* Jonathan Cape, 1987.

McGinn, Colin. *The Mysterious Flame: Conscious Minds in a Material World.* Basic Books, 2000.

McGuire, Meghan. *Gyres and Waves: Bergsonian Movement and Multiplicity in the Works of W.B. Yeats and Virginia Woolf*. University of North Carolina, Greensboro PhD thesis, 2017.

McNamara, Patrick. *Mind and Variability: Mental Darwinism, Memory and Self*. Praeger, 1999.

McRoy, Jay. "Case Study: Cinematic Hybridity in Shimizu Takashi's Ju-On: The Grudge." In Jay McRoy, ed., *Japanese Horror Cinema*. Edinburgh University Press, 2005, pp. 175–84.

Michaelian, Kourken. *Mental Time Travel: Episodic Memory and Our Knowledge of the Personal Past*. MIT Press, 2016.

Montebello, Pierre. "Matter and Light in Bergson's Creative Evolution." Translated by Roxanne Lapidus. *SubStance* 36, no. 3 (2007): 91–99.

Moore, F. C. T. *Bergson: Thinking Backwards*. Cambridge University Press, 1996.

Moore, G. E. "Proof of an External World." In Thomas Baldwin, ed., *G.E. Moore: Selected Writings*. Routledge, 1993, pp. 147–70.

Morin, Edgar. *Le Cinema ou l'Homme Imaginaire. Essay d'Anthropologie*. Les Editions de Minuit, 1956.

Morrison, Mark. *Modern Alchemy: Occultism and the Emergence of Atomic Theory*. Oxford University Press, 2007.

Mossé-Bastide, Rose-Marie. *Bergson éducateur*. Presses Universitaires de France, 1955.

Mossé-Bastide, Rose-Marie. *Bergson et Plotin*. Presses Universitaires de France, 1959.

Mourélos, Georges. *Bergson et les niveaux de réalité*. Presses Universitaires de France, 1964.

Moynihan, Thomas. *Spinal Catastrophism: A Secret History*. Urbanomic Press, 2019.

Mullarkey, John. *Bergson and Philosophy*. Edinburgh University Press, 1999a.

Mullarkey, John. "Bergson's Method of Multiplicity." *Metaphilosophy* 26 (July 1995): 230–59.

Mullarkey, John. "Creative Metaphysics and the Metaphysics of Creativity." *Bergson Now, special issue of the Journal of the British Society for Phenomenology* 35 (2004b): 68–81.

Mullarkey, John. "Forget the Virtual: Bergson, Actualism, and the Refraction of Reality." *Continental Philosophy Review* 37 (2004a): 469–93.

Mullarkey, John. "Introduction: *La Philosophie Nouvelle* or Change in Philosophy." In Mullarkey, 1999b, pp. 1–16.

Mullarkey, John. "Life, Movement, and the Fabulation of the Event." *Theory, Culture & Society* 24, no. 6 (2007): 53–70.

Mullarkey, John, ed. *The New Bergson*. Manchester University Press, 1999b.

Mullarkey, John. *Post-Continental Philosophy*. Continuum Press, 2006.

Mullarkey, John. "The Tragedy of the Object: Democracy of Vision and the Terrorism of Things in Bazin's Cinematic Realism." *Angelaki: The Promise of Cinema: Revisiting themes from Bazin* 17, no. 4 (2013): 39–59.

Murdoch, Iris. *Existentialists and Mystics: Writings on Philosophy and Literature*. Edited by Peter Conradi. Penguin, 1999.

Murphy, Timothy S. "Beneath Relativity: Bergson and Bohm on Absolute Time." In John Mullarkey, ed., *The New Bergson*. Manchester University Press, 1999, pp. 66–81.

Nail, Thomas. *Being and Motion*. Oxford University Press, 2019.

Neimanis, Astrida. *Bodies of Water: Posthuman Feminist Phenomenology*. London: Bloomsbury Academic, 2017.

Noakes, Richard. "Haunted Thoughts of the Careful Experimentalist: Psychical Research and the Troubles of Experimental Physics." *Studies in History and Philosophy of Science Part C: Studies in History and Philosophy of Biological and Biomedical Sciences* 48, Part A (December 2014): 46–56.

Noakes, Richard. "The 'World of the Infinitely Little': Connecting Physical and Psychical Realities Circa 1900." *Studies in History and Philosophy of Science* 39, Part A (2008): 323–34.

Ó Maoilearca, John. *All Thoughts Are Equal: Laruelle and Nonhuman Philosophy*. University of Minnesota Press, 2015.

Ó Maoilearca, John. "The Defragmenting Image: Stories in Cinematic Time Travel." In Daniel Rubinstein, ed., *Fragmentation of the Photographic Image in the Digital Age*. Routledge, 2019a, pp. 189–203.

Ó Maoilearca, John. "Metaphysical Alter-Egos: Matheson, Dunne, and the View from Somewhere." In Christina Rawls, Diana Neiva, and Steven S. Gouveia, eds., *Philosophy and Film: Bridging Divides*. Routledge, 2019b, pp. 356–73.

Ó Maoilearca, John. "Spirit in the Materialist World: On the Structure of Regard." *Angelaki: Journal of the Theoretical Humanities* 19, no. 1 (2014): 13–29.

Ó Maoilearca, John, and Charlotte de Mille, eds. *Bergson and the Art of Immanence: Painting, Photography, Film*. Edinburgh University Press, 2013.

Owen, Alex. *The Darkened Room: Women, Power and Spiritualism in Late Victorian England*. University of Chicago Press, 1989.

Owen, Alex. *The Place of Enchantment: British Occultism and the Culture of the Modern*. University of Chicago Press, 2007.

Papanicolaou, A. C., and P. A. Y. Gunter, eds. *Bergson and Modern Thought: Towards a Unified Science*. Harwood Academic Press, 1987.

Parker, Sybil P., ed. *McGraw-Hill Encyclopedia of Physics*. McGraw-Hill, 1982.

Pasi, Marco. "The Modernity of Occultism: Reflections on Some Crucial Aspects." In Wouter J. Hanegraaff and Joyce Pijnenburg, eds., *Hermes in the Academy: Ten Years' Study of Western Esotericism at the University of Amsterdam*. Amsterdam University Press, 2009, pp. 59–74.

Pattison, George, and Kate Kirkpatrick, eds. *The Mystical Sources of Existentialist Thought: Being, Nothingness, Love*. Routledge, 2018.

Pereen, Esther. "Specter." In Mercedes Bunz, Birgit Mara Kaiser and Kathrin, eds., *Symptoms of the Planetary Condition: A Critical Vocabulary*. Thiele Meson Press, 2017, pp. 167–71.

Perri, Trevor. "Henri Bergson." In Bernecker and Michaelian, 2017, pp. 510–18.

Phelan, Peggy. *Unmarked: The Politics of Performance*. Routledge, 1993.

Pilkington, A. E. *Bergson and his Influence: A Reassessment*. Cambridge University Press, 1976.

Pinch, Adela. "The Appeal of Panpsychism in Victorian Britain." In *Romanticism and Victorianism on the Net* #65 (2014–15), https://ronjournal.org/s/3363. Accessed June 28, 2020.

Plaisance, Christopher. "Magic Made Modern? Re-evaluating the Novelty of the Golden Dawn's Magic." *Correspondences* 22 (2014): 159–87.

Plato. "Theaetetus." Translated by M. J. Levett. Rev. Myles Burnyeat in *Plato. Complete Works*, ed. John M. Cooper. Hackett, 1997.

Podoroga, Ioilia. *Penser en durée: Bergson au fil de ses images*. Editions L'Age d'Homme, 2014.

Povich, Mark, and Carl F. Craver. "Mechanistic Levels, Reduction, and Emergence." In Stuart Glennan and Phyllis Illari eds., *The Routledge Handbook of Mechanisms and Mechanical Philosophy*. Routledge, 2018, pp. 185–97.

Prigogine, Ilya, and Isabelle Stengers. *Order Out of Chaos: Man's New Dialogue with Nature*. Bantam, 1984.

Ramey, Joshua. *The Hermetic Deleuze: Philosophy and Spiritual Ordeal*. Duke University Press, 2012.

Ramos, Filipa. "The Zoological Apparatus: Chris Marker, Simone Forti and Joan Jonas' Artistic Engagement with Animals." PhD diss., Kingston University, 2021.

Regardie, Israel. *The Golden Dawn: The Original Account of the Teachings, Rites, and Ceremonies of the Hermetic Order* (1937). Edited by John Michael Greer. Llewellyn, 2016.

Resurgam, V. H. Fra. Flying Roll No. V "Some Thoughts on the Imagination." In Mathers, King, and Gilbert, 1987, pp. 47–51.

Ricoeur, Paul. *Memory, History, Forgetting*. Translated by Kathleen Blamey and David Pellauer. University of Chicago Press, 2006.

Riquier, Camille. *Archéologie de Bergson; Temps et métaphysique*. Presses Universitaires de France, 2009.

Robbins, Stephen E. "Analogical Reminding and the Storage of Experience: The Paradox of Hofstadter-Sander." *Phenomenology and the Cognitive Sciences* 16, no. 3 (2017): 355–85.

Robbins, Stephen E. "On the Possibility of Direct Memory." In V. W. Fallio, ed., *New Developments in Consciousness Research*. Nova Science, 2006, pp. 1–64.

Robins, Sarah K. "Memory Traces." In Bernecker and Michaelian, 2017, pp. 76–87.

Russell, Bertrand. *The Analysis of Mind*. George Allen and Unwin, 1921.

Russell, Bertrand. *The Philosophy of Bergson*. Macmillan, 1914.

Santayana, George. *Winds of Doctrine: Studies in Contemporary Opinion*. Charles Scribner's Sons, 1913.

Sartre, J. P. *The Imagination*. Translated by Kenneth Williford and David Rudrauf. Routledge, 2012.

Sartre, J. P. *Sketch for a Theory of the Emotions*. Translated by Philip Mairet. Routledge, 2001.

Schechner, Richard. *Performance Studies: An Introduction*. Routledge, 2002.

Schneider, Rebecca. *Performing Remains: Art and War in Times of Theatrical Reenactment*. Routledge, 2011.

Seers, Lindsay. "Nowhere Less Now." https://www.lindsayseers.info/content/lindsay-seers-nowhere-less-now. Accessed June 17, 2020.

Shermer, Michael. *The Believing Brain: From Ghosts and Gods to Politics and Conspiracies—How We Construct Beliefs and Reinforce Them as Truths*. Henry Holt and Co., 2011.

Sinclair, Mark. *Bergson*. Routledge, 2020.

Sinclair, Mark, and Delphine Antoine-Mahut. "Introduction to French Spiritualism in the Nineteenth Century." *British Journal for the History of Philosophy* 28, no. 5 (2020): 857–65.

Sinnett, A. P. *Collected Fruits of Occult Teaching*. J.B. Lippincott, 1919.

Sinnett, A. P. *The Occult World*. Trubner and Company, 1881.

Smith, Anthony Paul, and Nicola Rubczak. "Cloning the Untranslatable: Translators' Introduction." In François Laruelle, *Principles of Non-Philosophy*, translated by Nicola Rubczak and Anthony Paul Smith. Bloomsbury Academic, 2013, pp. xi–xix.

Smolin, Lee. *The Life of the Cosmos*. Weidenfeld and Nicholas, 1997.

Smolin, Lee. *Time Reborn: From the Crisis in Physics to the Future of the Universe.* Houghton Mifflin Harcourt, 2013.

Sommer McGrath, Larry. *Making Spirit Matter: Neurology, Psychology, and Selfhood in Modern France.* University of Chicago Press, 2020.

Soulez, Philippe, and Fréderic Worms. *Bergson.* Flammarion, 1997.

ter Schure, Leon. *Bergson and History: Transforming the Modern Regime of Historicity.* State University of New York Press, 2020.

Steiner, Rudolf. *An Outline of Occult Science.* The Theosophical Publishing Society, 1914.

Szerszynski, Bronislaw. "Colloidal Social Theory: Thinking about Material Animacy and Sociality beyond Solids and Fluids." *Theory, Culture, and Society* (September 2021): 1–21. https://doi.org/10.1177/02632764211030989. Accessed October 5, 2021.

Tereshchenko, Nicolas. "Israel Regardie (1907–1985) and the Golden Dawn." *Aries* (old series), no. 4 (1986): 71–87.

Thurschwell, Pamela. *Literature, Technology and Magical Thinking, 1880–1920.* Cambridge University Press, 2001.

Tully, C. J. "Celtic Egyptians: Isis Priests of the Lineage of Scota." In Eleanor Dobson and Nichola Tonks, eds., *Ancient Egypt in the Modern Imagination: Art, Literature and Culture.* Bloomsbury Academic, 2020, pp. 145–60.

Tully, C. J. "Samuel Liddell Macgregor Mathers and Isis." In Dave Evans and Dave Green, eds., *Ten Years of Triumph? Academic Approaches to Studying Magic and the Occult.* Hidden Publications, 2009, pp. 62–74.

Tulving, Endel. "Episodic Memory and Autonoesis: Uniquely Human?" In Herbert S. Terrace and Janet Metcalfe, eds., *The Missing Link in Cognition: Origins of Self-Reflective Consciousness.* Oxford University Press, 2005, pp. 3–56.

Turner, Victor. *The Anthropology of Performance.* PAJ, 1986.

Underhill, Evelyn. "A Defence of Magic." *The Fortnightly Review* (November 1907): 754–65.

Valery, Paul. "Philosophy of the Dance." *Salmagundi*, No. 33/34 (Spring-Summer 1976): 65–75.

Valiaho, Pasi. *Mapping the Moving Image: Gesture, Thought and Cinema Circa 1900.* Amsterdam University Press, 2010.

Van den Broek, Roelof, and Wouter J. Hanegraaff, eds., *Gnosis and Hermeticism from Antiquity to Modern Times.* State University of New York Press, 1997.

Van der Tuin, Iris, ""A Different Starting Point, A Different Metaphysics": Reading Bergson and Barad Diffractively." *Hypatia: A Journal of Feminist Philosophy* 26, no. 1 (2011): 22–42.

Van Egmond, Daniël. "Western Esoteric Schools in the Late Nineteenth and Early Twentieth Centuries." In Van Den Broek and Hanegraaff, 1997, pp. 311–46.

Van Elferen, Isabella. *Timbre: Paradox, Materialism, Vibrational Aesthetics.* Bloomsbury, 2020.

Van Gemert, Ties, and Johan Eland. "Bergson and the Fringes of the Psyche: Psychical Research, Spiritualism, and Vitalism." Paper presented at "Bergson and Vitalism(s): An Online Workshop," at Ghent University—University Toulouse Jean Jaurès, April 29–30, 2021.

Wallace, Vesna A. *The Inner Kālacakratantra: A Buddhist Tantric View of the Individual.* Oxford University Press, 2001.

de Warren, Nicolas. "Memory in Continental Philosophy: Metaphor, Concept, Thinking." In Dmitri Nikulin, ed., *Memory: A History.* Oxford University Press, 2015, pp. 228–7.

Werning, Markus. "Predicting the Past from Minimal Traces: Episodic Memory and its Distinction from Imagination and Preservation." *Review of Philosophy and Psychology* 11 (2020): 301–33.

Wills, David. *Dorsality: Thinking Back through Technology and Politics.* University of Minnesota Press, 2008.

Wittenberg, David. "Bigness as the Unconscious of Theory." *ELH* 86, no. 2 (Summer 2019): 333–54.

Woods, Derek. "Scale Variance and the Concept of Matter." In Sarah Ellenzweig and John H. Zammito, eds., *The New Politics of Materialism: History, Philosophy, Science.* Routledge, 2017, pp. 200–24.

Yeats, W. B. *A Critical Edition of Yeats's a Vision* (1925). Edited by George Mills Harper and Walter Kelly Hood. Macmillan, 1978.

Yeats, W. B. *Letters to W. B. Yeats: Volume 1.* Edited by Richard J. Finneran, George Mills Harper, and William Murphy. Macmillan, 1977.

Yeats, W. B. *W.B. Yeats Online Archive.* https://my.matterport.com/show-mds?mls=1&m=CfD9eU6iPhf. Accessed November 24, 2021.

Zammito, John H. "Concluding (Irenic) Postscript: Naturalism as a Response to the New Materialism." In Sarah Ellenzweig and John H. Zammito, eds., *The New Politics of Materialism: History, Philosophy, Science.* Routledge, 2017, pp. 300–21.

Zukav, Gary. *The Dancing Wu Li Masters: An Overview of the New Physics.* William Morrow, 1979.

Index

For the benefit of digital users, indexed terms that span two pages (e.g., 52–53) may, on occasion, appear on only one of those pages.

Tables and figures are indicated by *t* and *f* following the page number